D0276792

Remarkable
People

Also by Dan Walker:

Dan Walker's Football Thronkersaurus:
Football's Finest Tales

Dan Walker's Magic, Mud & Maradona:
Cup Football's Finest Tales

DAN WALKER

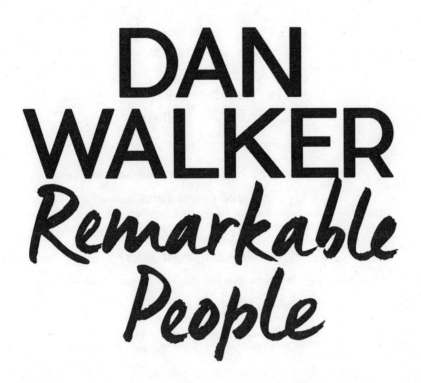

Remarkable People

Extraordinary Stories of Everyday Lives

HEADLINE

First published in 2020
by HEADLINE PUBLISHING GROUP

3

Cataloguing in Publication Data is available from the British Library

Hardback ISBN 978 1 4722 7889 0

Unless otherwise stated, all images are courtesy
of the author or the book's participants.

Typeset by CC Book Production

Printed and bound in Great Britain by Clays Ltd, Elcograf S.p.A.

MIX
Paper from
responsible sources
FSC® C104740
www.fsc.org

HEADLINE PUBLISHING GROUP
An Hachette UK Company
Carmelite House
50 Victoria Embankment
London EC4Y 0DZ

CONTENTS

INTRODUCTION

The first and most important thing to say is 'thank you'. I know it's traditional to put that at the end, but thank you for picking this up and for taking an interest in what is contained within these pages.

We've all been through a lot in 2020 and the global pandemic is not something we are going to forget in a hurry. That feels very current, but this book has been on my mind for a long time. I have been privileged over the years to sit down with some incredible individuals. I have interviewed some really 'important' people. I've shoved a microphone under the nose of the last six UK prime ministers, various members of the royal family and all sorts of sporting superstars in countries across the world. None of them appear in this book.

In my twenty-plus years in this job, there are some people who I have been unable to get out of my head. Their words, their stories or actions have really stuck and left me asking questions, being inspired or wondering what I would do in their situation.

I have always been far more comfortable talking to and talking about other people. This isn't one of those books where I feel I have a load that I want to get off my chest, but there are some things I wanted to share. I love hearing what makes people tick and it is an honour to share a huge variety of stories here. The other thing I am trying to do, is show you what I have learned from these people – how they have informed me and made a difference to the way I do my job and how I live my life.

The world that we operate in doesn't hang around for long. We hear a brilliant story, or a remarkable tale, and we might choose to share it. We might post about it on social media or tell our friends but, sometimes within hours, it has gone, and we are looking for the next one. That is why I wanted to take the opportunity to go back and revisit some of those individuals who have made a lasting impression on me.

I also want to take the opportunity to thank everyone who has agreed to be in this book. I tried to tot it up and I think I have spoken to about 45 people and each one of those interviews lasted over an hour – some of them were much longer than that. I have laughed, I have cried and I have learned a lot about myself and others.

Some of the people featured here made big headlines – Tony Foulds, Terrence, Maria, Gary Speed, Ken and Kia – but others may not be so well known to you. I trust that you, like me, will enjoy learning about them and seeing what you can take away for yourself from their extraordinary lives.

All this has involved quite a bit of soul searching for me too. I have discovered that there are some things I have hidden away, emotions I never dealt with and things I could and should have learned the first time around.

One of the other reasons I have written this book is that I am increasingly worried that we live in a hostile and toxic environment. I have thought long and hard about leaving social media behind over the last few years, but I still believe the positive outweighs the negative, and, let's be honest, where else would we get videos of dogs on surfboards or a granddad opening cupboard doors to the Phil Collins drum solo from 'In The Air Tonight'?

I see that toxicity every day when I sit on the *BBC Breakfast* sofa or in the BBC Sport studio. The debate over Brexit, the 2019 General Election and the coronavirus pandemic have all added to a situation where there is a constant assumption of bias – whatever your political persuasion. During the build-up to the General Election, after every political interview I was accused of being either a 'Corbynista' or a 'Tory boy'. There are insults, threats, accusations and slander and a growing feeling that any mistake is deliberate.

Some observers see every question or comment as either an attack on them or someone else. I fear we may be losing the ability to disagree with each other. In real life, I have always thought it possible to debate issues with friends or colleagues without falling out or losing respect. The same rules don't always seem to apply to social media land and we risk missing out on essential human discourse. We should not accept the argument that if you disagree with someone's lifestyle, you must fear or hate them; and, if you love someone, you automatically agree with all that they do and stand for. Both might be as dangerous as each other.

That is one of the reasons why I took up the opportunity to write this book . . . as an antidote to all that. I want to introduce you to some lovely, amazing, kind, generous people on these pages. They are not perfect. Some of them have gone through awful things in their lives but are willing to share how they came out the other side. So many of them are an essential reminder that finding life hard doesn't mean you are failing.

The other thing I need to do before inviting you to dive in, is to thank the 'remarkable people' I see every day. When I told my family I was thinking of writing this, my kids asked me what it would be called and Jessica – our middle child – was not happy with the title. 'Dad,' she said sternly, 'if you don't call it something a bit better, like *Remark at the Remarkable People*, then I'm sorry, but no one will buy it.'

My family are superstars. There are many times over the pasts few months when I have apologised to them and told them I had to go off and write this thing. My wife, Sarah, has been her usual amazing self and, without her, none of the things you read about in this book would be possible. She has given me so much sage advice over the years and I respect her wisdom almost as much as I appreciate the sacrifices she has made to allow me to keep doing the job that I dreamed of as a child and the job I still love.

This book is dedicated to Sarah and our three wonderful children – Susie, Jessica and Joe. I should also probably mention our dog Winnie. Without her, there would have been no flypast in Sheffield and walking her has given me plenty of thinking time in between all the writing and interviewing.

That's enough from me. One of the toughest jobs was whittling this down to just 10 chapters. Maybe I'll write Part 2 one day and let my children pick the title. In the meantime, I really hope you enjoy reading this one.

IT STARTED WITH A BOWL OF SOUP

'It seems strange to say this, but from the moment I met Winnie, I knew my life would never be the same again.'

In 2004, Lisa Ashton was a researcher working in television. She had been sent to Johannesburg, along with former British athlete Jonathan Edwards, to produce a mini documentary about post-apartheid South Africa.

They were filming in a place called Finetown, about 50 kilometres outside Johannesburg, when Lisa came across a woman called Winnie Mabaso. Winnie was a former nurse, now in her seventies, who had taken it upon herself to feed some of the underprivileged children who walked past her house every day.

'Winnie lived in this shack,' explains Lisa, 'and she used to watch children go past her every day with no food. She started making soup. As more children came, the bowl kept getting bigger and bigger. By the time we met her, she was feeding about five hundred children a day.

'I was so struck by the love and compassion of this woman. Once we had finished filming, we continued chatting to her and watching her. She told us it was "time to get the mattresses out".

She was preparing her front yard so that many of the children would have a safe place to spend the night.'

Lisa explained that many of the young girls found themselves attacked by men at night. HIV was rampant in Finetown and there was a strong belief that if you were able to sleep with a virgin, that would get rid of the virus. Winnie was protecting those young girls as best she could with food during the day and shelter at night.

'You know what it's like Dan, there are moments in your life when your heart is captured. I remember saying to myself, "I've got to do something to help this woman." I had no idea what that would entail, but I was compelled to do something. I couldn't get the image of her, or those children, out of my head.'

Lisa returned to the UK, but she and Winnie started writing to each other. Winnie would send long, beautiful letters and in one of them she mentioned that the house opposite her in Finetown had come up for sale and she thought it would be perfect for an orphanage.

'I knew nothing about charities,' remembers Lisa. 'I knew nothing about HIV, but I just told her I would do everything I could to raise the money we needed to help. I set up the Winnie Mabaso Foundation later that year. At that point in my life I thought, I'll raise the money we need and that will be my job done. I never realised it would take over my life.'

Lisa was still working as a researcher at the BBC at the time. She had a husband, Steve, and a daughter, Charlotte, who was five years old. The fundraising operation went into overdrive. Letters were written, emails sent, calls made, events organised and the donations came flooding in.

'I found out that I was very persistent and had no shame when it came to begging for other people's money,' explains Lisa. 'I would tell Winnie's story to anyone who would listen. I was just on it. I didn't miss an opportunity and, somehow, within about ten months, we had raised enough money to buy the house.'

It was such an exciting time for Winnie and Lisa. In 2005, Winnie and some of the children she looked after moved into the orphanage. This amazing woman, who had spent many years trying to protect vulnerable children in her community, had a place that she, and they, could call home.

'I used to ring Winnie every Friday to ask her how things were and see if there was anything she needed me to do,' explains Lisa. 'About three months after they moved in, I made my normal call, and a man answered. His English was poor, and he struggled to explain what had happened. I managed to work out that Winnie was sick and that she was in hospital.'

Lisa spent much of the weekend frantically trying to find Winnie. She looked up 'South African hospitals' and started calling them all to try and see if her friend was there. She was getting more and more frantic. Eventually, Lisa got through to the Chris Baragwanath Hospital in Soweto, at the time the biggest hospital in the world. The wonderful receptionist could hear the desperation in her voice. She connected her to a ward and Lisa managed to speak to the ward sister who confirmed that Winnie was there but explained that she couldn't give her any information because she wasn't a member of the family.

'I just broke down in tears,' remembers Lisa. 'The sister told me to wait for a moment. I stayed patiently on the phone for a few minutes and then I heard it rattle as someone on the other end picked it up. "Hello?" It was Winnie. She was totally taken aback by the fact that I had managed to track her down. She sounded frail and explained that she had an obstruction in her bowel but was feeling okay and looking forward to going home. I told her I loved her. She said the same thing back to me and that was the last time we ever spoke to each other. Winnie died later that day.'

Lisa went to South Africa for Winnie's funeral. It was a beautiful day. There were so many people there who had come to understand what she had done for others. The whole service was a celebration of her spirit of compassion and love. Just before she was buried, all the children from the orphanage stood hand in hand around her coffin.

Lisa stops talking as she remembers that moment. It is clearly still a huge, defining moment in her life. The tears are flowing again.

'I knew, looking at them, looking at those children, that I would end up doing whatever it takes to keep them safe. Just like the day I met Winnie for the first time, I had the feeling that I couldn't let them go. I knew they were going to turn my life upside down, but I knew for certain that I had to continue what Winnie had started.'

* * *

In 2010, I was given an incredible, once-in-a-lifetime opportunity to cover the football World Cup in South Africa for the BBC.

The plan was that, over the course of five weeks, we would drive a double-decker bus around the whole country visiting every one of the World Cup grounds. Our brief was to cover matches but, more importantly, to try and experience the culture and history of the 'Rainbow Nation' and bring that back to our viewers in the UK.

In total, there were fifteen of us who made the trip: a combination of presenters, reporters, camera crew, technical geniuses, producers, a driver, two security guards and a marvellous local called Jo. Jo is a filmmaker, producer, guide and fixer, and filled with enthusiasm for South Africa. I asked her what job title she would like me to put down for her in the book. She laughed in that mischievous way we had all become fond of. 'Storyteller and Mother of Dragons,' she said. Jo is mum to three-year-old twins Jack and Leo, but back in 2010 she was the fearless guide for a BBC film crew, and she was desperate to make sure we saw the real South Africa.

'I remember feeling quite emotional before you all arrived,' says Jo. 'Here was this big BBC crew and it was my job to show off my country. Everyone arrives in South Africa with preconceived ideas about what they will see and who they will meet. I was trying to show you what was special about South Africa and help you to try and understand what makes us tick. I could tell from conversations we had before you arrived that the BBC were understandably worried about security and about keeping you all safe on the bus. It was my job to make sure

5

that you felt safe enough to try and see the real South Africa. I wanted you to see our resilience. I wanted you to see that a broken nation was on the mend.'

The World Cup was a huge moment for South Africa. A chance to change perceptions. Wherever we went in the country people were so proud that the world was watching them. Jo told us about the significance of the Rugby World Cup in 1995, and President Nelson Mandela and Springbok captain François Pienaar united in triumph. That was a moment that brought together a nation, that bonded a delicate society. The football World Cup in 2010 was another opportunity to show the best of South Africa to the rest of the planet.

Jo was also aware that she was the only woman on the bus; it was five weeks with fourteen smelly blokes. 'I remember when I first met you all that you were all quite, how can I put this politely . . .' she laughs again and looks at me knowingly, '. . . blokey blokes, if that makes sense. What was lovely for me to see was that, over those weeks together, there were some wonderful moments when your hearts were broken, and I saw a real tenderness in all of you.'

Jo was right. To say the trip was an 'eye-opener' would be an understatement. We watched some amazing football, met some amazing people – from all walks of life – and experienced some real highs and lows. We attended a church service in Soweto, filmed at Rorke's Drift, learned about the brutal legacy of Cecil Rhodes' diamond business in Kimberley and sat down to dinner with a white supremacist.

Our five-thousand mile journey started in Cape Town

where, after our first match of the tournament, we visited a township just outside the city called Khayelitsha. Hundreds of thousands of people were forcibly relocated there back in the 1980s and, to give you an idea of the scale of the place, it is bigger than Birmingham. At the time, 1.3 million people called Khayelitsha home. It was South Africa's second biggest township behind Soweto, but it was the fastest growing.

As we drove around, we saw house after house stacked side by side. It was a kingdom of corrugated iron. Jo explained how those who were successful didn't tend to leave the township. They simply built an extra layer on their house. 'It's an easy way to find the doctors and dentists,' she said. Staggeringly, Jo also told us that an estimated 20 per cent of the residents of Khayelitsha were HIV positive.

We visited a scheme funded by Football for Hope and run by a company called Grassroot Soccer. The organisation offered a programme teaching kids football skills and educating them about HIV and AIDS. The guy in charge, who looked remarkably like Hulk Hogan, talked about some of the ignorance he encountered every day, the same thing that Lisa had learned from Winnie.

'It's hard to educate some of these kids about what is actually happening around them. Some of the lads here are taught that if they sleep with a virgin, that will rid them of the virus.' Those who did have the virus could find themselves ostracised immediately.

We heard about Siya, a young lad whose mother and father both tested positive. His friends immediately stopped talking to him and playing football with him. For months, he spoke to no one. Thanks to the scheme, Siya's friends were convinced he had done nothing wrong and was not contagious. Thankfully, he was now laughing and joking with his friends, playing football every day, and hoping that South Africa were going to have a great World Cup.

There were children everywhere. On the street corners, on packed pitches, outside shops – many of them staring at our ludicrously white double-decker bus. All the schools in South Africa had been closed for six weeks in an attempt to reduce World Cup traffic. We drove past one of the main high schools in Khayelitsha and you could see all the windows covered in bulletproof glass. There was a room on the ground floor with an enormous yellow dot on the door which opened up onto the main playground.

'Anyone know what the dot is for?' asked Jo. The bus was silent. 'Many of the kids can't read or write so they are taught, on their first day at school that, if they hear gunfire, or see anyone with a gun, they must run to the yellow circle as quickly as they can. The door is thick enough to stop anything.'

It was a very different existence, and Khayelitsha was an early reminder of the real challenge for that 2010 World Cup. FIFA had spent a lot of time in the build-up to the tournament talking about the importance of leaving a legacy in South Africa; of not just turning up and leaving the country as they found it. Many of the people we met on the trip said that, unless a lasting difference is made in townships like Khayelitsha, then the tournament would never be classed as a success.

Now is not the time for a detailed analysis of the legacy of that World Cup. At the time, the experience for many South Africans was overwhelming positive, as Jo explained, but many promises were broken after the final whistle of the final game. I remember speaking to a hotel owner in the city of Durban. FIFA had block-booked many of the hotels for World Cup requirements, but just a few days before the tournament started, the bookings had been cancelled and the hoteliers were told they could now fill their own rooms and fend for themselves. Most people had already booked their travel and accommodation by that point and there weren't as many international spectators as organisers had expected. At a time when businesses were dreaming of a bumper summer, thousands of hotel rooms lay empty.

'Listen,' says Jo, raising her hand to make an important point. 'The football was amazing. I still remember filming in a bar at the moment South Africa scored our first goal in the tournament. I was lifted up off my feet by this wave of emotion. That is the power of sport. But many people feel like FIFA let them down.' She continues, 'All South Africans look back on that time with great pride, but there are also painful memories. Stadiums built in the wrong places, projects not followed through and promised money that never materialised.'

We moved on from Cape Town and made our way along what is known as the 'Garden Route' which leads all the way from west to east and Port Elizabeth.

We had our fair share of bus-based drama along the way: tyre blowouts, generator failure, satellite issues and we even came under attack from a giant bird. A gigantic feathery friend flew straight through the front window of the bus, smashing the glass and causing some lasting damage to our mobile editing suite. Our driver-handyman-raconteur-all-round legend, Roger Walker, fixed the window in minutes.

It was one of those trips where, even though it was an amazing experience, every day I realised how inept I was, as I marvelled at the practical talents of the others on the bus.

Andy, our engineer, is probably the cleverest bloke I have ever come across. He could build, repair and redirect a satellite at a moment's notice. I just sat there hopelessly eating a ham sandwich one day watching him recalculate exactly where he needed to point the thing, five minutes before a live broadcast. He would occasionally swear at himself under his breath in his broad Lancastrian accent but, because of Andy's expertise, we never missed a technical beat in five weeks, whatever the weather or location.

Matching Andy in resourcefulness was our rigger, Micky. He didn't know much about satellites, but he could fix anything – like an East End MacGyver. It also helped that Micky looked like someone had blended together the faces of Ray Winstone and Sinbad from *Brookside*.

So, as we dashed around South Africa watching matches, eating in service stations, interviewing all sorts of interesting people, filming elephants and generally having an amazing time, there was one day that stopped us all in our tracks.

It had nothing to do with animals, nothing to do with football and everything to do with the moment we approached Johannesburg. We would be visiting a place called Finetown. Jo had organised for us to visit a little orphanage. Yes, that one. Winnie's place.

The house that Lisa and Winnie had set up was called the Zenzele Orphanage. I still think about that day regularly. None of us were emotionally prepared for it. It was a big day for those 'blokey blokes' Jo had laughed about.

'Give it a few weeks and Africa will get to you,' was one of the first things my fellow presenter Rob Walker said to me after we met at Heathrow Airport before flying into Cape Town. Rob had filmed on the continent a lot and felt that intoxication before.

It was on that Saturday in 2010 that I understood what he meant. Our double-decker bus drove into Finetown, some thirty miles outside Johannesburg, and pulled into the grounds of Zenzele. We were met by a wall of children with huge smiles on their faces. The white building behind them was home to about sixty children. The wall down the side of the orphanage was part breeze block, part brick, part wood and part mud. It was rickety and well-used but it was held together with love, and most importantly, it was safe.

Our plan for the day was to show this wonderful group of children their first-ever football match. We were going to rig up a few televisions to the satellite and allow the kids to watch Ghana take on Australia. When I say 'our' plan, of course I mean Andy and Micky's plan.

For most of the year, there was little or no electricity at the orphanage, and the vast majority of the children had never seen a television before in their young lives.

Jo remembers it well. 'I think I had a slightly different perspective because I had worked in those environments a lot over the years. When that white bus turned up at the orphanage, the faces on those children . . . wow! It was like a UFO had just landed. I actually had a ten-year reminder on my Facebook last month, you know, one of those photos. It was one of the little lads we met that day, pretending to drive the bus. His face was amazing. It's hard to explain just how excited they were to see us arrive that day. Here was a bus, mostly full of white men, who were interested in them and what they were up to.'

After the initial excitement, the children gathered in front of the main house for a performance. They sang us a song and some of them read us a script they had written. They explained what the orphanage meant to them and talked about the legacy of a lady called Winnie. Winnie Mabaso. Most of them had never met her. She had died in 2005 and yet, five years on, their faces beamed as they talked about what she had done for them, what it meant to live in her house and they explained what they understood as 'Mabaso love' – unconditional, inexplicable, unflinching and transformative.

They showed us a picture of Lisa and thanked us for all the help and presents they received from the UK. We gave them a rousing round of applause before a lady called Miriam, proudly wearing a South African football shirt, stepped forward to speak. She was one of the women who helped run Zenzele and she wanted to tell us a little bit about the children and the work of the orphanage.

She explained that all of the children we were looking at were HIV positive. All of them had lost their parents to the virus. She told us to look at their faces, to think about what they had been through and to watch them as they laughed and smiled and showed their love of life.

I will happily admit to you that Miriam's speech knocked me off my feet. I was aware that the children were watching us carefully. I was watching their gorgeous faces smiling back at us as the tears began rolling down my face.

Miriam went on to explain that there was very little help available for the children at Zenzele. Many of them weren't from South Africa and had no access to HIV medication. They looked after them by trying to keep them as healthy as possible, feeding them vegetables they grew in the orphanage garden and taking them to the local health clinic if things got serious. Finally, Miriam explained that she too was HIV positive and had lost her mother to the virus.

It is hard for me to put into words how it affected us all that day. I have never seen a bunch of grown men cry like that. We had to get the bus ready to show the football match but, before we did anything, we gathered behind the double-decker and wept.

We talked to each other about the mixture of anger, frustration and guilt at the life we all had back at home. We thought of our own children and I think we all felt that overriding feeling of helplessness and the pain of a system that just wasn't helping the most vulnerable. I think, above all, what was causing this wave of emotion, was the joy we saw in those children. Joy in the turmoil, laughter through the tears and a profound resilience in the face of despair. The children of Zenzele continue to inspire me to this day.

I can't really put it any better than Steve Lyle, our lead producer, who is one of the finest fellas you could ever hope to come across. He is adored by his colleagues who will all tell you that he has a reputation for going quiet and shaking his head. It doesn't really matter whether he's been told something happy, sad or a terrible joke, the reaction is always comically identical. That day Steve was shaking his head as the tears were pouring from his eyes.

'I've been thinking a lot about that trip since you asked me to speak to you for your book, and my overriding feeling is still one of being completely overwhelmed by it. It still feels so unreal to me. It was such an incredible story and I don't think any of us were ready for it. We had been travelling around South Africa and most of the stories had either been related to football or World Cup themed. This was totally different. It was raw, it was painful . . . but it was real life. My background was sport's journalism and sport's production – I remember watching those children and looking at the incredible people who were looking after them and feeling like an imposter.

'I think it was the happiness juxtaposed with the sadness and the grief,' he continues. 'I have seen poverty before. My parents are from Old Harbour in Jamaica. It is a rundown area. I've been there, taken our kids there, to show them where their grandparents grew up before coming to England. Old Harbour is poor, but Zenzele was another level. The children we saw had nothing. No family, no money, failing health and no prospects and here they were, delighted to see us and spreading joy with their smiles.'

Thankfully, treatment of HIV in South Africa has now vastly improved. Education programmes, combined with political will, have led to significant changes to access to care and clinics. The cost of HIV treatment has fallen dramatically, and the situation is so much better than it was in 2010.

One thing that became very clear that day, was that the children at Zenzele were the lucky ones. The statistics were stark: those with AIDS who live outside the gates are far more likely to die before they reach adulthood. That was why – during the day – there were children jumping the walls to get into the orphanage.

When we finally rigged the TV up, all the children gathered on a crop of rocks in the driveway. We showed them how to cheer if a goal went in – and they soon had the opportunity to practise when Australia took the lead. There was delight when Ghana equalised but the highlight was when they saw the advert for *Doctor Who* at half-time. 'What was that?' said El Rico, one of the young lads who was glued to the screen. 'I want to see that show,' added Thabiso. The conversation about *Doctor Who* lasted much of the second half. Try explaining what a Dalek is to someone who has never seen one before!

Once the game had finished, and our piece on the orphanage had been broadcast on BBC One, we showed it to them on the screens. Imagine seeing yourself on screen on the first day you had ever seen a TV. Dancing broke out and the occasional yelp was followed by pointing at the faces they recognised. Miriam broke down when she was told how many people were watching them back in the UK.

As the sun set, we left with warm hugs all round and promises that we would never forget the people we had met and the friends we had made.

I recall something Jo said at the time about admiring the resilience of the children. We heard some of their stories that day, heart breaking tales of abandonment and abuse, but here they were, making life work against all the odds. 'I am South African,' says Jo, 'but I come from a privileged background. You think about all the things you have been given, all the doors that are opened to you and the fights you don't have to fight and then you see people making the most of what they have, and what they have is nothing.'

'I remember that no one wanted to leave,' recalls Steve. 'We didn't want to go, even though we'd done everything and were late, and the children were desperate for us to stay. The emotion was so strong that I don't think any of us wanted to walk away and forget what we'd seen. I know I will never forget it.'

It was pitch black when we finally did depart. I read through a number of emails on my phone. It was packed with organisations and individuals who wanted to help. I think that Christmas, the children of Zenzele had quite a few gifts under the tree.

'I don't know about you Dan,' says Steve, 'but I keep coming back to that day when I speak to my own children.' Steve had a three-year-old at the time and now has two beautiful daughters. 'There have been several times, since returning from South Africa, where I have sat down with my children and used the example of Zenzele to remind them that they don't know how lucky they are. I talk to them about Winnie Mabaso, what she did, what Lisa is still doing and how fortunate they are to enjoy the things that we all take for granted.'

Just like Steve, I think that of all the trips I have made around the world, the things I saw in South Africa that summer have stayed with me the longest. We all knew it was a complicated country with huge social problems, but some of the people who were thriving in adversity continue to take my breath away.

It's difficult to find the right words at times like these. I remember talking about our visit on the television and radio at the time and some people accused us of saying, 'oh, isn't life hard for some people' and 'look at how poor they are'. My intention was, and remains, simply to describe what we saw and the effect it had on us. I don't have all the answers. I wish I could save all those children, and I am inspired by people like Lisa, and Winnie before her, who are having a huge impact on people's lives.

On the following day, we met a fella called Michael at a church service in Soweto. As a South African, his opinion carries far more weight than mine, and he managed to articulate exactly what I am trying to say.

'I have lived in South Africa my whole life. Over the last 40 years, I can barely remember a day when I haven't felt frustrated by what I see around me. I love this country. At times, it makes me laugh and cry in equal measure but I am confident that, before I die, I will live to see a better South Africa because there are so many people desperate to make a difference and change it.'

Winnie Mabaso was one of those people and Lisa Ashton is following in her footsteps. There is something beautiful in watching someone help another person simply because it is the right thing to do. When the motivation isn't praise, publicity or power then it holds an unparalleled purity. Winnie and Lisa knew that no one else was going to provide for those children, so they took it upon themselves. That is service. That is life-changing, both for those who experience it and those who are fortunate enough to witness it.

There are so many other things I could tell you about South Africa that I think I'd need another book to fit them all in. I haven't mentioned Moira, who we met in the town of Cullinan – about twenty miles east of Pretoria. She was a twenty-four-year-old who trained a marching band that played at the World Cup closing ceremony. The band members admitted that without Moira's help they would be struggling with drink, drugs and teenage pregnancy, just like huge numbers of the young people that live in their township.

I still think about an amazing lady called Georghina who lived in the shadow of the stadium in Nelspruit – one of those white elephants. All her money came from the meals she made for the construction workers at the stadium just a few hundred yards from her front door. She was worried about how she would provide for her family once the football left town.

Wherever you go in South Africa, the history both disturbs and inspires. The struggle against apartheid is well documented. I was transfixed by our interview with Lukhanyo Calata, whose father was one of the murdered Cradock Four. In June 1985, Fort Calata was one of a group of anti-apartheid activists from Cradock who were stopped at a police roadblock outside Port Elizabeth. The men were abducted, killed and the police burned their bodies. Their remains were found in dumps around the area and their eventual funeral was attended by thousands of people.

We were stalked by a miffed five-tonne elephant in Pilanesberg National Park. Thankfully, at the last minute the big unit decided he was more interested in a noisy bunch of Argentina fans in a Volvo. Everybody survived unscathed.

If you can remember the football, it was probably the worst England have ever played at an international tournament. The goalless draw with Algeria in Cape Town remains the worst game of football I have ever watched, and I've seen some stinkers.

There were enough memories from our trip to last a lifetime, but I so often come back to that day at the orphanage in Finetown and the children we met there. After the match that day, I remember a young lad called William who wanted to sit on my shoulders. He was the same age as my eldest daughter, Susie, and I still think about what he is up to now as my daughter has become a teenager. What are his hopes and dreams? What are his prospects? What is he dreaming of doing in later life?

Zenzele has changed since we were there in 2010. It has now become more of a community centre and is run by social services in Johannesburg. Many of the children from Zenzele are still alive and living in Finetown. I was overjoyed to hear that William and Thabiso are doing well and still attending events run by the foundation. Lisa's focus and attention has moved to another project less than a mile away called Ilamula House. Ilamula is now home to twenty-three young girls. The house is in the township of Meriting and that is where the Winnie Mabaso Foundation does all its project work.

'It is seventeen years now [speaking in 2020] since we set up in South Africa,' says Lisa, 'and we have made so many mistakes along the way. We had to make a decision to move our base from Zenzele.'

It was a near-impossible decision for Lisa to leave. She felt like she was letting Winnie down and wasn't sure it was the right move to make.

'Winnie's favourite flower was a rose. We planted one at Zenzele but when I walked into the garden of the new house, less than a mile away, there was a perfect rose bush in front of the house. I know it sounds daft, but I saw that as a sign we were doing the right thing. This was the place to continue Winnie's legacy.'

Lisa is rightly proud of what they've managed to achieve in the last few years. 'We have a pre-school for thirty children, we run a sewing school for twenty unemployed women, and we have a library full of books donated by people from all over South Africa. We started running reading classes for the children but then their parents started coming too. We've been able to help hundreds of people who couldn't read, fall in love with literature and it's wonderful to watch.'

A man called Fimo, who learned to read in the library, now runs courses for the next generation of students. The library is also where Lisa runs smear tests for residents of Meriting and there is a mother and baby group there every Tuesday.

Lisa has never been accused of being a 'white saviour' and I think there is a good reason for that. She never imposes her will on the people she works with. It's always about projects that they want to invest in and things that will affect them directly. It is always a collaborative process.

'We have always tried to take our lead from the community. Most of the projects we run are ideas or suggestions that come directly from the people we are trying to support, and everything we do is run past them before we go ahead. Winnie's dream was always to give people a hand-up not a handout.'

If you are ever able to see the work in Meriting, you will now find over one hundred individual gardens. This was a project which came directly from the residents. They asked Lisa to help them and teach them to grow their own food because of the indignity they felt at begging and not being able to feed their own children. They no longer have to rely on handouts. They now have a thriving market garden – hunger relieved, dignity restored.

There are nearly forty people working for the Winnie Mabaso Foundation in South Africa. Lisa is the only full-time employee in the UK. She works from home, covers all the running costs herself and a close friend sponsors her to do the work, so every penny raised goes to South Africa. Lisa now splits her time between her 'two homes' – a month in the UK, followed by a month at Ilamula.

What is it that continues to inspire her to work so hard?

'People ask me this a lot,' she explains, 'and I think it all comes back to Winnie. Her kindness and generosity made me fall in love with her instantly. I was always incredibly close to my grandmother when she was alive – she was a really important part of my life. I know this sounds a bit strange,' she says laughing, 'but I had a dream one night and in the dream my gran was with Winnie. They were both surrounded by children who were laughing and so happy. I woke up and I thought "that's it". My gran loved seeing children happy and Winnie was exactly the same. I was drawn to her because I saw so much of my own grandmother in her.'

Winnie felt the depth of that relationship too. Her own daughter was murdered in 2003, just before she first met Lisa the following year. She used to say to Lisa, 'God sent you to me after I lost my own daughter.' All the letters that Winnie sent to Lisa over those years are addressed to 'my child'.

Lisa's own faith in God is still there but it has been hit hard by some of the things she has seen over the years. 'I think, if anything, my faith has been challenged and tested and I would say I have more questions than answers. When you see the awfulness of life and the poverty and how hard life is for some people, I think that you have to ask questions and also accept that you won't always find the answers. Having said all that, there is so much goodness and light in the darkness. Everywhere I look I see the power of love and kindness to transform the world.'

Lisa has often wondered if Winnie knew she would continue the work they started together. Winnie was determined that, even though the children lived in an orphanage, the house would be filled with laughter, hope and joy. The children at Zenzele called it 'Mabaso Love' and that phrase appears on the uniforms of every member of staff at Ilamula.

'We have never moved away from that as our central message,' says Lisa. 'We want the children to feel that love and kindness every day. They are so young and have seen the very worst that life has had to offer. It is amazing to witness the transforming power of love. I cannot tell you what it means to see these frightened, bruised, damaged little girls come to life.'

Ilamula takes in girls from the ages of two up to sixteen. At the time of writing, the youngest is five and the oldest is nineteen. I ask Lisa what she hopes for these girls and, before she even starts to answer, she breaks down. She keeps apologising. I tell her it's okay and that it's lovely that it means so much to her. 'I just want them to know that it's okay for them to make mistakes. I want them to know that they are not to blame for the things that have happened to them in the past. I want them to be content, I want them to know that our love is unconditional and, my dream is, that they are able to grow up thinking that anything is possible for them.'

*   *   *

The oldest girl at Ilamula is called Palesa. She was born in Johannesburg in 2001 and arrived at the house in 2014. She is planning on going to college and dreams of being a hairdresser. 'I love it at Ilamula,' she beams. 'I wish I could stay here forever. I have learned so much and feel like a very different person to the one who arrived here. It took me a while but it's the first time I have been able to be myself and feel safe. I laugh and smile every day. I have twenty-two siblings here.'

Two of those twenty-two are Palesa's actual sisters – Lerato and Maki. Palesa and Lerato arrived together and their youngster sister, Maki, came to Ilamula a few years later. I ask Palesa what life was like before Ilamula and there is a long silence on the end of the phone. It is such a long time that I check the line to see if we've been cut off. I can hear the faint sound of tears at the other end. It is too hard to talk about, too painful to recall.

Ilamula is a home for girls who have been abandoned and abused. Palesa, like all the residents, has seen unspeakable things. She has lived through pain and suffering and watched her sisters suffer in the same way. Now they are safe. Eventually, she is able to continue.

'We didn't feel safe at home but now . . . now we are safe. We love each other, the three of us. Our old life seems a long way away now. Our mother left and we had to live with our father. This is a journey we are on together. They love me and we love spending time with each other.'

Unbelievably, she apologises for crying on the phone. I tell her it's alright. I try and tell her that I understand but I feel hopelessly inadequate when it comes to comprehending what she has been through. I ask her about Winnie and Lisa.

'I never knew Winnie but I know all about her. I knew she did amazing things and that we are here today because of her. Lisa is a special person to all of us.' You can hear Palesa relax as she talks at length about the impact that Lisa and the staff at Ilamula have had on her. 'Lisa is amazing. She is a very understanding. So kind, so sweet . . . she is the mother I never had. She always seems to know when you need a hug and she is a good listener. She tells us when we are wrong, which I know is important, and what a loving parent is meant to do. If it wasn't for Lisa, I would be like so many of the other children around. I wouldn't know how to speak to you in English,' she laughs, 'and I wouldn't be going to college. I wouldn't have a future at all. She has given me my childhood back. I am able to enjoy living.'

Birthdays are a big thing at Ilamula. On the day that Palesa's youngest sister, Maki, joined them at the house it was her eighth birthday. It was the first time in her life she had ever celebrated it. 'It was great day,' remembers Palesa. 'Maki had never had a cake or presents before. We danced and laughed for most of the day.'

Palesa knows it will be hard to leave the house eventually. That's one of the reasons why one of Lisa's next projects is to try and fund a halfway house for children like Palesa who are getting ready to work. 'Mandela always said that education was the way out of poverty,' says Lisa. 'We are just trying to make that possible for as many people as possible.'

'In ten years time,' says Palesa, 'I want to be cutting hair, working hard and trying to help other people. It makes such a difference to know that my sisters are safe. I have so many special memories. All the staff have been so kind and gentle. They treat us like their own family. I know that things won't always be easy but I now know how to deal with things when it doesn't work out how you plan it. I am free. My sisters are free. I have been given a second chance at life and I intend to use it.'

What does Lisa think Winnie would think make of all this?

'I think and I hope she would be enormously proud, and she'd be chuffed to bits that her name lives on. It's more than fifteen years now since she passed away [in 2005]. The vast majority of these children weren't even born when Winnie left us, but they all know who she was. That is part of my responsibility. Winnie built all this from one bowl of soup. Look where one bowl of soup can lead!'

And the work goes on. During the coronavirus crisis, the foundation has provided thousands of grocery packs to the people around Ilamula. There is still much to be done and that weighs heavily on Lisa and her team.

'My life was very comfortable before I met Winnie,' explains Lisa. 'I had never seen horror or hardship. I am still struck by so much of what I see. We had a young girl and there was a terrible smell coming from her room. She was hiding food everywhere. Each mealtime she would take some and put it under the bed, in the wardrobe, anywhere she could. Her life had taught her that food wasn't a guarantee and she never knew where her next meal was coming from. It takes time to build trust with someone like that, for them to know that you will protect them.

If you read some of the case notes and saw what some of these girls have been through, you wouldn't believe you were looking at the same person. I cannot understand how some of them can ever trust an adult again. When they do, that is incredibly precious.'

Lisa's family have supported her throughout this adventure. She used to use all her annual leave to travel to South Africa and her husband – known as Papa Steve to the girls at Ilamula – and her daughter, Charlotte, appreciate that it is a huge part of her life.

Lisa has always been someone who makes decisions quickly and goes with her heart. She grew up in South East London and later moved to Manchester. In March 1997, she met Steve 'over a murky swimming pool' on holiday in Tenerife. They got married six months later and Charlotte was born the following year. 'We got married on the day of Princess Diana's funeral,' says Lisa. 'You can imagine what that was like.'

The year 2013 was decisive for Lisa. She decided to leave her job at the BBC, she was awarded an MBE for her charity work and the girls moved into the new house at Ilamula.

If you spend any time with Lisa, you'll notice she has a little starfish tattoo on her wrist. 'Do you know that story of the starfish, Dan?' she asks.

'We were running a food service in the local squatter camp handing out meals. We had come to the end of our time there and we had given out all the food. There was nothing left. As we were driving away from the camp I looked out of the back window of the van and I saw two young boys running after us holding empty bowls. That is why the work will never end. There will always be a child chasing after a bus, holding an empty bowl.'

That image haunted Lisa until someone told her the story of the starfish.

One day, an old man was walking along a beach that was littered with thousands of starfish that had been washed ashore by the high tide. As he walked he came upon a young boy who was eagerly throwing the starfish back into the ocean, one by one.

Puzzled, the man looked at the boy and asked what he was doing. Without looking up from his task, the boy simply replied, 'I'm saving these starfish, sir.'

The old man chuckled aloud, 'Son, there are thousands of starfish and only one of you. What difference can you make?'

The boy picked up a starfish, gently tossed it into the water and turning to the man, said, 'I made a difference to that one!'

'That's why the starfish is there,' says Lisa. That's why we put the hours in. It's wonderful that we've been able to make a difference to some people. There is so much more we can be doing, but my responsibility, and the question for all of us, is who can we help?'

I am not sure Lisa realises the impact she has on others. The starfish story is an interesting one if you carry it on beyond the child throwing them back into the sea. The man tells his friends and colleagues as the boy continues his work at the beach. The story spreads and, after a few hours, others are helping him. Eventually there is a crowd, all carefully putting the starfish back in the sea. Pictures and videos are shared on social media, the local paper and TV station get involved. The 'human interest' story goes national and a marine biologist starts thinking about a way to stop the starfish all ending up on the beach. A local councillor starts a 'Save The Starfish' campaign and then other coastal towns around the country follow their example.

Change starts right where you are. For Lisa that was meeting Winnie and, as she said, her life has never been the same since.

'I have no idea what I'd be doing if I hadn't met Winnie,' says Lisa. 'All I know is that I met her for a reason. There has been so much heartache. We have lost children. We have seen them die. We have been through a lot but, alongside that, there has been so much fulfilment and joy. It's not a job, it's my life.'

I don't know about you, but I find Lisa, and Winnie, to be an incredible source of inspiration. They make me question all my priorities in life. We can all convince ourselves that we don't have the time to help others. Life is hard, life is busy but there is something truly wonderful about doing something that makes a difference to someone else.

I can still see in my mind all of those children we met at Zenzele. I will never forget scanning across their smiling faces as they sang their hearts out on our arrival. It was a great pleasure to speak to Palesa and hear her talk about a life transformed, hope renewed and trust restored.

There are thousands of Palesa's out there around the world, who need our help. It all starts with a bowl of soup.

'HE WAS MY DAD . . . I LOVED HIM AND I WANTED PEOPLE TO KNOW THAT'

'Ed, do you remember that goal at Manchester United when he was playing against Ronaldo?'

'Yep, we were both there weren't we? I think we were with Mum in the away end. Everyone always used to say a "trademark Gary Speed header" and that was it: flick on from Abdoulaye Faye, and there was Dad at the far post.'

'He made it 1–1, didn't he?'

'Yeah. United won in the end but we were so proud that day. Seventy-odd thousand people inside Old Trafford and our dad scored. I think I must have been about six or seven at the time, but it was amazing.'

Ed and Tommy Speed are both in their early twenties now. Ed was fourteen and Tommy had just turned thirteen when they lost their dad under tragic circumstances.

'Dad was the glue that held the whole family together,' says Tommy who is now studying business management, and playing football, at Adelphi University in New York. 'He was always the one who was running family barbecues, getting people together, telling jokes, organising games. He loved being around people who he loved, and he loved us.'

'We both know that things would be different if he was still here,' says Ed. 'He was everything to us, but we also know we have to get on with life. Tommy and I will never have that father–son relationship but that doesn't stop us loving him and missing him.'

Gary Speed's two sons have never spoken publicly about their dad's death before. I loved working with their dad. I enjoyed interviewing him as a player and he was a friendly, kind and insightful pundit. At the time of his death he was the manager of Wales. He was trying to change the fortunes of his country, and he was turning things around. All that changed on the morning of Sunday 27 November 2011.

The day before his death, Gary had been a pundit on *Football Focus* on BBC One. He was in the studio alongside his good friend and former Leeds United team-mate, Gary McAllister.

Over the course of this chapter, I want to tell you about Gary. I want to tell you about the man that I knew and loved spending time with. His two sons and two of his close friends have agreed to talk about him for the first time since he died.

I want you to know about the man that he was and the hole he left in many people's lives. I want you to hear from the people who loved him, looked up to him and who still struggle with the fact he is no longer here. I want you to know that sometimes, even though you spend years looking, there are no answers.

* * *

'I've got a white shirt or a sort of dark navy one, Dan. What do you reckon?'

'Go with the dark one, Gary. White never looks good on our set.'

'What is Gary Mc wearing? Probably one of those terrible cardigans.'

'Don't know, I'm afraid.'

'Okay, well, I'll see you nice and early and definitely no tie or jacket, right?'

'Definitely. Keep it casual, big dog. See you in the morning.'

Gary Speed would always ring the night before we worked together to check what the dress code was. I think it was because we did a gig at Wembley together many years ago and he had come in jeans and everyone else was in a suit.

I had always found Gary a great person to spend time with. He cared about other people. He was interested in you.

I had first met him when he was at Newcastle United in the 1990s and I started covering football. I interviewed him on the day he arrived at Bolton Wanderers in 2004 and then on his move to Sheffield United four years later. We worked together at various corporate events and we had often shared a studio together covering the game we both loved.

Gary was a wonderful footballer. He could play anywhere down the left side or in central midfield. He was tactically brilliant, renowned for his aerial ability and never seemed to get injured. He took great care of himself and continued to play until he was thirty-nine years old, before eventually moving into management.

Gary McAllister first played with Gary at Leeds. He signed for the club in the summer of 1990, just after they had been promoted to the old First Division. 'I had just turned up from Leicester for a million pounds,' says Gary Mc. 'Gary was the effervescent youngster along with David Batty. Gordon [Strachan] was the leader of that midfield and the four of us formed a great partnership. He was blossoming into a brilliant footballer. I have always been a fan of lefties because you don't see many of them. He was young and fresh and played with this amazing confidence. We got on straightaway.'

The two Garys were part of a brilliant Leeds side that won the First Division title at Elland Road in 1991–92, the season before the start of the Premier League. Gary left Leeds in 1994 to spend a few seasons at Everton before joining Kenny Dalglish's Newcastle United in February 1998 for five-and-a-half million pounds. It was at St James' Park that he became great friends with Alan Shearer.

'I'd played against Speedo many times before but never knew him until he turned up at Newcastle,' remembers Alan fondly. 'I knew he was good, but you could tell from the first training session that his attitude was amazing. He was a brilliant player, but what really stood out was his work ethic and his professionalism. We had a noisy, boisterous dressing room and he fitted in straightaway.'

It didn't take long for Gary and Alan to become good friends. 'We both took our kids to school every day and then we went to the training ground early and had breakfast together,' explains Alan. 'Every day we would sit and talk. He loved Ed and

Tommy. I cannot imagine what those boys have been through. Gary would be very proud if he could see them now. By the way Dan, prepare yourself if you haven't seen Tommy for a while . . . he is the spit of Speedo.'

Alan was right. Tommy looks exactly like his dad. Jet black hair, piercing eyes and incredibly handsome; just like his dad when he was winning the title at Leeds in his early twenties.

'Dad was always around. Every spare minute he would spend with me and Ed. He wanted us to play sport, but it wasn't just football. He supported us in everything. Ed was into his football, but I loved boxing.' Tommy laughs and looks at his brother. 'Dad didn't want Ed to box . . . he was too pretty.'

Ed is the older brother and, as Gary used to say, 'He's like a granddad in a boy's body.'

'Things always came easy for Tommy,' explains Ed. 'He's got all this annoying natural ability and I have to work hard to get anywhere. Dad demanded that of us. He was always there for us both and would tell you straight up if you did something wrong. He had a huge positive influence on the family.'

'Dad used to love coming to watch me box,' says Tommy with a beaming smile. 'He was desperate to win everything he did, but he never put that pressure on me. He just wanted me to try hard. When I was ten or eleven, I was totally into my boxing and Ed was playing football at Wrexham.'

'Guess what, Dan?' Ed jumps in. 'I hate to say it but,' he continues laughing, 'Tommy was really good. I remember we went to this sports hall to watch Tommy once. There was a big undercard but, because Dad was there, there was a real buzz when Tommy was fighting. Lots of people were crowding round and Tommy was taking on this massive lad. He looked like an animal, but Tommy took him to pieces. It was brilliant and Dad loved it.'

There are of course perks when your dad is one of the big stars of the Premier League. 'We used to love watching him play,' explains Ed. 'We started going with Mum [Louise] when he was at Bolton Wanderers. It was amazing to watch your dad play. I watched his goals back on YouTube the other day.'

Tommy supports Arsenal because once, in the tunnel at Bolton, his dad introduced him to Thierry Henry.

'Do you remember that free kick against Liverpool?' chirps Tommy.

Ed nods. 'Yeah, when [Pepe] Reina handled it outside the box. I remember that because I was watching it in the Peacock on the telly. I was playing that day and, after the match, we went to the Peacock to watch the match on the Sunday afternoon, just like always. Ivan Campo tapped the ball to Dad, and he smacked it low, past Reina. It's another one of those moments where everyone looks at you, cos it's your dad, and you just have to smile.'

Gary was a manager's dream. Never injured, always reliable and a leader on and off the pitch. 'He was at least a seven out of ten every week,' remembers Alan Shearer. 'I can't tell you how hard that is, to never have a bad game. That's why every manager loved him. He worked so hard to get the best out of his ability.' Alan chuckles as he remembers pre-season training. 'We all hated Speedo on the first day back because he was always so fit. Always at the front. Always looking round at the rest of us and laughing.'

One of the reasons Gary and Alan got on so well was because they were both meticulous timekeepers. At the World Cup in Brazil in 2014, I was due to meet Alan in our hotel reception at 10 am to walk to the BBC Sport office which looked out over Copacabana Beach. At 9.57 am I was stuck in a long queue for the lift. My phone started ringing and before I even looked at it, I knew who it was.

'Daniel!'

'Yes, Al.'

'Do you know what time it is?'

'Yes, Al. I'm just waiting for the lift. Down in a mo.'

There was a pause on the other end and a low Northeast groan. I knew what was coming.

'Daniel, to be early is to be on time. To be on time is to be late and to be late is unacceptable.'

Gary had the same chronological DNA as Alan. He was early for everything we ever did together. The morning of our final *Football Focus* together, both he and Gary McAllister arrived about an hour before they were asked to be there.

'I was keen to get there early,' says Gary Mc, 'because we hadn't seen each other for a while. Within a few seconds we were back where we left off. Everyone got on with Gary because he was always interested in what you were up to and ye cannae fake that. He was ripping into my cardigan and we were talking about family.'

I ask Gary Mc if he has ever watched that show back.

'No, Dan,' he replies with certainty. 'I don't think I ever could. I can't watch it back. It would be too weird, too hard. Everything about the day felt normal. I've thought about it a lot and the man I talked to that day was Gary Speed. It wasn't an awkward Gary Speed. It wasn't a different Gary Speed. He was there in the room with us. I knew him well enough to know if something was wrong. That was the same guy who loved football, whether it was playing it or talking about it.'

I once had the pleasure of playing against Gary Speed in a charity match. It was an England v Wales 'Legends' game held at Pride Park two months before his death. It was a combination of footballing greats and a few numpties from TV. The whole game was live on ITV4.

There were a couple of things I remember vividly about the game. Harry Redknapp was our manager and told me before the match that I would get, at most, 45 minutes. There was some serious talent in the England team: Dion Dublin, Chris Sutton, Stan Collymore were alongside a number of other well-known pros. I would be sharing the right-back position with none other than Idris Elba.

'What are you like, Dan?' Harry asked, with his arm round my neck in the dressing room beforehand.

'I'm okay, Harry,' I said tentatively. 'I can run a bit and I know which way I'm playing.'

'Did you play a bit as a lad? For a club?' Harry said with interest.

'I played county level, boss, but that's it. I was six-foot-six at the age of twelve so that helped.'

'He's useless, Hazza!' shouted Robbie Savage from the Welsh end of the dressing room. 'Like Bambi on ice.'

Harry laughed and looked at me and Idris thoughtfully, with his hand on his chin: 'Right . . . I'll start with Idris at right-back because he was in *The Wire* and you weren't, Dan. Okay?' It sounded like as good a reason as any to start me on the bench.

Next to Savage in the dressing room was Gary Speed. I remember looking over at him and laughing because, while my pre-match snack was a Mars Bar and a Drifter, Gary was eating a banana and some sort of weird-coloured nutrition drink. Timekeeping wasn't the only thing Gary was meticulous about.

'He trained every day, and I mean every day,' says Gary's eldest son Ed. 'He was so careful about what he ate and that was one of the things he drilled into me and Tom.'

'Yeah,' remembers Tommy. '"You can't be eating takeaways, lads" he used to say to us. It was always protein after we'd done any exercise and so much water. Water, water, water!'

When Gary got the job as Wales manager, Ed was playing in the Under-16s. 'He would always come to our games, not because I was playing, but because he wanted to see and know everything. He was really big on the sport science side of things and was trying to change the culture.'

Alan Shearer never had any doubt that Gary would become a manager. 'You always get asked that, don't you? Did you think so-and-so would be a manager and Gary was always going to go down that road. He was a student of the game. He worked a lot with Sam Allardyce at Bolton, who was a great innovator, and Gary was all over the stats. He had a good rapport with players and was great at the man management side of things. He was a natural leader.'

'It was always salmon, jacket potato and peas, wasn't it, Tom?' recalls Ed. 'Tommy was a little pasta machine, but Dad used to say, "You can't live off pasta."'

Tommy continues, 'I remember getting weighed for a fight once. I was meant to be forty-two kilos and I came in at forty-three-and-a-half. Dad was not happy. I had to work my butt off for a few hours to get the weight down. I think I got a pasta ban after that.'

It's lovely to watch the boys laugh as they remember their dad.

'I always remember what he was like after a game,' says Ed. 'If you didn't play well, he would tell you, but he would help you get better. It was never just negative. One of our coaches at Wrexham, one day he got all the lads together and he told us we had to stop listening to our parents and listen to him instead if we wanted to get better. I told that to Dad and he laughed and said, "Shut up, listen to me." He was always there if there was something you needed. He would tell you how it was.'

'It wasn't just sport though, was it, Ed?' recalls Tommy. 'I was always the smarter one and Ed would always try hard at school.' Ed acknowledges his brother's playful tongue in cheek with a big smile on his face. 'Seriously though, Ed would be getting the top grades, ones and twos, and I got a run of threes once and got grounded for weeks. Dad demanded that we worked hard.'

Ed jumps in. 'I used to love parents' evening,' he chuckles. 'Mine would always go well and Dad's face was always different after talking about Tommy. I used to enjoy that.' This time it's Tom's turn to laugh and nod knowingly.

The brothers are great friends. It's obvious how well they get on and, despite the gentle sibling jabs, they clearly love each other deeply and they both know how hard it is to lose a father who was such an integral part of their lives.

I ask them about how their dad's advice affects them now, after nearly a decade without him.

'We have both learned so much from him and Mum,' continues Ed. 'I'm always thinking "what would Dad do?" or "how would Dad deal with this?"'

'That has helped us a lot,' Tommy nods in agreement. 'Definitely.'

'When I get criticism, I listen to it,' says Ed, 'but it doesn't drag me down. I can shrug it off. I learnt that from Dad. He was tough but always positive.' Ed smiles and looks up. 'I can still hear his voice in my head. That will always be a part of us.'

We are ten minutes into England *v* Wales at Pride Park and Harry Redknapp wanders over to the bench. 'Get warmed up, Dan. Idris is getting torn a new one by big Joe [Calzaghe]. He looks like a massive spider. You're on.'

After trotting on, my first job is to take a throw-in. I distinctly remember being berated by Stan Collymore for not giving it straight to him and instead choose to go safely back to Dion Dublin at centre-half. Such is the ferocity of Stan's language that a significant swathe of the East Stand at Pride Park lets out an audible gasp.

These charity matches are always interesting. You get two types of 'celebrity' playing in them. I am in the first category: those who are happy to be there, love the game, but aren't going to take it too seriously. The second category is for those who fancy themselves as a player, think they could have made it, and want to try and put on a show against the professionals.

Normally in these games, the pros potter around at about 10 per cent capacity, occasionally showing a touch of class or pinging a pass that only comes from someone who has spent a lifetime perfecting the skill.

Gary Speed is doing exactly that in the middle of the Welsh midfield. He is having a giggle, pulling down Robbie Savage's shorts and hardly getting a sweat on. Our midfield is made up of angry Stan and TV star Jeff Brazier, who is a quality footballer.

Jeff is keen to show off a few little tricks and flicks. On one occasion he manages to flick the ball between Gary's legs. Gary laughs. About a minute later, Jeff tries it again and is again successful, only this time he shouts 'megs' and laughs as he does it. I look across our defence and Dion Dublin is sucking his teeth. Jeff has crossed the charity match line and Gary is understandably a little miffed. At the next set-piece he jogs over.

'Dan, tell your man there that if he tries that again, it won't be pretty.'

*   *   *

'That sounds like Speedo,' chuckles Shearer as I re-tell him the story of that day. 'I don't know many pros who would have given him a warning, Dan.'

That game was one of the first things that Gary mentioned on that morning we did *Football Focus*. He asked me if I'd recovered from marking Joe Calzaghe. (If you're interested, England won the game 6–0 and I managed to successfully stifle the Welsh wizardry of Calzaghe.)

I have been over that Saturday morning with Gary thousands of times in my head. I have woken up in the middle of the night on many occasions. I have been driving down the M1 or up the M6 and missed my junction.

I have pored over everything that was said before, during and after that show. I've talked it through with Gary Mc but still we both have so many questions. 'I've thought a lot about what he said that day,' he told me. 'I have gone over it a lot and I can't get away from the fact that he was just the same Speedo I had known for twenty years.'

Like Gary Mc, I have over-analysed every pause, every look, every question, every conversation I can remember. I recall asking Gary how he was dealing with the stress of management while we sat enjoying a cup of tea. He took about five seconds to answer. Why did he take so long? Was he stressed about work? Did he want to talk about it? Could I have helped him that day?

He made a joke about how uncomfortable the sofas in the green room were. They were vile. There was a big wooden strip that ran through the middle of both of them and you could feel it digging into your bum no matter where you chose to sit.

The conversations from that day have been rattling around my head for the best part of a decade. Gary Mc asked him how life was treating him, and he answered quickly and then changed the subject back to ask about Gary Mc's family. (Gary Mc had lost his first wife, Denise, to cancer back in 2006.) That was Gary's way. He was always more interested in talking about other people.

We talked about golf – a lot – about how his boys were developing as footballers, about Tommy's boxing and his dreams of taking Wales to a major championship.

Part of Gary's charm was that he cared. 'How are you finding Sheffield, Dan? I loved my time there. Are you and the kids settling in okay? I bet Sarah [my wife] loves being back home, right?'

As we wandered into the studio for the show, one of the camera operators on the floor of the *Football Focus* studio said 'hi' to Gary and mentioned that he went to the same school as him in North Wales. The pair of them were laughing and joking about the day the Queen turned up. Apparently, there is a picture of Gary, fellow alumni Michael Owen, and Her Majesty still proudly on the wall in reception.

The two Garys were brilliant that day. Once *Focus* had finished, we recorded a ten-minute piece with Speedo talking about Wales' qualifying campaign for the next major championships. He spoke with passion about each fixture. He talked in great detail about the various teams they would face. His hope was that the upturn in form would see his team playing in front of a full crowd again. Wales were on a great run under Gary and he joked about Team GB and how Scotland would be an easy game, as McAllister giggled.

He was so hopeful about Wales' future and he sounded so proud that he was the man leading the team. At the time, no one had pulled on the red shirt more than Gary and he was desperate to take his team to a major championship for the first time in what seemed like an age.

'I'm just popping upstairs to see Al [Shearer], Dan. I'll see you up there in a mo,' he said after the show.

'Yes, Gary. I'll be with you in a minute. I think he's going to Old Trafford to watch Newcastle, but he'll be around for a bit.'

About ten minutes later I followed Gary up the one floor to the *Match of the Day* production office. He and Gary McAllister were in there chatting with Shearer and Mark Lawrenson. They were having a laugh and watching the early game that day – Stoke City against Blackburn Rovers.

'So, will you call me next week, Gaz and we'll try and meet up next Friday?' said Alan as he started putting his coat on to get to Old Trafford in time for the game against Newcastle United.

'Yes, Al. I'll bring Louise.' The Speeds were going to Newcastle to attend Alan's foundation dinner. Gary was always there when Alan asked him. He was Mr Dependable.

'He came every year,' says Alan. 'He was a good friend. He was someone you could rely on to be somewhere if he said he would. He always supported my foundation and that meant an awful lot to me and the people we look after.'

They shook hands and then Alan put on a rather ridiculous hat. It was part disguise, part essential clobber, on a particularly chilly November afternoon. As was dressing room etiquette, Al was mercilessly ribbed for his headwear, before firing off a few insults of his own and leaving. There were broad smiles on everyone's faces.

'I'd better get back to Sheffield too, lads,' I said, gathering my things. Gary gave me a long, warm handshake, looked me in the eye, and said, 'Thanks for today, Dan.'

'We might even have you on again soon,' I joked.

Gary giggled. 'I'll call you on Monday and we'll organise a game of golf, okay?'

'Great,' I responded. 'You can come over to Sheffield or I'll come to you. Let me know Monday.'

And that was it. Monday never came for Gary. We never saw him again.

'I texted him straight after the show finished to say that it was the best I had ever seen him on TV,' says Melissa. 'He was relaxed, comfortable and he looked like he was really enjoying himself.'

Melissa Chappell was Gary's agent and always spoke to him after a show. She and Gary trusted each other from the start. Mel knew her football, was well connected and opened doors for Gary straightaway.

'Gary was desperate to take Wales to a major tournament,' she says, 'but he wasn't always happy with the way things were going away from the pitch. He was all about the detail and wanted the best for his players. When he first went into the job, he was frustrated by a lack of professionalism from those in charge and was keen to make sure that the infrastructure matched his ambition. There were a lot of battles about hotels, flights and simple things like players' diets. Gary was very popular and could have easily walked into a coaching role in club football. Newcastle, Everton and Bolton were all potential options at the time. TV companies were also keen to sign him up on a contract if he wanted to be a pundit. He had the footballing world at his feet.'

Gary had spoken to Mel on the Thursday of that week to change the dates of a family holiday to Dubai at Christmas. He had asked her to book an extra week as a treat for the family.

'I sorted that out,' explains Mel, 'and the only other thing I told him was to remember to smile when he went on *Focus* on the Saturday. I always said to him that he should do more of that when he was on TV. He had a great smile and it helped people engage with him. I texted him after the show to say "well done". I thought he looked like he'd had a great time. It was the best performance of his TV career.'

Gary never responded to that text. He always responded. Mel went to a friend's house for dinner that night in London. She left her phone in the back room but popped out to check for a message from Gary.

She knew that Gary had spent the afternoon with his family

and was out for a meal with Louise and some close friends. 'I didn't want to disturb him. By the time the night had finished it was midnight and, even though I was concerned he hadn't responded at all, I knew it was too late to call, and I left it.'

His two boys, Ed and Tommy, will never forget that weekend.

As usual, they had spent the Saturday afternoon playing football. 'I remember it vividly,' recalls Ed. 'Mum and Dad went out for the night and me and Tommy had a few friends over. As they left, Dad reminded us to make sure we were in bed by midnight and that was it.

'The next morning, I was woken up by Mum screaming for me, or just screaming, I can't quite remember. She was outside and she had seen Dad through the window of the garage. I ran downstairs and she was struggling to breathe and talk. You know, you don't want to see your mum like that. No one does. She was just in shock. She told me not to look in the garage but . . . ,' he pauses, 'it still haunts me what I saw . . . Dad suffering like that.' Ed is composed and calm as he goes through that awful morning. Tommy is watching him intently.

'I went back out to Mum and we called the ambulance. I wasn't really thinking about what was happening, I just knew I needed to help Mum. We were in the kitchen speaking to the person on the other end and they talked us through what to do. It was just so unexpected. A complete and utter shock. I couldn't really comprehend what was going on but at the same time I had so many questions.'

'Is that when you came upstairs to see me?' asks Tommy.

'Yes,' replies Ed. 'Mum and I knew we had to go and tell Tom.'

Tommy jumps in, 'They came into my bedroom and woke me up. Ed just said, "Dad's gone" and we all hugged. Ed told us that we had to stay strong.'

It's worth remembering that Ed was just fourteen years old.

'I get lots of bum dials,' explains Alan Shearer. 'My name starts with an "A" so I often get people calling me by accident. That's what I thought it was. I had fifteen or twenty missed calls that Sunday morning. In the end, I answered. It was one of Gary's pals. I asked him if he was drunk and had sat on his phone. I must have said, "I hope you're winding me up" hundreds of times. He wasn't.'

Like everyone else who got the news that morning, Al was in total shock. 'I didn't really know what to do so I just started calling people. I honestly can't remember who, or how many people I called, but I was on the phone for ages. Shay Given, Steve Harper, Steve Bruce, I called you a few times, Dan, and Gary Mc because I'd seen him the day before.'

Gary McAllister always says he has a terrible memory, but some things stick in your mind forever. 'It was early. If you're getting a phone call at that time on Sunday morning you know something isn't right. I'll be honest with you, Dan, I lost my legs a little. It hit me hard. My memory is actually vivid in that moment. I can remember looking at the phone, I remember walking out of the bedroom with the phone and answering it in the front room. I don't think either of us knew what to say. We just couldnae believe it.'

I was sat in church in Sheffield. My phone was on silent, but it just kept ringing. I looked across at my wife and mouthed, 'I'm going to have to get this' and strolled to the front door of the building. As I pushed the door open, I saw I had fifteen missed calls and six of them were from Alan Shearer. I thought it was weird and remember going over to the wall by the side of the church. Just like Gary Mc, I could take you now to the exact spot where I was standing when I called Al back. I was next to a waist-high brick wall, overlooking the Porter Brook river in Sheffield. I had left my coat inside and it was freezing so, as the phone rang at his end, I shuffled around to shelter from the wind. Al answered the call quickly.

'Dan. Have you heard about Gary?' He blurted out his words before even saying hello.

'What's happened, Al? Was the show okay?' I was assuming he was talking about Gary Lineker and the previous night's *Match of the Day*.

'No, Dan, it's Speedo,' Alan gasped desperately. I had never heard him so emotional before. 'He's gone, Dan. He's killed himself.'

We talked it through for a few minutes in disbelief. What was happening? I must have asked Alan ten times or more if he was sure it wasn't just a sick joke.

Alan says he can't actually remember a single call that morning. He knows he spent hours on the phone but has no idea what he said. 'I must have just said the same thing to everyone. It was almost like I needed to find someone who would tell me it wasn't true, so I just kept ringing people, almost to check.'

I said goodbye to Al, told him I'd try and ring him later, and trudged home. When I got there, I called Mel Chappell. She couldn't speak. It was one of those conversations where two people just cry down the phone at each other. 'I was at the gym when a friend texted me to let me know. At first, I assumed that, because he was in the car so much, he'd died on a road somewhere. I spoke to his sister Lesley. The family were in tatters. The day still makes no sense to me. The whole thing makes no sense,' recalls Mel.

I was getting loads of messages from the BBC and other news organisations. I needed to get my head straight. 'Mel, what should I do? They want me to write something about Gary. They are asking me to go on the news to talk about yesterday.'

'Right,' said Mel. You could almost hear her pulling herself together and thinking it through. The tears stopped. 'You need to do it, Dan. You need to explain what happened and talk people through what he was like yesterday.'

That's what I did. I kept telling myself I was okay. I was interviewed on the *One O'Clock News* and spent hours writing and rewriting a blog, for the BBC website. I wrote the whole thing, deleted it, wrote it, deleted it, again and again. In the end, it was just a stream of consciousness. At about 4 pm the phone rang. It was Gary McAllister.

'What's happened, Dan?'

Neither of us could explain so we just went through the day in our heads. We were both stunned – a feeling shared by many who heard the news that day.

Gary had a seemingly perfect life. The unusual death of the

modest man of football was impossible to explain. His loss had a massive impact on his peers and his profession, but the ripples were felt far beyond that.

It was front and back page news for the whole week. The entire nation mourned him. His friends and family were crushed. At the centre of that family were his two young boys, Ed and Tommy.

In the immediate aftermath things felt claustrophobic. There were cameras, reporters, questions everywhere. What looked like a wonderful life from the outside had ended far too soon and nobody had the answers.

The assumption was that Gary had taken his own life. The coroner would eventually rule that there was not enough evidence to sufficiently determine whether his death was intentional or accidental but, whatever happened, he was gone.

'I read a lot of the tributes, but I didn't look at anything else. I still don't know why he did it,' ponders Ed as Tommy nods and adds that 'there was just so much support. Craig Bellamy took us to Liverpool's training ground at Melwood for the day and that was a great opportunity to get away. But you never stop thinking about Dad.'

Do they feel any anger towards him?

'I am angry at him sometimes,' says Ed with an understanding look on his face. 'But that is quickly replaced with love. I listened to Kieron Dyer's podcast once and he was asking how Dad could do what he did to us. How he could kill himself with two young boys to look after. I am not angry at Dad though. He filled our life with love and happiness. A lot of kids never get that from their father. So the anger never lasts long. I just miss him. I miss my dad.'

'It feels mean to say I'm angry at him, but sometimes . . . yeah,' adds Tommy. 'But you can't look back and let that eat you up. I still ask questions. We both still ask those questions. We'd be mad not to. Did he know how much suffering he would leave? Did he think about how many lives he was turning upside down? I felt really sad for two years after he died, but I have come to learn that there is nothing we could do.'

Everyone was asking 'why?' There were rumours, claims, stories and experts all over the place claiming that Gary must have been depressed.

'He wasn't depressed,' says Ed with a degree of certainty that has been absent from much of our conversation. 'There was just something in his brain. I have always said I can't quite put my finger on it. Dad had the perfect life, but something was going on, or something happened and, for whatever reason, he didn't look for help. That wasn't him. He would always talk about things but, when it came down to it, he didn't and I don't know why. I can't explain it now because he just had so much to look forward to.'

Tommy is watching and listening to his big brother's every word. This is something they rarely talk about together.

'He loved us,' says the younger sibling. 'That's it. He loved taking us to school, playing football with us, talking about football with us. It was great because he could get us into games. He had so much in his life, and he loved sharing it with me and Ed.'

Tommy stops talking. Neither of the boys speak for a moment.

None of the family spoke about Gary's death for many years. Louise, his widow, just like Ed and Tommy, has spent plenty of time looking for answers. Was it depression? How long had it been going on? He'd written her a letter when he was 17 and a youngster at Leeds United. He'd explained that even though he loved her so much, he sometimes hoped he would never wake up from his sleep.

I still think about Gary a lot. I still wonder if I missed opportunities to talk to him. Would he have wanted to talk? As a friend, I wonder if I could have helped him. As a Christian, I ask myself if I tried hard enough.

I think Gary's death has affected me much more than I have ever allowed myself to see. I think writing this chapter, speaking to his family and friends has shown me that quite clearly.

He has changed the way I think about my job, particularly when it comes to interviewing. His death opened my eyes to the huge subject of mental health in sport. We are far more aware of the issue now but, back in 2011, it was not on the agenda in the same way.

I spend time with a lot of people who must feel a pressure to put on a brave face, to look and feel their best at all times. I remember interviewing Robbie Williams about that pressure many years ago, after he had left Take That. He talked about the need to maintain the façade and make sure people couldn't see the cracks. That has always stayed with me.

Gary's death remains a constant reminder of what can sometimes be going on under the surface. A reminder that wealth and fame do not insulate you from struggle. A reminder that we never know what someone else is feeling behind the smile.

I think he has made me far more careful about the way I interview people. I don't always get it right, but Gary's death has made me very aware of the possibility of inner turmoil. I am not sure I am any better at spotting the signs, but I'm better at looking for them. I often think that when I say goodbye to someone, that might be the last time I ever see them. I know that might sound a little morbid, but I like to think that helps to make me less judgemental and a better listener.

Things have changed a lot in football. I spoke to Frank Lampard recently and he talked about football being in the 'dark ages' on mental health when he was a young professional. Gary McAllister, currently Steven Gerrard's assistant at Rangers, recalls life in a dressing room in the 1990s.

'We just didn't talk about what was going on in our heads. If you did voice any concern, it would have been seen as a sign of weakness. The message from fellow pros was almost always to just "deal with it". It is so different now. Player welfare is a huge part of football and there is so much help around a club. I'd like to think that if one of our players had an issue, they would know they can talk about it and get help. That's the way it should be.'

Gary Mc has also struggled with the loss of someone so close. For the last decade he has steered clear of trying to rationalise what happened. 'You can easily get wrapped up in horrible thoughts and I don't think that helps anyone,' he says. 'The thing is, it's simple really, Dan. I just miss him. I miss seeing him. He was good for me, he was good for football.'

Gary was a natural leader. He played over five hundred Premier League matches and, as he matured as a footballer, he took time to look after the next generation of players coming through.

Alan Shearer saw that develop at Newcastle. 'Gary was the one that people went to. He was always there to talk. He would always listen. The younger lads would spend lots of time with him and he saw that as an important role in the team. When he got angry, you knew it was with good reason.'

Alan tells a story about a Newcastle away match down at Portsmouth where Gary lost his temper. I looked it up. It was in March 2004. Newcastle were looking for their first away win in five months and were leading 1–0 going into the last minute.

At the start of that season the Premier League had approved a new loan system which allowed clubs to lend players to each other during the season. At the beginning of February, Newcastle had decided to loan the Congo international, Lomana LuaLua, to Portsmouth and, for some reason, not insisted that he then didn't play against his parent club when the two sides met. Guess who scored the equaliser in the dying seconds? Gary went ballistic in the dressing room, furious that the club allowed LuaLua to play against them and that Newcastle had been denied all three points.

'Like all of us,' explains Alan giggling, 'he hated losing. Football, Scrabble, golf, anything. You don't get to his level without being a winner. He was furious with the club because for him, preparation was everything. That's why he lasted so long as a pro, he left no stone unturned and, in contrast, the club had dropped the ball with LuaLua. He was fighting our corner and we loved him for it. No one had a bad word to say about Speedo. He would never let you down.' That was to be Gary's last season at Newcastle.

Alan shares Gary Mc's view as to what happened that night in November 2011. 'If he was depressed, he was very good at hiding it. We spent a lot of time with each other, talked a lot, and the subject never came up . . . ever. I just think, for whatever reason, he decided to end it all in that split second. I don't think we will ever really know. He was such an energetic personality. He lit up every room. He was happy-go-lucky but serious when he needed to be. He was just a great lad.'

Those who knew Gary best, his close friends and family, seem united in the belief that what happened that night was the result of one bad decision. Gary Mc, Alan and his former agent Mel, all feel that if someone could have got to him that night things could have been different, and Gary would still be here. It was a moment where something snapped and, if someone or something had interrupted that snap, he might never have gone there again. They feel that something misfired, and Gary believed that, for whatever reason, his only way out was to take his own life. That fills them all with a great sadness.

Alan is still close to the family. They used to go to Portugal together and Alan has called Roger Speed, Gary's dad, who now suffers with a form of dementia. When I asked Alan if he was okay to talk about Gary for the first time since his death, he checked it would be okay with Gary's mum, Carol, Louise, and Ed and Tommy. That is his way.

Does Alan feel he could have helped him when he was still alive?

He is thinking, deliberately not wanting to rush his answer. 'I wish I could have helped him. It plays on my mind a lot. It's still tough to comprehend. The last thing I said to him was, "I'll call you on Monday" and I fully expected to see him the following Thursday. I went through a lot of emotions: sadness, loss, anger, guilt . . . everything. In the end, I came to the conclusion that it wasn't about me; that I couldn't explain it. At that moment I switched to thinking about his family. They became my focus.'

I spoke to Alan before I spoke to the boys and he told me they were amazingly level-headed. He reminded me how much they had been through and asked me to tread carefully. He also reminded me that Ed spoke at his Dad's funeral. 'I still don't know how he did it,' remembers Alan. 'What he said was incredible. He was fourteen!'

'I felt like I had to say something,' says Ed when I ask him what that day was like.

'You like being centre of attention, don't you?' laughs Tommy. 'I can't really remember you talking, Ed.'

Ed shrugs off the brotherly dig and continues to explain that his mum asked him if he wanted to say something and it didn't really cross his mind not to. 'He was my dad. I loved him and I wanted people to know that. I wanted to thank him for everything he had done for us and tell people that me and Tommy would make him proud one day.'

I remembered what Gary had said about his eldest son, about him being a granddad in a boy's body. That maturity was shining through. No fourteen-year-old should ever have to address the congregation at his dad's funeral.

At the end of the funeral Grandma Marge – Louise's mum – spoke to the boys and told them that the worst day of their life was over.

There was huge media interest in Gary's funeral and the cameras were on the family again at a memorial match for Gary at the Cardiff City Stadium in February 2012. Wales were taking on Costa Rica. Gary's dad, Roger, spoke to the Wales players before the game in the dressing room and Ed and Tommy led the team onto the pitch that night. At half-time, the family joined friends in one of the large executive boxes overlooking the pitch. There were about two hundred people packed into that room and, at half-time, Ed stood on one of the tables in the middle of the room and someone clinked a glass. A blissful silence fell over the room. You could hear the low hum of crowd noise bleeding through the huge glass windows and the occasional blast of the tannoy system.

'I knew I needed to speak for him,' says Ed.

I have heard some impressive speakers in my time but, I have to say, what I heard in that room that night took my breath away. I know it must have been fuelled by emotion and the occasion, but Ed lit that room up.

The teenager on the table had a piece of paper in his hand but he never looked at it.

'I had read it over and over again to make sure I knew what to say. I wasn't nervous but I wanted to make sure I got it right. I needed to speak for him and for the family. That's what Dad would have done. When I stood on that table, I thought, "Can I show these people how strong me and my brother are?" It's okay to show weakness and cry, but this was about showing that we'd be okay, that we were strong. There was a strength I had inside me and I wanted to let everyone see that and not worry about us.'

'That sounds like a good speech,' says Tommy as he breaks the emotional tension of Ed's recollection. Ed shakes his head at his brother in mock disbelief that he went there. 'Do you remember it?' he asks.

'I missed that one too. I think I was in the toilet,' Tommy giggles. 'I am surprised you were that good because you're normally rubbish in public.' Tommy is pressing for a reaction but the twenty-three-year-old 'granddad' refuses to rise to it.

'It's a good job we get on, isn't it?' adds Ed, after composing himself. 'We've always had a strong bond, especially after Dad died. There are some brothers who aren't like that, but we feed off each other. We've also always been competitive, desperate to beat each other, but that changed without Dad. We both have to be strong for each other.'

One thing that really strikes you when you talk to Ed and Tommy is that they don't feel sorry for themselves. They are both aware that there are many people in a far worse situation than them.

'Lots of people have had a tough time losing members of their family,' says Tommy. 'We are not alone in that. People grow up without parents all the time. Mum lost her husband. Les lost a brother. Roger and Carol lost a son they adored. It's horrible. They have been through so much. They supported him through everything and loved him to pieces.'

The year after Gary died, Ed's best friend also lost his dad and that again hit Ed hard. For a while he stopped trying at school the way he always had. Nothing seemed to matter. He went from the being the kid who always grafted, to the one who didn't bother and messed about. He just scraped the grades he needed to continue his studies in America.

I am keen to know what the pair think about their dad now and ask them to reflect on some of the lessons he taught them.

'I learned everything from him,' says Tommy. 'We have to accept that we will never have that father–son relationship, no matter how much we want it. We know that things would be so different if he was around, but . . .'

Ed jumps in. 'We've got to get on with it, with life. It's hard. You often think, "would he be happy with what we've done?" or "would he be proud?" Sometimes, if I've played a good game of football, I want to look at my phone and see that it's my dad calling to say "well done". When I graduated with a degree in economics in the summer, I would have liked nothing more than my dad to call me and tell me how proud he was. I know he would be. That's all he wanted for us.'

Ed and Tommy are sure that if we were as aware of mental health issues ten years ago as we are now, then their dad would still be here. They both talk about a recent programme they watched which featured Tyson Fury and the former footballer Dean Windass discussing their own struggles.

'With Tyson Fury, you could tell he wasn't healthy mentally. Dad was completely different. He was fit, healthy, social . . . there were no signs. It just wasn't him.'

I wonder if they speak to each other about their own mental health.

'Of course,' says Tommy. 'It's rare for anyone to feel 100 per cent all the time. I would always encourage people to come out to someone, to be honest.'

'I think Dad made me more open,' adds Ed. 'Sometimes, we all need to speak to someone. I know when I'm not feeling myself, I think we all do.'

Tommy asks Ed if he remembers the letter that the deputy head from their school sent to their mum. 'Oh yeah,' says Ed, 'what was his name?'

'It was Mr Hargreaves,' says Tommy. 'He sent Mum a letter when we left school to say that me and Ed were the living legacy of our dad. I think that meant a lot to all of us. It's little things like that, they really make a difference.'

I think Mr Hargreaves hit the nail on the head. When I was first asked to write this book, I was unsure whether I should include Gary Speed or not. When Ed and Tommy agreed to talk about their dad for the first time, that made the decision even harder. Could I do their dad justice? Could I convey their sense of loss and pain but at the same time reflect their love for him? Could we, by telling their story, help someone else going through the same thing?

I started off determined to focus on Gary but, through spending time with Ed and Tommy, it has been my pleasure to discover that they are every bit as remarkable as their father was. His positive traits shine out of the pair of them, they are a credit to their family and talking to them has helped me to come to terms with what happened.

'It would just be nice Ed, wouldn't it,' says Tommy, 'to thank him for all that he did for us both.'

'Yeah,' nods Ed, 'I'd love to know if he thinks we've done okay without him.'

You have, lads. You have.

'ON BEHALF OF THE METROPOLITAN POLICE ... SORRY'

John Sutherland is one of life's encouragers.

He is the sort of person who knows you've had a tough day and sends you a text message at just the right time.

He is a man who always seems to have the right words for the right occasion.

John joined the Metropolitan Police in 1992 and rose quickly through the ranks. He retired in 2018, after a quarter of a century of service.

In 2013, John suffered a nervous breakdown and battled depression.

John Sutherland is one of those people who, even though I don't see him that often, has a regular impact on my life. I love John's Twitter feed. He is a voice of calm in a storm. He is insightful and careful where others are opinionated and brash. John always has an interesting take on some of the most important issues that affect us as a society and, as a police officer, sees the best and worst of us. John is one of those who is often left picking up the pieces. He knows that he has one of those jobs that when he tells people what he does, everyone has a question.

Before joining the police in 1992, John was a roadie for the alliteratively pleasing group called Fat And Frantic. Imagine a cross between The Housemartins and Madness. He started off selling T-shirts and eventually became the stage manager. They were decent, but never quite made it. If you ever want to see them in their element, go on YouTube and type in 'Last Night My Wife Hoovered My Head'. I think you'll be intrigued. That snippet will give you a good idea of what they are all about. Unsurprisingly, John doesn't get asked many questions about his time with Fat And Frantic but the questions never stop when he mentions his time as a copper.

'Children want to know if you've arrested any baddies and adults want to know what the worst crime you've ever seen is. People want to hear your stories. As a society we are captivated by the police. Look at the television schedules, books, documentaries. The work of the police is constantly in the public eye. We are fascinated by it. Everyone's interest is my love.'

John has plenty to talk about. He has seen a lot. Crimes of every colour, hostage negotiations, public meetings, bureaucracy, terror attacks, trauma, distress, all of life and all of death. John joined the force just months before the death of Stephen Lawrence.

Stephen was a black teenager from southeast London who was murdered in a racially motivated attack while waiting for a bus in Eltham on 22 April 1993. After the initial case, five suspects were arrested but not charged. The case called into question both the actions and prejudices of the police and wider society. It eventually led to the partial revocation of the rule against double jeopardy and two of the perpetrators were convicted of murder in 2012.

'I have worked on some high-profile cases which have led to severe criticism of the police – Victoria Climbié, Damilola Taylor and many others – but no case had as much of an impact on my profession as the murder of Stephen Lawrence in 1993. When the findings of the inquiry were published in 1998, it was decided that the Metropolitan Police force was "institutionally racist". I wasn't the only one shaken to my core by that. I spoke to colleagues who felt, "But I'm not a racist and they are telling me that I am." That verdict left a lot of people angry, sad and confused but we had to listen, and we had to learn. How do you rebuild relationships with communities? Were they really "hard to reach"? I remember that, as a force, we started talking about people who were "hard to hear" instead of "hard to reach" but that was also missing the mark. They weren't "hard to hear" . . . it's just that we simply weren't listening.'

I have interviewed hundreds of police officers during my career about everything from basic road traffic accidents to huge court cases and terrorist incidents. John seems to have been blessed with the ability to see the job of a police officer from both inside and outside the force. He loves the job, feels it is essential to a functioning society but is aware of the issues, flaws and misconceptions which surround it.

'You realise very early that policing happens in the hurting places and that in almost every part of society there is injustice and inequality. Look at the racial mix of those stopped, questioned or arrested. Look at the economic background of those who end up in jail. Why is it that more Covid-19 tickets have been handed out to black people than anyone else? As a civilisation, we still have so much to learn and for many years I was on the front line of that.'

Right back at the start of John's police career, on his first day on the job, he made a promise to serve. When you speak to him, all his examples keep coming back to that principle: service.

'That is the word that gets to the heart of what we do,' says John. 'Police officers can't have a bad day, because when they do there are terrible consequences.

'Many in the force feel they are damned if they do or damned if they don't. They are taking a hammering from every side. A copper's lot is to be caught in the middle. You have to remember that beneath that uniform they are people and it can really hurt. Away from work they say, "the only reason I come to work is because I want to help".

'We call it a job like no other and, although so much about the job has changed, fundamentally, the ultimate goal remains the same: to save lives. Whenever I gathered the team together, I would always ask them, "why are we here?" That's what it's all about. The vast majority of officers are with you all the way. Sadly, those are not the voices given great prominence until an officer is killed or a terrorist strikes. You get sympathy and appreciation for about a week and then it all returns to normal.

'When policing gets it wrong it is so damaging and we must always hold it up to the light. The profession must be under the tightest scrutiny and I think every officer understands that, but for all the negative stories I could tell you one hundred tales of heroism and courage under fire that would take your breath away. I would love there to be a better sense of balance in how we look at the police.'

John Sutherland is one of those people who provide balance. I see him a bit like Yoda in a uniform – just a little taller, with more hair and smaller ears.

I first met John when he was in a pulpit and I was in the front row of a church. We were both speaking at a carol service at St Michael's Church in Chester Square in London. It was 2012. John was giving the main address and I had been asked to give one of the readings. One of the other people giving a reading that day leaned over and said, 'I don't know about you, but I haven't been in a church for about fifteen years. Not entirely sure why I've been asked to do this.' They did look a little uncomfortable as they made their way to the pulpit to read an extract from Luke's gospel. It is difficult, even for the best actors, to feign sincerity when the words they are reading, which mean so much to some, have very little personal resonance.

I have sat in a lot of churches over the years. I have heard a lot of amazing preachers deliver amazing messages. When John was invited to the pulpit, I was intrigued to know what his take on the Christmas message would be. I had read in the blurb that he was a Christian and I am sure he was aware that, of the hundreds of people in the congregation, only 20 or 30 per cent would be of the same religious persuasion as him. So how was this former hostage negotiator going to pitch it?

'I remember someone sitting me down before I signed up for the force and saying, "John, you can either be a police officer or a Christian . . . but you can't be both." I like to think that everything I have done has proved that person wrong. The job I was being asked to do was entirely consistent with the job I was trying to do to the best of my ability: save lives, stand up for justice, defend the weak, protect the vulnerable and keep the peace. Those values sounded exactly like what I was taught as a child and what I read about in the Bible each week. I know that some Christians have struggled in the job but for me, it was always in perfect balance. My faith is fundamental to who I am.'

John had the congregation in the palm of his hand that evening. It was perfect. He retold the Christmas message from a police perspective.

'I have always taken to upfront roles. I suppose it started out as a youth leader and then as an officer there were lots of public meetings. I spend much of my life giving briefings to fellow officers and I never feel intimidated by a crowd. I've not had any training as a public speaker, I've just learned as I've gone along. I love interacting with people in the room. I have always found that people respond to honesty and empathy.'

John's address that night was filled with both those things. It was inspired, heartfelt and meaningful and, with his kind permission, you can read it too.

BETHLEHEM POLICE DEPARTMENT
Daily Crime Bulletin (Date obscured)

Briefing for Operation Census

Substantial number of migrants arriving at border during past week – Limited community tension reported – no incidents of note – Large crowds expected in Bethlehem this evening – No intelligence regarding any pre-planned disorder – Terrorism Threat Level remains at 'Severe' – 12 officers on duty – Road Worthy Chariot in for repairs – no replacement available.

1400 hrs

Start of shift. 2 PCs to fixed post at main Town Checkpoint. 2 PCs to ongoing crime scene at Herod's Palace Nightclub (it's next door to Caesar's but a bit rowdier). 2 PCs to constant watch in the cells. Remaining officers out on foot.

1500 hrs

Routine patrols on Bethlehem High Street. Town Centre crowded but peaceful.

1630 hrs

Call to Civil Dispute in the foyer of the Judea Travelodge. Apparent misunderstanding regarding double booking of two suites. Situation deteriorated as it became apparent that there are no other rooms available – anywhere in the neighbour-hood. Couple leave peacefully. Mother is heavily pregnant. 2 other suspects became violent. 2 arrests. We have given them a room for the night here.

1715 hrs

Suspect detained for theft of wine from the Bethlehem Bras-serie. Evidence consumed prior to police arrival. Suspect unfit for interview until tomorrow morning.

1800 hrs

Reports of possible UFO sighting. Claims of a bright light – moving East to West at height of several thousand feet. Area Search – No Trace. Possible Nuisance Call.

1830 hrs

Multiple calls to disturbance on hillside a mile outside town. Reports of strobe lighting and loud music. Initial suspicions of an illegal rave in progress. On arrival, met by gang of shepherds and a large quantity of sheep. Shepherds claiming to having been visited by angels. Despite lengthy enquiries and hillside search, no sound system or lighting equipment found. Thorough search of shepherds revealed no evidence of alcohol or illegal substances. Not even a spliff. Initially threat-ened shepherds with arrest for wasting police time – but settled for a Verbal Warning when they explained that they were leaving anyway. Shepherds last seen running towards Bethlehem Town Centre.

1900 hrs

Call to an impromptu protest outside Bethlehem Town Hall. Discovered a small crowd carrying banners, chanting slogans and demanding Judean independence from the rule of Rome. Dispersed at request of officers without incident – though something tells me we haven't seen or heard the last of them.

1930 hrs

Call from Judea Border Patrol. They have stopped a group of travellers who claim to have come from 'afar'. Have yet to establish where this is. The 3, who appear to be in charge, are well dressed and claim to know something about the earlier UFO report. Search of luggage has revealed a quantity of gold and a container filled with an aromatic and suspicious looking resin. They claim it's not dangerous. Enquiries ongoing.

2015 hrs

Update from Border Patrol. Travellers able to prove ownership of gold – and the resin turns out to be something called myrrh. Checks confirm this isn't a controlled drug. Allowed on their way.

2100 hrs

Call to believed Child Protection case. Reports of newborn baby being cared for in wholly unsuitable circumstances – apparently in a stable, surrounded by livestock and with no heating or running water. Unmarried teenage mother with no obvious means of support aside from someone claiming – without documentation – to be her 'betrothed'. On arrival, found earlier group of shepherds in street outside. Initially threatened them with arrest for Obstructing Police – then saw expression on their faces. Decided to see for myself what was going on.

I've walked this beat for more than 20 years and I've seen most things that this line of work puts your way – but I have no words to describe what I saw last night.

No arrests necessary.

No explanation adequate.

But everything is different now.

By the time you read this, I'll have finished my shift. If you have any questions about this report, you'll find me back at the stable door.

It was one of those pin-drop moments when he finished. I have heard hundreds of Christmas messages, but John's came from a totally fresh perspective. I sought him out afterwards and was keen to let him know that his words were wonderful. Those who populate the pulpit are accustomed to the occasionally meaningless 'thanks for your message' as people leave a church, but I wanted John to know that I was truly thankful.

I can't really explain why, but I asked John for his email address. It is very rare to come across people who are wise, kind, interesting, intelligent; people who have seen a lot, experienced the heat of the battle and are still able to rise above all that froth and see the bigger picture. I knew John would be an invaluable contact. I was right.

John has written two books on his life as a police officer: *Blue* and *Crossing the Line*. If you ever get a chance to read them you will see the story of a man who, despite the world in which he operates, never sees himself as the judge. One of the things I respect about John is that he always tries to understand the story behind the front page. The reasons behind the crime. The person behind the prisoner. John recalls:

'I remember right at the start of my career I was an interviewee on *Songs of Praise*. I was a probationary PC and I went to the scene of my first arrest. I was saying to the film crew that everybody has a story. There are reasons why all of us have ended up where we are. So often, as police officers, we concentrate on the symptoms rather than the cause. Crime is a product of many deep lying factors. Crime is a cry of the heart.

'It is so easy to define a person by the worst thing they have done. I fundamentally believe that what they have done isn't who they are. We have to ask how people get to where we find them. I think it's essential to search for humanity and hope in the worst situations.

'One of my best friends is a twice convicted murderer, Erwin James. I met him at a literary festival. In his book, *Redeemable*, he talks about how a prison psychologist helped him to change his perspective. He was taught that he was born precious and his life was redeemable. There was no excuse for what he had done, for the murders he had committed, but there is a difference between excusing and understanding.'

I ask John how you can find 'humanity and hope' when you turn up to a murder scene and the perpetrator is an eleven-year-old boy?

'All you can do is deal with the crime. There are some young men who are so dangerous that if you don't confront them, someone will die. Society's idea is to lock them up and punish them for life. I have no choice but to confront them, challenge them, sometimes kick their front door down, but I can still do that with humanity. On occasions the job demands that you are physically rough, but you can always be personally decent.

'None of these crimes take place in isolation. There are so many people caught up in it: victims, families, witnesses and the wider community. I have investigated knife murders where there are dozens, sometimes hundreds, of people affected. My mind often goes back to the death of Ben Kinsella.'

Ben Kinsella was a sixteen-year-old student at Holloway College who was stabbed to death by three men in Islington in 2008. His murder led to a series of anti-knife demonstrations and a review of sentencing. The case also received plenty of media attention because Ben's sister, Brooke, was an *EastEnders* actress.

'One of the days I will never forget was sitting in my office with Brooke and Ben's dad, George, moments before the press conference on national TV. How on earth do you find the words to say in that situation? You have to be instinctive. You try to be kind. I was there desperately trying to find the right things to say. I remember looking up at them and they were grey with grief. I looked at George and told him that I was so sorry and that no parent should ever have to bury their son. The only other thing I said to them in that time was to make them a promise: I promised to do everything in my power to make sure no other family had to go through the pain they were currently feeling. They are both very good friends of mine now.'

And those final few words sum up all you need to know about John Sutherland. Even though he met Brooke and George Kinsella at their lowest point, broken by grief, John gave them what they needed. John, as he always seems to, found the right words at the right time. That is his superpower.

It is always a pleasure talking to John but, thankfully, I have not had many regular run-ins with the law over the years. I have, to my shame, a few points on my driving licence for thinning tyres and doing 55 mph in a 50 mph zone. I was once chased down a train by Chinese police officers, a story briefly mentioned elsewhere in this book, and had a gun pointed in my direction in Brazil and South Africa, but I have only once come close to arrest in the UK.

The year was 1996 and I was walking home from a mate's house in Sheffield after a party. I was a student there at the time and the party had been at the home of a few future dentists. I have no recollection of how we got on to this conversation, but there was an argument going on, among the dental students, about whether it was better to brush your teeth with a normal toothbrush or one of those fancy electric ones.

It was one of those pointless arguments you tend to have in the early hours when strong opinions come out about stuff that doesn't really matter. One of the students appeared with a large box of supplies they had recently received from Colgate. There were hundreds of toothbrushes in there and, as someone whose tooth hygiene wasn't impeccable, I jumped at the kind offer of taking a dozen of the fresh brushes back home with me.

I left the house shortly after and started the twenty-minute stroll back to my halls of residence. As I got to Hunters Bar roundabout in Sheffield, I was desperate for a wee, so I quickly jumped into Endcliffe Park to seek relief behind the wall just inside the main gates. I emerged from behind the wall to a flashlight in my face. 'Police ... raise your hands!' came the shrill cry. I did as requested and asked what the problem was.

'What are you doing in the park?'

I explained that I had taken a leak behind the eight-foot wall and was on my way home.

'Is there anyone who can confirm where you have been for the last few hours?' asked the officer.

'I've been at a house party in Greystones since about 9 pm. I can tell you the address,' I offered tentatively.

It transpired that the officers were searching for someone who had been breaking into a series of shops along Ecclesall Road in Sheffield. A number of witnesses had called the police and told them they had seen a man running into Endcliffe Park.

He was wearing a beige coat. I was wearing a beige coat. And one of the shops he had stolen from was a pharmacy . . . .

'What's that in your pocket?'

I couldn't see the officer's face because the light was still in my eyes. I assumed he was referring to the large bulge in my inside coat pocket.

'Can you carefully, with one hand, show us what that is?'

I cracked an awkward smile. 'You're not going to believe this but it's a twelve-pack of toothbrushes.' As requested, I cautiously removed the dental aids from my coat pocket, and carefully placed them on the floor. I was in the middle of giving a detailed, painful and, judging by their reaction, remarkably unconvincing account of who had given me the toothbrushes – and why I hadn't nabbed them from the pharmacy around the corner – when their radios went. Another pair of officers on the other side of the park had found the man they were looking for hiding in a bush. He was also wearing a beige coat and had a lot more dodgy gear on him than me. The light was lowered, and I was allowed to continue my stroll home.

My meetings with John have been a lot more positive and the second time we crossed paths came in the build up to Christmas in 2015. I was hosting the afternoon show on BBC Radio 5 Live and we were working on a special programme which was dedicated to the problem of knife crime in London. The whole show was going to be coming from a community centre on a housing estate in Hackney in London. Fifteen teenagers had been stabbed to death in London that year. Across England and Wales, assaults involving knives were up 15 per cent on the previous years. This was a huge problem and, over the course of a few hours of live radio we would be speaking to reformed gang members, survivors, mothers who had lost their sons, community leaders, affected residents and John, who was representing the police.

It was an emotional afternoon. I was really struck by a young man called Abraham who had survived an attack and had the huge scars to prove it. The only thing he thought about while he was lying in hospital was revenge. He was annoyed he hadn't been carrying a knife before, annoyed at the people who told him there was 'another way' and, in his own words, desperate to 'bring that same sharp pain' onto somebody else. Abraham painted a really clear picture of why it was so hard not to fall into the knife-carrying culture and why so many of his peers never left home without one. It was 'keys, wallet, phone, knife.'

Thankfully, Abraham spent some time with a youth leader who changed his life and he saw that there was another way that didn't lead to prison and is now trying to help others.

One of other guests was a mother who had lost her son to knife crime. It was heart breaking to hear her story of how her son had been 'taken away from the life he wanted to lead.' She was understandably angry and, over the course of a few minutes, that rage poured out. She was angry with her son's friends, with him, with his school, with the leaders in the community, with the government, with the local council and with the police. At so many steps along the way she felt her son could have been saved or the situation could have ended differently. She was also angry that things weren't changing, and her son's death felt pointless and meaningless and that made the pain even deeper.

John was also in our circle of guests that day. I was watching him carefully while she was speaking. His eyes never left her. He was oozing empathy. He cared. At the end of her impassioned speech he looked at me, gently raising his eyebrows, asking to respond.

'First of all, and most importantly, on behalf of the Metropolitan Police . . .' There was a pregnant pause as he waited for eye contact. 'Sorry.'

He said it slowly, powerful, purposefully. It wasn't followed by a 'but'. The emotional tension in the room suddenly lifted. The broken mother bowed her head and started to cry. That was the one word she hadn't heard from anyone in authority since her son had died. That was the one word she was desperate to hear. It didn't take the pain away or make things any easier, but it showed that John was not only listening, but that he heard what was being said and he understood what she was going through.

The subject of knife crime is something I have covered a lot over the last few years on both TV and radio and that afternoon was, by some distance, the most constructive time I have witnessed on the subject. That was down to John and he remembers that day well.

'We live in a world that is hopelessly adversarial. We are consumed with trying to win an argument or land a blow. That poor mother didn't need to hear a defence of police methods.

The last thing she needed was to hear me pontificate on the various reasons why her son died. He wasn't around anymore, and she was suffocating in that loss.

'A few months ago, I was on *Newsnight* talking about domestic violence. The whole piece was about the mistakes made by police in the build-up to a particularly awful incident. Emily Maitlis, who is brilliant at her job, was in the presenter's chair, and I could tell that the tone of the interview was going to be: the police have failed, what have you got to say about it? That was essentially her first question.

'She expected me to go toe to toe. I think that's why I was there. I responded by saying, "How could the victim feel anything other than anger about how her case had been dealt with?" I think I successfully diffused the situation and prevented the interview from becoming the normal argument about mistakes made. An argument that never seems to end.'

In a world where so many of us are interested in building walls, John is carefully building bridges. 'It doesn't always work,' he says honestly. 'During the London riots of 2011 I was keen to go and meet community leaders to try and listen to them and answer questions. I was speaking at the front of one of these meetings in Camden and a man stood up and yelled at the top of his voice, "I HATE YOU. EVERYBODY HATES YOU!" I think about that a lot. He was referring to my uniform, and what that represented, but it was heartfelt hatred. The following week I was at another community meeting but, this time, there were a lot of vicars and pastors in the room. I was retelling the story of what was shouted at me and one of them stood up and shouted, "I LOVE YOU. EVERYBODY LOVES YOU." It's about the voices that we amplify and it's often the voices of hate that we give too much prominence to. The good stuff doesn't make the airwaves. The positive voices don't make as good a story and that concerns me.'

Domestic violence and knife crime are two of areas where John Sutherland has particular expertise. However, in recent years, like every other police officer, terrorism has come into a much sharper focus for him too.

My next interaction with John came in the weeks after the Westminster Bridge attack of 2017. Five people, including PC Keith Palmer, were killed that day after a car driven by a terrorist mounted the pavement on the bridge and drove into pedestrians. The car then crashed into a barrier outside the Palace of Westminster. The knifeman got out and began running towards Parliament. He was confronted by PC Palmer, who was wearing a protective/stab vest but was not armed. The police officer was attacked and killed with a knife before his assailant was shot dead by armed officers.

Along with PC Palmer, Aysha Frade, a British national, and US tourist Kurt Cochran, were killed in the attack. Leslie Rhodes, from Clapham in south London, died from his injuries the next day and Romanian Andreea Cristea, who fell from Westminster Bridge into the River Thames, died more than two weeks later.

Ever since I first met John, I have read a lot of what he writes.

His books, his blogs and his social media updates. They are particularly pertinent when the police are involved in a major incident.

That attack took place on 22 March 2017. Two weeks later, I was asked to host what was called the 'Service Of Hope' live on the BBC. It was to take place in front of 2,000 people, including all of the families of the victims, at Westminster Abbey on 5 April.

The programme was scheduled to run for just under an hour. There would be a pre-recorded piece to camera outside the church, which we'd film in the morning, but the rest of the service would be voiced live from one of the tiny rooms at the side of the main chapel. This was a huge responsibility. There would be millions of people watching at home and every word had to be perfect.

It could never sound rushed or hurried and had to fit in perfectly with the speakers, the readings and the carefully chosen music. It had to frame an incredible solemn national event. There are many jobs that I do where you can get away with a stray word or a phrase that doesn't quite hit the mark. This was not one of them. Everything was perfectly timed to the nearest second, everything had been carefully choreographed and everything would be ruined if I got it wrong.

I needed assistance from someone who always found the right words for the right moment. I went to John. Early in the service I read these words from his blog on the attack on Westminster Bridge.

They are brave. Dear God, they are brave. They are the headlong rush of blues and twos: the first to the scene; the first to the chase; the first to confront; the first to protect. They are the first into harm's way. And, sometimes, they pay the greatest price of all.

I had been struggling for a few days to find the perfect words to finish the programme. I knew I couldn't better what John had written so I asked him if I could use his.

This is what I wrote to conclude the service:

And as the Royal party leave, the rest of the congregation will soon be departing the abbey too.

Even though the events of Westminster bridge are still raw, today was all about looking forward with hope. We have heard powerful words from the lectern and, our cellist was playing from the nave where you'll find the Winston Churchill memorial.

Churchill often has a quote for an occasion like this: 'My hope is that the generous instincts of unity will not depart from us.'

I don't think they did hashtags in Churchill's day, but you could easily imagine a 'We Are Not Afraid' hashtag being added to that.

The Duke of Cambridge has reminded us from Luke's gospel of the Good Samaritan. The lesson of the good neighbour was 'the one who showed mercy' and we are all encouraged to 'go and do likewise'.

Today has been about remembering those who lost their lives a fortnight ago, but also paying tribute to those who saved others from death and injury . . . those who ran towards the trouble when instinct tells us to run away.

We heard earlier from Chief Superintendent John Sutherland who wrote in his blog about the police officers he works with. He concluded with this:

'Policing offers a repeated invitation into the darkness – and a consequent challenge to give up on hope.

'There are still lives to be saved. And lost folk to find. And vulnerable people to protect. And men of violence to be faced down.

'Two weeks ago, in the face of the unthinkable, we discovered and expressed a renewed sense of appreciation for the men and women who stand on the thin blue line.

'As we watch this today there are still questions to answer, investigations to run and people who need protecting.'

I hope this service of hope has given you the opportunity to reflect this afternoon.

The light shines in the darkness, and the darkness did not overcome it.

Thanks for watching.

Goodbye from Westminster Abbey.

John texted me that evening to say that his mum was one of those watching and she was in tears knowing that his words were used on such an important occasion.

'It was a real privilege that you included me in that day because Keith Palmer was one of those people, I never met him, but I knew him. Police are a family. You feel a loss to the very depths of your being. I can't watch the footage from that day. I can't even look at the photographs. I find myself thinking a lot about the first armed officer on the scene that day. He arrived after PC Palmer had been fatally stabbed. He gave CPR to the terrorist. Imagine being in that situation. Imagine being that man. Trying to save the man who had done that. That is the job of a police officer. To serve.'

If you ever get the opportunity to speak to John Sutherland, you'll realise that his empathy is both a blessing and a curse. There is a reason why he can't look at the footage or the pictures from the Westminster Bridge attack: trauma affects him deeply. His job became a huge part of his life from the moment he started.

John loved his early training at Hendon. He talks about everything feeling like it was heading in the right direction, like there was a purpose, but he was desperate to start doing the job, walking the beat. The first eighteen months of his career were the only time he didn't love and that was because it wasn't a professional challenge. He then got sent to Brixton, and that is where what he calls 'the adventure' began. He loved every moment of it. It became both a duty and a joy. Did it take over his life?

'To an extent, yes. The shift patterns, the early starts, I rarely had more than one weekend in three off. My friends would be heading off to parties and I would be heading off to work. You can't be a half-hearted police officer. The job is an affair of the heart and the soul. It fills your thoughts almost constantly. I was speaking to a GP friend of mine recently and she has an interesting theory about compassion and empathy. From watching many colleagues over many years, she believes that, in a profession like that, if you are compassionate you survive. If you are empathetic, then you take far more upon yourself and, from her experience, those are the ones who are crushed by the job. Those are the ones who leave early. You almost can't help yourself. That sounds a lot like me.'

It all became too much for John in 2013. Eventually he was away from work with depression for seven months and has never been able to return to the same job.

'At the point I broke, I had been a police officer for just over twenty years. There had been a long, slow build-up of trauma and sadness; things I had seen, things I had heard, situations I had been in. Much of my understanding of what happened to me is retrospective because, at the time, I didn't know what was going on.

'The final, serious stage of the illness was two months of crippling anxiety and exhaustion. In that time there were extraordinary panic attacks and night terrors. I'd had anx- iety on numerous occasions in my life, but it was always the normal healthy feeling over an exam, a presentation, an arrest or something like that; this was totally different. I was off for seven months. I spoke to a colleague who had joined the police from the military. He had already suffered from PTSD before he came to the police and he said he "learned to live alongside it". I think that is how I see it too. I am not the same person I used to be seven years ago. I loved being a hostage negotiator, I loved being in charge of operations, but I can't do any of those things anymore. I still struggle really badly with trauma. That is the legacy of mental illness.

'You could offer me all the money and wealth in the world and I wouldn't volunteer to go back and go through that anxiety and those panic attacks again, but I also wouldn't give up what I have learned as a consequence of going through all that.'

Every conversation with John has taught me something. I have learned so much from him and he makes a difference to the job that I do, the questions I ask and the way I see my role in the media.

I have learned that we owe a remarkable debt to police officers. I have a better understanding of the job they do and the high standards they are required to keep.

I remember studying Robert Peel, the man behind the modern police force, at school many years ago. He always envisaged that the police are the public and the public are the police. As John says, 'You do what you do with the consent of the people that you serve. Every day we are standing shoulder to shoulder with Mrs Miggins at number 23. Never forget that.'

I've also learned that the police feel austerity has hit the force hard. John is not one for excuses but he is also aware of the figures. Between 2010 and 2018, there were around 21,000 officers cut from police numbers. John points out that if you add in other police staff, community support officers, crime intelligence analysts and researchers, that total rises to 44,000. 'You have to ask yourself,' says John, 'if you can take that many people out of a public service and think it'll be unchanged.'

John will also passionately tell you that, whatever walk of life you are in, you can make a difference. 'Look at domestic violence,' argues John passionately. 'Domestic violence is the other pandemic. So much of our attention has been on coronavirus but some of the most vulnerable are more vulnerable than ever before and it is ripping families apart. Coronavirus is not causing domestic violence, but it is showing us the stark reality of it all. How do we even begin to tackle a huge problem like that? People say it costs too much, that we can't afford the investment needed. I would argue that we can't afford not to invest in these things. We are always saying things are too difficult and that change will demand too much of us. We need to be prepared to do whatever it takes, whatever the cost. It is not that people don't care about what happens outside their own lives and family, it's that they don't know. Policing offers a view of the very worst and the very best of people. If more people knew, I think they would want to make a change.'

If you ask John what his favourite word is, he'll tell you it is 'hope'. That sums him up. Despite all he has seen and all he has been through – both personally and professionally – John Sutherland is a man who concentrates on the positives. For every life lost, John will point to the many lives which have been turned around.

I have also learned from John that the police know they have a problem. When I spoke to him for this book, it was a few weeks after the death of George Floyd in America, a death that sparked protests all over the world and the Black Lives Matter movement. John found himself agonising over his death. Part of his agony was that, as a white man, it was seemingly impossible to say the right thing.

'There must be a way of saying something that simply expresses humanity,' says John passionately. 'So many of us look at the death of George Floyd, and many others, and know that things need to change. I hope that will be the case. The fallout from his death took me back to a conversation I had with a friend after my breakdown. He told me my problem was that I cared too much. I still can't see how that can be a problem. I still care, I will always care, but I try and do it now without it taking over my life.

'We sometimes use force and get it wrong,' he says with a heavy heart. 'When police officers get it wrong there are huge consequences. There are sometimes immediate consequences, but they can also be generational with huge numbers of people having a poor opinion of policing. We need to listen to their views. We might just learn something. We also need to ask, "Who is standing up for policing in this country?" We have a relentless focus on the negative, but we shouldn't shy away from acknowledging the times when the police officers get it right.'

I will leave the final words in this chapter to John. I asked him about his time as a hostage negotiator and why he was drawn to the role.

'The coordinator would call you if there was a job and, without saying anything else, he would ask, "Are you ready to save a life?" As someone who believes in solutions, I always found that inspiring. Being a hostage and crisis negotiator was a great privilege. Much of it was mundane. It was very rare that you came across a bank robbery gone wrong. Normally you were dealing with people who had gone through the worst day of their lives.

'The hostage training course was the best thing I have ever done in my life. You are involved in the greatest duty that a police officer could ever have. The greatest privilege is to save a life. Nothing compares to that.

'In that moment, adrenaline takes over and your sense of professionalism kicks in. Your view narrows and you learn to just focus on the track in front of you, like a sprinter. The crowd, the stadium, the ambient noise all becomes irrelevant. You just focus on the job in hand. You have to conduct a negotiation through a closed door. While talking is important – the thing that really matters is listening.

'We live in a world where we are beginning to lose the art

of listening. We have divided ourselves and we spend our time just shouting at each other from further and further apart.

'Listening is the beginning of hearing, hearing is the beginning of understanding and understanding is the beginning of hope.'

DANGER: CIVILIANS IN CAMP BASTION

December 2013 was a strange month. It started for me in Brazil and ended in Afghanistan. It began in the resort of Costa do Sauipe, in Bahia, where the draw for the 2014 World Cup in Brazil was taking place. The hotel was packed with international luminaries and famous faces from football.

Aside from the draw itself, there are two things that I remember vividly from that trip. The first was the announcement of the death of Nelson Mandela. We had come so close to getting an interview with the former South African president during the World Cup in South Africa in 2010 but, sadly, we couldn't make the logistics work. I recall sitting on my hotel bed reading through thousands of tributes to Mr Mandela.

The other thing which sticks in my mind was a trip which we had been planning for months. While we were in Brazil, the final confirmation came through from the Ministry of Defence that we would be able to fly to Afghanistan over Christmas to film a special programme with British troops in Camp Bastion.

I don't think *Football Focus* has ever been presented from a war zone before, so you can imagine there were quite a few security hoops to jump through and forms to fill out in order to make it happen. Eventually we were ready to go, with pundits John Hartson and Kevin Kilbane in tow.

We had already gone through a rigorous regime to make sure we were fit for travel. John, Kevin and I, along with producer Dave Purchase and cameraman Mark Thorne, had been physically assessed by the army and had attended a 'Hostile Environment Training Course' to prepare us for the worst-case scenario, such as one of us getting shot or being captured.

It was an eye-opening few days spent running round the woods with fake guns, getting held up at gunpoint by Hartson – who was very convincing as a member of the Taliban if you were willing to ignore his Welsh accent – and learning how to tend to various wounds. Obviously, a real-life scenario would be entirely different, but we managed to successfully treat all the victims of a helicopter crash, and Kevin and I saved a man from a fake gunshot wound to the chest with a credit card and some gaffer tape.

The most sombre part of the course was the session we had with a man who had twenty years plus experience of life in the SAS. His insight was both humbling and mind-blowing. Every time I watch a TV show or film now and someone takes cover from gunfire behind a car, I annoy my wife by telling her 'there is no way that would give you any protection in real life. The bullets from an AK-47 would go straight through that'.

My biggest takeaway was that Kevin Kilbane is remarkably calm under pressure. If I ever wanted a former footballer to apply a tourniquet to my leg while taking fire and being shouted at by a superior officer, he'd be my first choice. As for John

Hartson, as much as I love the big fella, he would not be on the list. I still can't get the image of him trying to stop the flow of fake blood from our instructor's groin out of my head. Despite that, he was a wonderful travel companion.

Our five-man crew left early one morning from Brize Norton airfield in Oxfordshire. We had all been given air force accommodation the night before and been briefed on what to expect from the flight and our subsequent arrival in a war zone. It's always a little daunting when the final thing you check before you close your eyes at night is whether your armour-plated vest is a snug enough fit.

'Don't really think I'm sleeping,' was the text message I received from Kevin Kilbane at 00.45 on the morning of our flight. 'I was. Thanks Kev,' was my reply, knowing that the alarm was set for 02.55 in order to get to the airfield in time to catch our flight to Afghanistan via Cyprus.

I remember ringing John about the prospect of coming on the trip some months before and he had signed up within seconds of picking up his phone. 'When I was diagnosed with testicular cancer, I got hundreds of letters from troops in Afghanistan,' he told me. 'This is my chance to say thanks in person. I'm in.'

On our flight was Brigadier Neil Marshall, who had a pivotal role in the training of the Afghan National Forces in Kabul. He spent much of his time looking after high-ranking officers. 'One of the first things I tell them,' said the Brigadier, 'is to make sure they never underestimate the importance of football in a soldier's life.'

That is certainly something we discovered from the moment the journey started. The troops on the plane were asking Kevin and John about their predictions for the season and were desperate to hear stories about their careers and some of the stars they had played with and against.

'We stuck out like a sore thumb,' remembers John Hartson. 'The five of us stepped on the plane packed with hundreds of servicemen and women who all knew the drill. I was trying my best to act cool, but it was a little daunting.'

I knew what John meant. The flight attendants, from Squadrons 10 and 101, were so accommodating but there was a real mixture of excitement and nerves as we started to taxi down the runway. 'The take-off is the easy part,' said a voice from the row behind us, 'it's coming down you want to worry about.' There was a ripple of laughter. I looked at Kevin. Kevin looked at me. We both gulped.

'When we fly into Bastion,' said the Brigadier, 'you'll have to put your body armour on, and they'll turn all the lights off. Prepare yourself for a dramatic descent.'

'It's okay,' joked Kevin. 'I have to fly on Ryanair quite a bit back to Ireland.'

The brigadier gave him a look. 'You never forget the first time you fly into a war zone.' I looked at Kevin again. Kevin looked at me. We both gulped . . . again.

We were well looked after on the way. The flight attendants were even able to get the weekend's football results sent through on some sort of military vidiprinter while we were several thousand feet above the Persian Gulf.

Big John can sleep anywhere and was able to get some rest. As for me, at six-foot-six, I don't think I have ever slept on a plane so I was just chatting to Kevin and trying to plan out what was going to be a hectic few days. Our schedule was incredibly tight. We had two TV shows and a one-hour radio documentary to make in just over a day and a half.

During one of John's rare, non-snoring moments, he managed to get us all an invite into the cockpit of the aircraft – which was a real highlight – before we were told we had to re-take our seats for landing.

'Time to get tooled up fellas,' came the warning from the flight attendants. We all put on helmets and bulletproof vests for the 'drop' into Camp Bastion. 'I know you're all trying to scare us and make it fun,' I whispered to a flight attendant, 'but just how dangerous is this?'

'No plane carrying civilians has ever been shot down while trying to land in Afghanistan . . . yet,' came the not entirely reassuring reply. When you are used to a regular, gentle landing on a civilian aircraft, a military style landing can come as a bit of a shock. It's a bit like comparing a children's tea-cup ride at a fairground with a giant drop from the top of a rollercoaster. I was glad I hadn't eaten a large breakfast.

It probably didn't look as dramatic as it felt. I'm not a nervous flier at all, but I did leave ten little dents in the armrests at the sides of my seat.

'I think I've pooed my pants,' said John is his wonderful Welsh accent, laughing with the flight crew, as we finally touched down. As we exited the aircraft, we were met with the news that, even though we were classed as VIPs, there was a VVIP who was a few hours behind us.

About forty-eight hours before we arrived in Afghanistan, we'd had a call from the press team at Number 10 Downing Street, asking for confirmation that our trip was definitely going ahead. They also enquired if there might be some space on *Football Focus* that weekend if a certain somebody turned up. Approximately five hours behind us was a plane carrying Prime Minister David Cameron and a contingent from the English Football Association. They were aligning with our trip to launch a campaign to try and get the Afghan National Football League up and running the following year.

We had organised a training session and a game between British forces and British-trained Afghan troops for later that day and, by the looks of it, our kickabout had just taken on an extra slice of international significance. The big boys were in town.

At Camp Bastion the days were hot, the nights were freezing cold, but everywhere we went we were given a wonderfully warm welcome and, just as the Brigadier had told us, there was also that love of football at every turn. John was asked to autograph countless Celtic, West Ham and Arsenal shirts while Kevin quickly ran out of signed pictures. 'Have you guys heard the news about AVB?' shouted Captain Nick Nugent from the Royal engineers, as we were being shown around an Apache helicopter. Apparently, André Villas-Boas had just parted company with Tottenham and Nick was keen to get some instant pundit reaction.

It was just after the conversation about the vacant top job at Spurs that I managed to drop the BBC Sport iPad out of the aforementioned £40 million helicopter. When we returned home, I had to fill out a damage claim form to get the cracked screen repaired. On the section of the form where it said, 'How was the damage sustained?' I put down 'I dropped it out of an Apache helicopter in Afghanistan.' It is the coolest BBC damage claim form on the planet. I remember several 'The Administrator has denied your claim' responses before being able to get it repaired.

Bastion was in the northwest of Afghanistan, just outside the city of Lashkar Gah in Helmand Province. It was first established in 2005 and we were there for the final Christmas before the base became Camp Shorabak in October 2014. It is now home to the Afghan National Army.

The first thing that hits you is the size of the place. 'It's a bit like walking around Reading – if Reading was in the middle of the desert,' said one of the troops as we made our way to our quarters. The camp was four miles long and two miles wide and capable of housing thirty-two thousand troops. It was the biggest military base built by the British since World War II, but it was also home to a number of other international troops, including the Americans and the Danish.

All the streets were lined with huge blast-walls to protect from rocket attacks. There was concrete everywhere, much of it daubed with regimental graffiti. 'We are not allowed to paint on the planes like we used to,' said one of the engineers at the airfield, 'so we cover the concrete instead.' Batman was at one end of the blast-wall, some Transformers at the other and Marilyn Monroe was in the middle.

You can imagine in that intense atmosphere everything becomes competitive, even Christmas. 'We definitely try and get one over on the Americans,' laughs one of the regimental sergeants. 'Our trees have got to be taller and our baubles have got to be bigger. Having said that, we are in the middle of the desert and the local shop doesn't really have much in the way of baubles, so you just have to make do.'

The 'local shop' was called Boris's Haberdashery. The only currency accepted was US dollars and you could pick up everything from a toothbrush to a dish-dash – the Afghan national dress.

Boris did stock a few baubles but they were covered in dust. Everything was covered in dust. We walked into a gym filled with rowing machines, stationary bikes and gigantic dumbbells. They were so large I didn't even attempt to lift them for fear of looking puny. Every surface had a few millimetres of dust on it. It got in your bag, your clothes, your shoes, your hair, your eyes . . . into creases you never thought you had.

It was just a few days before Christmas so there were decorations at every turn. Even the little eight-seater vans, which acted like buses to get you around the base, had a tiny Father Christmas and tinsel hanging from their rear-view mirrors.

As we jumped in for our first little trip, we heard gunfire. It sounded a lot closer than was comfortable and the driver could tell we looked a little surprised. 'Don't worry. You'll get used to it. It's the firing range. They are at it all the time.' It's was amazing how quickly we did get used to the new sounds and smells.

We made our way past the barracks, the hospital, the shops and the football pitches. It quickly became eerily normal and it was easy to forget where you were. 'Does anyone go outside the base?' asked John. 'You know, other than on patrol?'

We were told a number of cautionary tales about those who had met a grizzly end on the wrong side of Bastion's heavily fortified fence. There was laughter, fun and an incredible sense of comradeship and camaraderie, but everyone was there to do a job, and they took that job incredibly seriously. They had to.

While we were there the Afghan moon was huge and provided plenty of light throughout the evening. That was a good job because there were no streetlights. You had to either carry a torch or wear a bright sort of cycling proficiency vest, so you were visible at all times.

There was no alcohol and a strict ten-o'clock curfew for everyone. It was never quiet though. The rattle of gunfire during the day was replaced by the hum of aircraft at night. The airbase was almost constantly in use. The noise was something everyone had to learn to live with.

During our trip we were looked after by Lieutenant Matt Weetch from the Media Operations Centre. It was Matt's job to point us in the right direction, answer any questions, find us people to interview and make sure we didn't get shot. This was not the job that Matt had dreamed of.

After starting his professional life as a travel agent, Matt joined the Navy as a mechanic back in 1990. He had it in his blood. His grandfather was a submariner and had been involved in the early stages of the development of sonar technology. He had to leave the armed forces after being hit by shrapnel at Dunkirk. Matt always wanted to follow in his footsteps.

'I was nineteen years old and this quiet, naïve little Cornish lad going off into the big, wide world,' remembers Matt. 'It was much harder than I ever thought it would be. I was incredibly shy but joining the Navy turned my life around. It gave me an air of confidence. Everyone who knew me before that would have seen a huge difference in me after a few years in the Navy.'

Matt spent time as a weapons engineer and a mechanic in far-flung corners of the world on ships like HMS *Sirius*, HMS *Argyle*, HMS *Montrose* and HMS *Sheffield*.

He was working his way up through the ranks and was on course to fulfil his dream of being a flight deck officer. That all came to an abrupt end when he was diagnosed with Ménière's disease in 2013. It is a condition which affects the ear and can cause vertigo, a spinning sensation, and cause you to lose balance and feel sick. Out of nowhere, Matt was unfit for naval service. Heartbroken, he applied for an operational tour, and was given six months in Afghanistan. He arrived in Camp Bastion in October 2013.

'I joined the forces to be in the Navy and I joined the Navy to go to sea. It was a crushing blow to have to leave, but those six months in Bastion were brilliant. It was the first time in years that the landscape had changed from blue to beige. It was the first time I stayed in one place for six months. I had never done that before in my life. It also gave me the chance to look after Gary Barlow and the team from *Football Focus.* What more could you ask for?'

Mr Barlow had been out to entertain the troops in Matt's first month and, aside from the 'marquee' guests, like members of Take That, Matt was constantly entertaining journalists from some of the biggest media outlets in the UK.

'The combination of jetlag and a hostile environment does strange things to people,' smiles Matt. 'It was always interesting to see how different individuals deal with the stress of being that close to war. Emotions can become very raw very quickly. I have seen people desperate to go home after twenty-four hours. I have seen people break and I've seen people share some of their deepest and darkest secrets with a bunch of strangers.'

We would see some of that ourselves before the end of our time in Camp Bastion but, before all that, we had a game of football to organise. Our arrival had caused quite a stir among the British contingent and there was a significant crowd gathering at the makeshift pitch in the middle of the camp.

While we were sorting out the teams and fixing the holes in the nets, there was a flurry of activity and, in a huge dust cloud, the Prime Ministerial party arrived. Out of the dust strode David Cameron alongside former England striker Michael Owen and a few tracksuited officials from the Football Association.

John Hartson can no longer play football since surgery to

remove a brain tumour, so he watched from the sidelines as Kevin danced about the pitch showing off his silky skills to his adoring team-mates. I lost count of the score when it got to about nine-all, but I do remember that it ended in the same way that most football adventures do on foreign soil ... an Englishman missed a penalty.

He might not have been officially 'playing' but Big John couldn't resist getting involved when the ball came anywhere near him and his interventions provided the highlight of the match.

'I did enjoy meeting the Prime Minister,' remembers John. 'I know everyone was roaring but, I've got to tell you, both times I hit him with the ball were a total mistake.' John is struggling to contain his laughter but is adamant. 'The first one was a really clean one on the shoulder. It was my first touch in the match, and I think I just misjudged the flight of it. It was very windy! The second time, well, I don't really know. I was never that good at the forty-yard crossfield pass. That got him on the back of the head.' At the time, the PM was deep in conversation with the head of the Afghan Football Association and the highest-ranking British officer at the base! 'He took it really well,' offers John, still seemingly oblivious to how close he came to causing an international incident.

We were filming the whole time we were at Camp Bastion, and when the programme eventually went out on TV in the UK, this is how it started:

'Welcome to Football Focus. We have a slightly different show for you this week. We are in Camp Bastion for Christmas with Kevin Kilbane and John Hartson. We'll talk to these two in a moment but first I need to introduce this man. The Prime Minister is also here. Now . . . don't take this the wrong way but . . . what are you doing here?'

We only found out later what a perilous position we were in at that precise moment.

'Did you notice how twitchy everyone was?' asked Matt with a smile. We hadn't. 'I can safely tell you that that is the most danger you have ever, and will ever, be in in your life. You were standing less than two feet away from the fella who was second on the Taliban kill list after the President of the United States.'

Matt went on to explain that there were members of the Afghan national team who, although they had been checked, were 'unknowns' when it came to their allegiances. By all accounts, there were an awful lot of nervous security officials with their hands within touching distance of their firearms that day.

'Thankfully, you didn't ask me if you were safe,' says Matt. 'I would have had to tell you the truth . . . and the truth is you weren't.' I'm quite thankful that I was oblivious to all this at the time, but I do remember the PM's close-protection team taking a particular interest when someone from the FA suggested that we all gather together for a group photograph.

It was, though, a timely reminder of the gravity of the situation our troops live with every day. 'I never once told my family that I would be going outside the wire,' says Matt, deadly serious. 'Every time we left the base, the padré would bless the vehicles just in case. Thankfully, I always came back.'

Despite the heightened security, we were keen to speak to the locals. Most of them spoke little or no English but they could reel off the names of virtually every famous face from the Premier League.

One conversation, with a member of the Afghan National Guard called Antaz, was a clear indication of the universal language of football.

Me: 'You like football?'

Antaz: Enthusiastic thumbs up and nods.

Me: 'Have you heard of Crawley Town?' (I wasn't expecting much of response to this one, but they were my team, so I had to check.)

Antaz: Deeply blank expression.

Me: 'Arsenal? Chelsea? Manchester United?'

Antaz: (with a huge smile) 'Rooney! Rooney!' (Pointing at me.)

Interpreter: 'He wants to know if you've met Rooney.'

Me: 'Yes.' (Big smile and thumbs up.)

Antaz: 'Cantona?'

Me: 'Yes.'

Antaz: 'Henry?'

Me: 'Yes.'

Antaz: 'Van Persie?'

Me: 'Yes, and him too.'

What followed was about five minutes of Antaz running me through all the players he knew. He was amazed that I had met most of them. I explained to him through the interpreter about the pedigree of John Hartson and Kevin Kilbane, but I think I lost him somewhere between Sunderland and Hull City.

All the filming went well, I broke the camp record for the number of profiteroles eaten in a single sitting (very proud of that one) and by the end of our time there, we were left with some incredible memories.

For all of us, the trip to Afghanistan was a real eye-opener into life in a war zone. What struck us all was the warmth of the welcome and the resilience of those who called Camp Bastion home for four, six or sometimes nine months. It was meant to be all about football, but it developed into much more than that. We met some amazing people in Camp Bastion. People from all walks of life.

There was Sergeant Ernest Tabi from the Engineers Regiment. When we bumped into him, he had been in camp for three-and-a-half months. It was his second tour and this time he was responsible for sorting out the squadron's pay. Sergeant Tabi was an administrator.

'My job is to put a smile on people's faces,' he said with a huge one of his own. 'As a family man, things are always tough out here. The way I look at it, I have one family at home and another one here. I miss my wife and my two children enormously but for me, and for them, it is a matter of pride.

'Your family are proud of you and they understand the job that you are doing out here. I am serving my Queen. I am serving my country. I am representing the Army and I am representing my family. I try and make people happy out here. I like to organise events, whether it's a football match, church events . . . I am even the local hairdresser!'

Chief Barber Tabi told us the important thing he tried to teach his children was to add value wherever they went. He was an administrator, paymaster, part-time chaplain, party organiser, hairdresser and a half-decent footballer too. Ernest played football in the same team as former Chelsea midfielder Michael Essien as a teenager before choosing a different path.

'My parents wisely advised me that football might not work out and they were right,' explained Ernest. 'I find my job now incredibly rewarding. I know some people have a problem with the Army and what we do, but we are fighting for a good cause and it is not in vain. People will always have their different opinions, but I see the good we are doing . . . the difference we are trying to make.'

Wherever we went around Camp Bastion it seemed that people dealt with being away from home at Christmas in a very personal way. Some filled their space with decorations, some with little gifts from home, others took part in the Secret Santa. And for some others, home felt like an eternity away and so they simply ploughed on through Christmas, as if it is was just another day.

'I have written Christmas off this year,' explained Lieutenant Weetch. Matt is husband to Tracy, and father to three daughters: Amber (thirteen at the time), Ellie (nine) and Millie (three).

'I'd be lying if I told you it didn't pull at the heart strings.

I want them to have a great Christmas back in the UK, but I want to just get on with it. I'm looking forward to ringing my family for an hour or so after they've had lunch, but I'll just try and crack on with my job.'

It's something everyone in the forces seems to have become accustomed to.

'This isn't my first Christmas away,' continues Matt. 'I am a servant. This is part of my job at the British armed forces.' He smiles. 'Suck it up, buttercup.'

One evening, Matt and I went on a stroll to the Camp Baston memorial. It was the place where everyone who died was remembered. There were no streetlights in the camp, so the beautifully lit stone tablets stood out in an otherwise pitch-black night.

Above the memorial flew the Union Jack and upon it were written the names of the 446 members of the British armed forces who – up to that point – had lost their lives in Afghanistan.

'Every member of the British forces here will be able to tell you the name of Warrant Officer Fisher,' says Matt proudly. He was the last British solder to die in Afghanistan, the month before we had arrived. No one forgets. Back in the UK, his death was the fourth story on the news. Sadly, we had got used to it.

'When you hear about fallen soldiers when you're back in the UK, you can understand the pain that a family feels, but it's very different when you are here. We all feel it deeply,' explains Matt as we stare at the memorial. 'It touches you in a way that is indescribable. I come here often . . . lots of us do. It's a chance to reflect on the sacrifice that all these men and women have made and also to think about their families back home.'

As we lay in our beds that night, Kevin and John both talked about how being in Camp Bastion reminded them of being back in the dressing room. They both realised how much they missed it. There was a common goal that brought everyone together. There was respect, hard work and a desire to win – at all costs. It also became very clear, to us all, that the bond between the various members of the armed forces was essential to survival. They don't just enjoy the camaraderie; it keeps them going.

Private Dan Lynch was responsible for Willie the black Labrador. The dog's job was to search for enemy explosives. Dan had started his six-month tour of duty in August of 2013. As a 'six-monther' he was able to apply for a little R&R. 'You put your preferences in,' said Dan, 'and hope for the best. Everyone asks for Christmas off, but you have more of a chance if you have a partner with young children, it's your first tour, or you're a low rank. I think I hit the sweet spot with all three. The more experienced you are, or the more stripes you have on your arm, the smaller chance you have of going home.'

Dan would get to spend Christmas back in Liverpool with his two daughters, Chloe and Rosie, after five months apart. 'You can never switch off,' he says. 'That's all part of the job. Willie the dog will stay here. We have got a job to do so, as soon as I get back, we'll crack on again.'

Dan was one of those who counted down the days. He explained how one of his friends on a nine-month tour approached it by dividing the months into different food groups.

'It helps to make things go faster for him. He won't eat any meat for the first month and then no bread for the second month. Then he has no pasta for a month, followed by another month without dessert. It sounds stupid, but that is his way of ticking off the days. You get into a routine and the routine gets you through the tough times.'

Willie was a huge help to Dan. He couldn't imagine doing a tour without him. 'We do everything together. His training never stops. Every day we are working on something else. I see more of Willie than anyone else in the world. I'm not sure either of us could survive without the other. Once we're all finished here in Afghan, I will ask if I can rehome him. I think the girls would love him and I'd miss him too much.'

Nine per cent of the troops in Camp Bastion were women. One of them was Corporal Amy Foster from the RAF. She had been a weapon's technician for over a decade.

'There are three types of helicopter in Bastion. The Apache (don't mention the iPad), the Chinook and the Sea King. My job is to make sure that, as soon as they land, everyone is safe and it's ready to fly again as soon as possible.'

The next time you are about to complain about your shift pattern at work, spare a thought for the Amy Fosters of this world. She worked every day, seven days a week, from midnight until midday, for four months, without a break.

'It is a strange shift pattern, so I decided to give myself a challenge to complete in my down time,' explains the outrageously fit Amy. 'I thought it would be a good idea to raise some money for charity by cycling the distance back to my home

base – RAF Brize Norton. That works out as three-thousand-
five-hundred miles and the only way I can fit that in is to do
two hours a day on the bike, every day, busting out thirty miles.
As soon as I finish a shift, I head straight to the gym and jump
on the bike.'

Amy was raising money for a charity called Veterans Aid
back in the UK. 'I firmly believe that no ex-service man or
woman should ever be homeless and that is why I keep getting
on the bike. That drives me on every day.'

Like everyone else, Amy was entitled to two hours of call-
time back home each week. She had not been using her full
allocation in December so that she'd be able to spend plenty of
time on the phone to both her mum and her husband, Mark,
on Christmas Day. She laughed and wisely refused to answer
when I asked her if she wanted to reveal which one she would
ring first.

'I try not to think about what I'm missing out on. I will ring
home, try and be full of Christmas joy, and then just see it as
another day out here. My husband is in the RAF too, so at least
he understands the mentality you have to have. He has a dog
to keep him company and I got him a day of stunt driving as a
present so that should keep him happy.'

Amy was going to start work at midnight on Christmas
Day. The team would all get there ten minutes early, open their
shoeboxes from home, and then start their twelve-hour shift.

'I don't think I'm hard, but I do think I have learned to
deal with it. The RAF teaches you that, but I know others find
it much more difficult. There will be a lot of people who find

Christmas Day the hardest day of the year and it's our job, as their family out here, to protect them, look after them and remind them they'll hopefully get to go home soon. I know it sounds daft, but a good Bastion Christmas dinner goes a long way.'

Amy wasn't the only member of the armed forces who understood the importance of turkey and trimmings.

'You do get a great feed on the big day,' says Leigh Buttel who was a Regimental Sergeant Major and a massive fan of Spurs and stuffing.

'You get turkey, cranberry sauce. They could do better with the stuffing, if I'm honest, but they make up for it with a few Christmas crackers. A little wine would go a long way, but you can't get a drink around here.' He winks. 'Believe me, I've tried.

'I think you can enjoy Christmas but it's just different to what happens at home so the more you've been through it, the more you get used to it. It's just a military Christmas. I'm one of those who tries to make the best of it. I have two young boys at home – Tom and Ollie. I miss them like crazy which is why any break from the norm is a welcome one.'

Part of Leigh's Christmas regime was a heavy involvement in the organisation of the Secret Santa. 'We have very strict rules,' he explained. 'It's ten dollars a person and you have to shop in the local Afghan shops, so you are guaranteed some tatt. I have become very skilled at finding some terrible Afghan tatt. No one wants me when it comes to Secret Santa.

'I know some people find it hard. I'll Skype home for an hour on Christmas day – I'll wish them all the best. The wife has done the lion's share of the present buying, if I'm honest . . . well, all of it really. I have sent them back a little shoebox of gifts. Some of the lads here will get emotional. Some suffer more than others. Christmas is a particularly hard time to swallow. We give the guys as much time off as possible. Some will choose to sit in their tents and contemplate and others will get involved in the things we try and put on. We give it a go with the decorations in the barracks but, if you want to really see how it's done, get down to the British Fire Station.' Leigh laughs. 'It's like a proper grotto down there. They've got a nativity scene and everything. Even the yanks are jealous.'

We did make it down to the Fire Station and Leigh was right. They had made an effort; both inside and out. Jesus, Mary and Joseph were in full nativity regalia by the entrance and there was a beautifully built fake fireplace inside, complete with stockings and mince pies. This was the home of the infamous Blue Watch.

John, Kevin and I had the privilege of spending a few hours with them. We filmed the final segment of our *Football Focus* programme in front of their fake fire, but that's not the reason those men stick in my mind. I often recall the conversation we had with them and, whenever I hear a helicopter, I am instantly transported back to their dusty little office in the middle of the desert. Let me explain.

I don't know about you but hearing a helicopter as a child was an incredible experience. I can still remember the day that one landed in our school field during a PE lesson. I remember hearing one flying over Sheffield, when I was at university, and running out of the house with giddy excitement.

The noise of a helicopter meant something completely different to the men of Blue Watch. It signified that casualties were about to arrive. It was their signal to scramble to the airfield and prepare for the worst.

Because of the nature of the job, Blue Watch worked a twenty-four-hours-on/twenty-four-hours-off shift pattern. Everyone agreed it was the best way of doing things, but it meant they were all susceptible to tiredness and the occasional burst of heightened emotion.

Sometimes, thankfully, days would go by without any emergencies to attend. That's why they had time to work on their fake fireplace and craft a series of animals to accompany the Saviour of the World and his earthly parents outside the front doors of the fire station.

But, when the alarm sounded, they had to be ready for anything. They were trained to get to the airfield as quickly as possible and were all aware that, once the doors of that helicopter opened, anything was possible.

None of them wanted to be named here but they were happy for me to recount what they told us.

'When the doors open. That's when your training kicks in. Some of the things, the injuries, the people we have seen would stay with you a lifetime. Our job is to get them to hospital as quickly as we can.'

The hospital at Camp Bastion was something else. State of the art equipment, world leading surgeons and the very best medical care on the planet.

They are understandably proud of what they do. 'This is

what it boils down to if numbers make it easier to understand,' explained a member of Blue Watch. 'Once we open those helicopter doors, whatever state you are in, as long as you have a pulse, we have a ninety-nine percent chance of keeping you alive.'

The men of Blue Watch might have time on their hands to make a nativity scene but, when they are called upon, their job is one of the most important in the whole base.

One of the most poignant moments of the trip took place on our final full day at Camp Bastion. We had brought some gifts over with us – an Xbox, a PlayStation and a few other bits – and we gave them out at a gathering of the troops under a large camouflaged gazebo near one of the dining halls.

John and Kevin also agreed to do a Q&A session with about thirty British soldiers. We told them that, even though we would film it, no question was off limits. We explained that we would just edit out anything that we thought might be a bit too fruity for a Saturday lunchtime audience on BBC One.

Our two pundits were asked all the normal questions about most difficult opponents, worst tackle they'd been on the end of, training ground bust-ups . . . that sort of thing. Kevin gave a hilarious answer about an on-field tussle with Roy Keane and retold the story of the infamous moment at the 2002 World Cup where Keane left the Republic of Ireland camp after a huge row with the then coach, Mick McCarthy. After a steaming, furious discussion between captain and coach, Keane shouted some unrepeatable insults and stormed off. There was complete silence in the team room. Nobody knew what to say. Nobody except reserve goalkeeper Dean Kiely who offered, 'I am available if you need someone to do a job in midfield, gaffer.'

We were nearing the end of the session when one of the squaddies asked John what he'd learned from his recovery from cancer and addiction to gambling.

I have known John a long time. I have heard him speak incredibly powerfully on the subject before. I had seen him reduce a room of people to a sea of tears as he described how addiction ripped his life apart and how cancer nearly killed him.

John looked across at me as if you say, 'How long have I got?' I gave the internationally recognised referees' sign for 'play on' and that's exactly what John did. There was total silence for about forty minutes.

In 2009, John found a number of lumps on his testicles. 'It was like a little nut sized lump to start with. Every bloke knows when something feels different. It gradually grew from a nut, to a bit more like a baked bean and eventually to a Malteser. I showed my wife Sarah. She couldn't believe I hadn't had it checked out and told me I had to go and see the club doctor immediately. I was playing at West Brom at the time and I assured her that I would do it as soon as I got in the next day. I lied.'

John was scared of what might be happening to him and convinced himself everything would be okay. When he got home the following day, he told Sarah that he'd seen the doctor and that everything was fine. He said she had nothing to worry about.

'The truth was, I never went anywhere near the doctor that day and, while I was being stupid and ignoring it, the cancer was spreading up through my lungs and into my brain.'

John's wife couldn't understand why he needed so much sleep. He'd come home from training in the early afternoon and sleep until 7 pm. He'd have to be woken up for his tea and then he'd feel exhausted, return to bed, and go straight through to the following morning.

'It was awful,' John told the troops, 'and it was starting to have a massive impact on normal life. I would have headaches that lasted for days on end and I even started falling asleep at traffic lights on my way home from training. I had to do something, but I was terrified I had left it all too late.'

John was eventually taken to hospital and spent six weeks fighting for his life. 'If I'd just gone to the doctor when I first felt the lump, he'd have diagnosed it and all of what happened to me would have been avoidable. I was stupid. Please don't be as stupid as I was. Please don't put your families through what I put mine through.'

John had two emergency brain operations, two emergency operations on his lungs and sixty sessions of chemotherapy. John published a book about his fight for survival called *Please Don't Go*. Those are the words his father uttered at the hospital when it looked like his son had gone for good.

'I had stopped breathing,' says John, 'and my wife tells me that my dad just collapsed on the floor and screamed, "PLEASE DON'T GO! PLEASE DON'T GO!"'

John didn't go. He came back. The NHS staff saved his life.

He has permanent scars to remember the ordeal which he showed off to the troops. If you see Big John these days, you'll see a deep dent on the right of his head from the brain surgery and a large scar on the other side.

'That looks worse, doesn't it, Dan?' he says feeling the long scar with his fingers. 'That came from when a mate lost control of a golf trolley and crashed it into a tree. I smashed my head open and there was blood everywhere. It's a good job I'm so good looking,' he says, roaring with laughter, 'or I'd be in all sorts of bother.'

Cancer was only one of the challenges that John has had to overcome. He spoke about his divorce from his first wife but also about the gambling addiction which came close to wrecking his second marriage.

'I stopped gambling on my mother's birthday in October 2011.' When he spoke to the troops, he was two years clean. He has now survived nine years without placing a bet.

'I am a recovering gambling addict. I still go twice a week.'

John recently relocated his family to Edinburgh and the first thing he did was join his local gambling anonymous group. 'It has been huge for me. Without their help I have no idea where I would be. Probably in jail or dead. They were there when I was at my lowest point.'

John recalls the day when everything came to a head. 'Our baby girl, Paige, was two years old and not very well. I decided to go out with the lads in Swansea and it was one of those all-day benders. I got home in the early hours of the morning and snuck into the spare room so that I didn't wake anyone up. The next morning, my head was banging, and I can hear all sorts of noise coming from upstairs. It was my wife packing cases. She burst into the bedroom. "Leave me alone!" I shouted, and she said, "I'm going to leave you alone for good." She told me that she had booked flights and that she was on her way to the airport to go back to Scotland with the kids.

'The thing that broke my heart was that she told me she felt she had to do it because she loved me so much and she couldn't bear to see me hurting myself like I was. She couldn't stand to see what I was doing. The gambling was taking over my life.'

John broke down. His wife and kids were in the room with him and he was a sobbing heap on the carpet. John had hit rock bottom. His wife said that his only chance to keep the marriage alive was to get himself clean.

'I looked for a gambling anonymous group right there and then,' remembers John. 'There was a session that night in Swansea. I went along. That was the hardest night of my life. I'm a famous face in Swansea. Everyone knew me but I was as low as I had ever been. The group was run by a little fella called Jimmy who was twenty-seven years clean. I spoke to him on the phone and he told me I'd be more than welcome and that no one would judge me. I was finally ready to admit that I was an addict, but I cannot tell you how hard it was to say the words, "Hello everybody. My name is John and I am a compulsive gambler." Walking into that room was so tough. Admitting I was out of control was heart breaking, but I knew it was the only chance I had of winning back my wife, my kids and my life.'

John was in full denial. He can see that now. Managers,

team-mates, friends and his parents had all tried to talk to him, but he had become a brilliant and compulsive liar, spinning stories to protect his secret life. It had taken over John's entire world. It was the first thing he thought about when he got up and the last thing he did before he went to bed at night.

'I managed to beat cancer and I hope I've got the better of this too,' says John with a sigh of relief. 'I now chair some meetings of GA, you know, Dan. I am the fella who starts things off and welcomes everybody. Can you believe that? If you'd told me that ten years ago, I would have laughed in your face. It is such an amazing feeling to be helping others in the same way that I was helped.'

John's foundation has raised over a million pounds for charities that raise awareness of testicular cancer and help those who struggle with gambling addiction. Once he'd finished talking to the troops that afternoon, there was almost a stunned silence at the camp. There was a rare beautiful moment that occurs when someone who you assume has the perfect life is brutally honest about their failings, their flaws and their struggles. John got a weight off his shoulders that day and it was amazing to watch. I think that is why he says that trip to Afghanistan was one of the most amazing experiences of his life.

There are so many things that I still look back on from that trip. From a practical point of view, I now have very detailed knowledge of the different facial hair you are allowed in the

forces. There are simple rules which allow you to quickly identify people.

In the Army, a beard is not permitted. You are only allowed
a moustache, but it can't fall below the top lip or extend beyond
the width of the mouth.

If you are in the Royal Navy, then a moustache is on the
banned list, but a full beard is permitted.

Those in the Royal Air Force are only allowed a moustache
but aren't restricted by the Army regulations. Wax is permitted
and the 'tache can be as wide as you like.

John Hartson occasionally flirts with a beard, but our trip
made him think about much more than his choice of facial hair.
'This is going to sound strange but, at times, I found it quite
embarrassing,' says John. 'It made me feel guilty for the stupid
things I worry about at home. I remember going into the cafe-
teria and some of them were clapping and cheering and calling
me "a legend". I wish I could go back and stand on the table
and tell them all how amazing they were. I found that part of
it quite overwhelming.'

It was an intense trip for John for many reasons. 'I've played
in massive games of football. I've played in cup finals and scored
important goals and yet, these guys were putting their lives on
the line – every day – and they are thousands of miles away
from their loved ones.'

The biggest eye-opener for me was being surrounded by that
many can-doers. In my experience, the armed forces seem to
be packed with those types of people.

'You will never find a better breed of people,' says Matt

Weetch. 'You just have to get on and do it, even when the times are tough. Everyone is tired, everyone is bored, so you don't tend to complain about things.'

Matt left the Navy in 2015 and now works as the Defence Business Development Director for A&P Group; a ship repair and building organisation. 'One of the greatest takeaways I had from the armed forces was my attitude to problems,' says Matt. 'When I first started working as a civilian, I noticed that so many people, when faced with issues or problems, would respond with "No, because . . . ." The Navy taught me that "Yes, if . . ." is a far more productive way of thinking. It takes time to change a mindset but once you get to "yes, if" rather than "no, because" it is so liberating.'

Matt is definitely a glass three-quarters-full type of guy but, like so many, he found life outside the forces extremely challenging.

'I had to leave because my dream was to be at sea and, because of Ménière's disease, that was just no longer possible. I didn't want someone to tell me I couldn't go to sea, so I just decided to go and be the captain of my own destiny. It was a lot harder than I thought. It is only once it's gone that you realise how important that sense of duty is to you. You also forget the highs are so high, but the lows are so low. That's why the troops were so excited when John and Kevin came into the mess tent, or into their quarters. Sometimes the only thing that punctuates the boredom is trauma . . . losing a friend, losing a comrade. Seeing your smiling faces was wonderful for so many of us and you gave us all a lift. I ended up going to see a doctor a year after leaving the forces because I felt like something was missing. That feeling of being relied upon, and relying on others, is something you can't replace. I think you just have to learn to live without it.'

I have no military connections in either side of my family. I did think about joining the Army for a while when I was about seventeen but, in all honesty, that's because we didn't have any money and the Army offered a brilliant bursary scheme to get you through university if you signed up afterwards.

Our trip to Afghanistan was only a few days but it really allowed us all to get a clearer understanding of how the military mind works.

I don't want to preach, or give an extended lecture, about how we should view our armed forces because I'm aware that my experience was a very personal one. I am sure that some of you reading this still feel that the war in Afghanistan, maybe all war, is futile. I came away from that trip knowing that, whatever you think about conflict, you cannot question the dedication of our armed forces, the pride they have in doing the job and the respect they have for the various badges and stripes they wear and the people they serve with and under.

'I think any bad feeling towards the military is almost always directed towards the government,' says Matt. 'The military is just the fighting arm of foreign policy. You can disagree with public policy but still love and respect the people who are carrying the weapons.'

All the people I spoke to at Camp Bastion were aware of some of the negativity around the conflict from back home, but all had that feeling that they were doing good; that they were making a difference. That came across really powerfully in every conversation. 'When you are young, you do things because you are told to do them,' reflects Matt. 'Over the years, I have heard three or four different reasons as to why we were in Afghanistan. I am not sure it's my job, our job, to argue the rights and wrongs of it. You have to believe in what you are doing and, even more importantly, you have to support your brothers and sisters in arms because all your lives depend on it. Imagine a workplace where the number one priority is to look out for each other. Imagine a workplace where the driving force, in every employee, is to want to be the best at what they do. That is the military mindset. That is what I miss.'

Leaving Camp Bastion was strangely emotional for all of us. 'I will never forget this. It's been an honour to have met you!' shouted Kevin over the noise of a landing Chinook, as we made our way back to the airfield.

'Apart from the birth of my five children this has been one of the most amazing experiences of my life,' added Big John Hartson, with a smile. The troops were not only surprised by the size of John's family but also the tears in his eyes.

This is going to sound stupid, but I will never see helicopters or Christmas in the same way again. Every time I hear a helicopter now, I am instantly transported back to our conversation with the men of Blue Watch. Every time I sit down to my Christmas dinner, I have a thought for those who would love to do the same with their family but can't.

When I'm tempted to complain about the state of Christmas

TV, I try and remember that there are many people, thousands of miles away, who would love nothing more than to sit on the sofa, next to their loved ones, and watch *Back To The Future III* . . . again.

'GEORGIA'S NOT COMING BACK.
I NEED TO TALK TO YOU'

There is something about hospitals. I have huge admiration for the people who work in them, but I don't have many happy memories of time spent there.

I was a regular visitor to hospital in my early years and my mum is often keen to fill in the details of a few stories of which I don't have that clear a memory. I've limped into accident and emergency departments all over the UK with cracked teeth, damaged knees, arms and pride. Most of them were of my own doing – apart from a bathroom fight with my brother which ended with him smashing my head against the sink.

I've dislocated my right knee five times, broken an ankle and leg playing football, snapped an Achilles on a five-a-side pitch and spent three days on an isolation ward because the doctors thought I had a rare form of meningitis.

More recently, there was the forty-eight hours my amazing wife spent in labour with our first child, and the horrible situation we experienced when Susie was just nine months old.

I was covering a football match in Blackburn. It was early 2008 and I received a phone call from my wife earlier in the day to say that Susie had been suffering with a high temperature for about twenty-four hours. She was lethargic and struggling to eat and drink.

Sarah called me back as I arrived at the ground to tell me not to worry but that she had organised with a friend to drop her and Susie off at A&E. She was going to go to the minor injuries clinic, but Susie seemed distressed and now couldn't keep anything down. Sarah just wanted to get her checked out.

The phone call I received at half-time was far more distressing. Sarah had gone to A&E and started to worry when she couldn't wake Susie up. When she eventually got to see the nurse, there was a worryingly red stool in her nappy. Sarah was ringing from the back of an ambulance. She was being blue-lighted to the children's emergency unit at the Chelsea and Westminster Hospital across London. Susie was strapped to her chest on the stretcher. The wonderful doctor, who had quickly spotted the gravity of the situation, was with Sarah in the ambulance even though her twelve-hour shift had already ended. Something was seriously wrong. I called the office and told them I had to leave the game immediately.

I picked up my things, ran down the stairs at Blackburn's Ewood Park ground and sprinted the five-hundred yards to the press car park. My car was hemmed in. The steward on the gate was lovely but there were three other cars blocking my exit. There was no way out. It was one of those times in life where you just want to throw your head back and scream at the top of your voice.

I called Sarah who, by this time, was in an understandable panic. She had arrived at the Chelsea and Westminster Hospital and Susie was surrounded by doctors, surgeons and nurses. They were inserting lines into her body, desperately trying to rehydrate her and asking my wife for Susie's medical history. I knew she needed me. My daughter needed me. I needed them . . . but I couldn't leave.

I went back into Ewood Park with the number plates of the cars to see if there was any way I could persuade the owners to move their vehicles. Two of them belonged to people who were commentating on the match and the second half had already started. I am not normally the sort of person who gets too stressed about anything. My family will tell you that losing my car keys sends me into a flap but that's usually the full extent of my panic. That second half was excruciating.

At the end of the game, I persuaded the owners to move their cars as quickly as possible and off I went to London with the tears streaming down my face, convinced I was never going to see our daughter again.

Two-hundred-and-forty-two miles south from Ewood Park, surgeons at the Chelsea and Westminster Hospital were trying to re-inflate Susie's bowel. She had suffered something called intussusception, where the bowel collapses in on itself and causes a blockage. The plan was to try and blow air at high speed through the bowel and re-inflate it. They would try this three times over the course of a few hours and then they would have to operate.

I arrived at the hospital just as they were trying the procedure for the second time. It failed again. Sarah and I were in pieces. There was that helplessness that washes over any parent with a sick child. There is nothing you can do other than trust the skill of the medical staff and pray. That's what we did.

At times like this you are thankful for small mercies. A month before, Susie was prescribed penicillin by our local GP and we had discovered that she was allergic to it. That saved her life. We were told by the doctor that the treatment, upon arrival at hospital, would normally have been penicillin. An allergic reaction at that point would have probably been too much for our little girl.

My wife and I were allowed to sit outside the operating theatre as they tried for a final time to re-inflate her bowel and avoid surgery. We had already been warned about how important it was that this worked, because the surgeons are never keen to operate on a child if they don't have to. When the fella in the mask walked through the double doors and said, 'It's good news', I cannot explain to you the relief that flowed through us. Susie stayed in hospital for another week, but she was on the mend.

As a family, we are eternally grateful to not only the staff at Chelsea and Westminster who took care of her but, most importantly, the A&E doctor at West Middlesex Hospital who spotted how ill she was, and hours earlier acted quickly and almost certainly saved her life.

I much prefer going to hospital when my only responsibility is to interview someone who works there. I would happily never be in a situation like that again.

*   *   *

Back in 2015, I was hosting the afternoon show on BBC Radio 5 Live and the plan was to present the entire programme from the Queen Elizabeth Hospital in Birmingham. I would be based in the hospital for the afternoon and co-host, Sarah Brett, would be back in the studio in Salford. The Queen Elizabeth remains one of the busiest hospitals in the UK. Over one million patients pass through its doors every year, and one of its specialisms is heart transplants.

The whole point of the show was to talk about how, as a nation, we feel about the issue of being a donor. Our plan was to meet people at various stages of the 'transplant journey' and look at some of the moral and ethical issues around the subject.

In the year before our show, there had been twenty-nine successful heart transplants carried out at the hospital. The operation has been available since the 1970s but it remains complicated, incredibly expensive and so difficult to get right.

There are about two-hundred and fifty people on the heart transplant waiting list in the UK at any one time. One in five of those are likely to die. The key fact, which we were pinning the whole show on, was that while 85 per cent of us would accept a donor organ, only 40 per cent of us would actually donate one.

I remember feeling a little nervous about the programme before we started. I knew we had some fantastic guests lined up, but it was the whole hospital thing that had me slightly on edge. The place was packed with people. The Queen Elizabeth, at that time, was a new building right next door to a crumbling, concrete old one. The new site had one of those vast open atriums, but the smell remained the same: a complicated mixture of sanitiser and bleach with the occasional whiff of chocolate custard.

The first family we met were the Halseys. Steve, Denise and their sons Jason and Stefan. Steve was a complicated case. He had suffered with cancer for years and now needed a heart transplant. He and his family had to make regular trips from their home in Lewes – a 350-mile round trip away.

'Family is the only thing that keeps me going,' explained Steve. 'It's a really difficult head space to be in because, for me to live, someone else has to die. I don't wish anyone any harm obviously, but it's the only hope I have of living.'

Steve said that it was an easy decision to go on the list for a fresh heart, but he constantly thinks about what other people and families have to go through for him to get better.

His wife struggles to lift her head as Steve describes the emotional turmoil that they are all going through. 'This is a family journey,' she offers, squeezing her husband's hand tightly. 'I have to try and hold it all together. There are lots of people who we wouldn't have met if we weren't on this journey. I think a lot about the donor programme. I wasn't a donor before. This has put a different light on all of it. I can't bear to think of people in the same situation as Steve.'

Their eldest son Jason explains how he has had to step in to lead the family in the absence of his dad. 'There are times when you have a collective family cry, but you have to think past the operation and look at what the future holds.'

I am not sure what sort of patient I would be in that situation. Laura Grocott, the Transplant Coordinator, explained that there were generally two types of transplant patient: those who wanted to know everything and those who wanted to know nothing.

'I don't want to be a scientist,' says Steve, 'but I do want to know what is going on. I wish I understood what all the beeps mean but, I suppose, as long as it's still beeping . . . I'm still here.'

Steve was on the urgent waiting list at the time. His family knew that his heart could give up and stop at any moment and he could also go into theatre as soon as a donor organ became available.

'The dark moments creep up on you sometimes,' admits Steve. His wife hasn't let go of his hand for the duration of our chat. She squeezes even tighter as he struggles to speak without getting emotional. I can see the whites of her knuckles. I reach out to hold her other hand as Steve continues.

'I can deal with those dark moments. I know I'm in a good place. This is the only hospital in the country that can deal with my condition. I need a heart transplant and I need a full stem cell transplant after that. It's a long road ahead for all of us.'

Their other son Stefan, who slept most of the way to the hospital that morning, just wants life to return to normal. 'I see this as a blip. I am looking forward to Dad feeling better, this all being behind us, and we can just get on with our lives.' (Steve did eventually get his transplant, but sadly he passed away in 2018. His family were keen for his story to stay in this chapter. I want to wish them all the best for the future.)

Laura is one of those looking after patients like Steve and his family. She is part of a team who are on call twenty-four hours a day. As Transplant Coordinator, she receives referrals from doctors for assessment to go onto the transplant waiting list, manages the waiting list and coordinates the transplant when a suitable donor organ becomes available. 'We filter all the information coming in about the organ and speak to the surgeon. They ultimately make the call to see if the transplant will go ahead and hopefully be successful. You want it to work out for everyone.'

Laura's is the sort of job that is hard not to take home with you. 'We are used to being on call 24/7 but the ability to detach is so important; otherwise it becomes all consuming. I've got to say, it's the most rewarding job I've ever had. It's lovely to see the patients before, and after, and see the life-changing difference that organ donation makes. We see them every six months to make sure that everything is working well. We encourage them to have "transplant goals" like holidays or walking a daughter down the aisle and it's wonderful when you see that happen.'

The risks are significant but 50 per cent of Laura's transplant patients survive ten years or longer and, as technology leaps forward, those statistics are constantly improving.

One of the steps forward comes in the form of the LVAD machine. The left ventricular assist device is a mechanical pump which pushes the blood into the aorta and then around the heart. It's an amazing device, but it does come with a large battery which you have to carry around with you the whole time.

We met Ian, who was the proud owner of an LVAD machine. 'I was going for a transplant but because of the condition of my heart, I was told this machine was the best chance for me to survive and see my family'.

Ian is in a wheelchair pushed by his daughter Rosie. Ian explains that his battery lasts for about fourteen hours and that you have to be careful because – he laughs – it's not the sort of thing you want to run out.

'It was a family decision,' explains Rosie, looking lovingly at her dad. 'It was a big thing for us all to get our heads around but, from our perspective, we are just trying to support Dad and let him do the things he wants to do – play the guitar and mess about in the kitchen.'

Ian's family are doing all that they can to make his life as comfortable as possible. Rosie has ordered a vest from America which has pouches to hold the batteries to help her dad's mobility.

The pair are joined by Dr Lim, Ian's cardiologist, who is hopeful that, in the future, someone like Ian won't need to order a vest from abroad. 'We have already come an incredibly long way with this device, but it's exciting to think where we might be able to get to. In the future, all these things,' he says pointing at Ian's wire and boxes, 'will be inside the body and you won't need batteries and wires outside at all.'

Ian was waiting for a heart transplant – an operation which

costs between thirty and forty thousand pounds. The machine currently keeping him alive costs seventy thousand pounds.

Ian had no idea how long he would be on that list. The youngest person given a heart transplant in the UK was five days old and the oldest was seventy-one. One of the real perks of that day in the QE Hospital, was getting to watch an operation take place.

The theatre was packed with people. There was a surgeon in there, a registrar, a student doctor, two runners and a scrub nurse. The surgeon was working at the 'business' end of the body, and at the other end someone else was taking a vein out of the right leg. It was about the width of a washing line. That vein would eventually be used to bypass a section of the heart.

The smell is difficult to get used to and even harder to forget. 'Is that burning?' I foolishly ask. It was burnt bone. They were using an instrument which coagulates the blood vessels while you cut. The skill of the surgeon means that the plan is to complete the entire operation without the patient requiring any extra blood.

I was never a strong scientist at school. I understood chemistry for about fifteen minutes, and I had a purple patch with physics around the time of my GCSEs but, outside of that, I was severely limited. That said, even I could appreciate the amazing nature of what I was watching. I asked the surgeon to explain what was happening for someone who had a very basic grasp of biology.

'The patient is hooked up to a machine which essentially takes over the function of their heart and lungs. The heart is stopped during the operation. If we can then keep it cold enough, we can stop it beating and reduce the energy requirements. We can then keep it alive without a blood supply. At the end of the operation, we take the clamp off, the solution is washed out of the heart and hopefully it starts to beat again.'

My mind was suitably blown. 'There is no such thing as routine heart surgery,' said the man who was showing us around. 'One technical error and the patient can die.'

With that thought rolling around my head I asked one of the heart surgeons, Neil Howell, how he managed to remain level-headed in those circumstances.

'Training' he says calmly. 'You look at it as a series of problems that need to be solved. You compartmentalise everything to remove the complication.'

The surgeon was an expert problem solver. If I was the bloke holding the scalpel, I would be terrified of making a mistake and harming the patient. Neil always took the patient out of the equation to streamline his decision making.

'People work differently but, for me, it's important not to see their face. I see the draping process (covering the patient) as part of the dehumanisation. I have trained for years to solve these problems. I have worked my whole life to be the best at that job that I possibly can be. I am paid to solve a technical problem. If I was a mechanic, it would be fixing a car. I am a biological mechanic. I fix bodies.'

Surgeons do have a tendency to be a little cocky, but, if I was the dehumanised body under the drape, I'd want to be operated on by someone who didn't allow doubt to fog their thought process. I'd want someone with that heightened sense of confidence.

When we met Eileen Wright that day, she was forty-two years old. At the age of thirty-one she became one of only six people in the UK (at the time) to have a heart and lung transplant.

'I remember the day clearly,' said Eileen. 'I could hear someone having a panic attack next door to me. They were screaming and I thought, "that's going to be me". I was told it would take twelve hours and then, all of a sudden, it was happening. Under I went.'

Eileen's operation was a success. 'I am so incredibly thankful . . . every time I breathe. I could breathe in deeply for the first time in my life. It is a wonderful feeling. I feel so fit compared to how I used to be.'

After a year, you're able to write a letter to the family of the patient who donated you the organ. Many choose not to as it is such an intensely emotional thing, not only for the person on the receiving end, but also for the donor's family.

'I didn't want to know too much about the person,' says Eileen. 'If I visualise them, I would start to feel guilty. Imagine if it was a mum who had a daughter? I have to, in my head, think about it as a spare part. I want to write the letter – I think knowing that a part of their loved one is keeping someone else going is truly remarkable.'

I don't know how you feel about the subject of organ donation. I don't know if you have ever discussed it with your friends and family. I don't know what you would do if you were in the situation that Steve, Ian or Eileen found themselves in.

I am going to introduce you to a woman who I think about a lot. Speaking to her opened my eyes to this subject. She was our final interviewee on the show that day in Birmingham and I will never forget our conversation. There are many people I have interviewed over the years who have made a lasting impact on me; some of them are featured in the pages of this book. There are very few who have reduced me to a sobbing wreck. Ilse Steyaert-Fieldsend did exactly that.

Before I tell you about this remarkable woman, I must ask you something. As you read her story, please try not to judge her, or the decisions she has made. This is a woman who has stared grief in the face and come out the other side. This is a woman who has been to a place that every parent dreads. This is a woman who has survived. This is her story and the story of her daughter, Georgia.

It is Christmas 2013. Ilse Steyaert-Fieldsend and her husband James had decided they were going to celebrate Christmas early that year. They were going to take their three-and-a-half-year-old daughter, Georgia, and two-year-old son, Joshua, on a last-minute family break to Egypt to avoid the vile British weather.

'We celebrated Christmas Day on 22 December, and it was wonderful,' remembers Ilse. 'The kids were none the wiser. They were just happy with their toys. I know it sounds a bit clichéd but Josh got a train set and Georgia got a doll's house. They played with them and we just left it all in the living room because we had to pack. I remember it was so cold and wet that December. We had booked flights to Sharm El-Sheikh the next day.'

Georgia was a particularly happy child. I know that every parent thinks their child is special, but it seems that Ilse and James had been blessed with what they describe as an 'easy' child. I asked Ilse to describe what Georgia was like.

'Her smile was infectious. She was great fun to be around. From the age of three months she would sleep through the night. We were very fortunate parents. She breast-fed from day one and the first night after she was born, Georgia slept through. We were in a packed ward with eight other mothers with noisy babies. Despite all that, Georgia had an amazingly peaceful night.'

'She was a good eater, a good sleeper, she just got on with it,' says her proud mum. 'People would say there was something magical about her. She was always smiling. She was a really good walker from as early as thirteen months. We used to walk everywhere. I love animals and love nature and she was the same. We talked about animals a lot. I remember taking her to pre-school on the first day. She saw her friends – Honor, Imogen and Nicky. She just ran off and enjoyed herself, leaving her sobbing mother at the gate. I cried my eyes out. She was fine. Not a care in the world.'

Just after her third birthday, Georgia told her mum that her head was hurting. 'I would rub her head and ask how it was.

Less than a minute later, she would just tell me it was fine and go back to dancing or jumping. A few weeks passed by and then she told me again. I remember speaking to James and saying that something was wrong. We agreed that I would take her to the doctor. Georgia just giggled and laughed through the whole thing and the doctor said she might not be drinking enough and told me to treat it with Calpol. It seemed like the right thing to do.'

A few weeks later, Ilse took Georgia to the doctor a second time, but again Georgia was fine, and her concerned mum was reassured that everything was normal.

Fast-forward to Christmas Day 2013 and the family holiday in Egypt. Georgia was playing on the beach with Ilse. They were running about in the sand and dancing. Georgia was always dancing. 'She asked me if she could go in the water,' recalls Ilse. 'We both went in together. She was playing with her shadow and I was taking pictures. She took off her little skirt to go swimming and then she screamed, 'MAMA! MAMA!' As she shouted my name a second time, she sounded in real distress . . . then she collapsed on the beach.'

Ilse caught her daughter but she was struggling to breathe. Georgia was rushed to the local hospital but one of the doctors there was unsure how to treat her. He was convinced Georgia was just sleeping, so while Ilse was screaming for help, still in her bikini, trying to give her daughter mouth-to-mouth, she was alone. The family later found out that Georgia had suffered from a ruptured brain aneurysm.

The next twenty-four hours were impossible. They couldn't

get a medical flight back to the UK without a guaranteed hospital bed and they couldn't get a hospital bed without a flight number. Eventually, after a series of desperate phone calls, Dr Akash Deep, from the Children's Intensive Care Unit at King's College Hospital in London confirmed there would be a bed available and, on Boxing Day 2013, the family made their way home.

During that flight came the conversation they had been dreading. The doctor who travelled with them confirmed the worst possible news. Their baby daughter was all but dead. They were unable to do the necessary tests in Egypt but there was no brain function. The only thing keeping Georgia alive was the machine she was strapped to.

They arrived at Luton Airport at one o'clock in the morning on 28 December. Ilse and Georgia went to the hospital in the ambulance and James and Joshua followed behind in a taxi. The tests over the next few hours confirmed the news they had received on the flight. Georgia had died on Christmas Day. There was nothing that could be done to save her.

'A parent never gives up hope,' says Ilse through the tears. 'If there is a one per cent chance, you cling to that one per cent. I believed with my whole heart that somebody would be able to save our child but, everywhere I turned, I was told that was impossible. The staff were exceptional. Their care for us was incredible, but they couldn't do anything for Georgia.'

This wasn't the first time that death visited Ilse's family. When she was fourteen years old and growing up in Belgium, her world was shaken by the death of her cousin – nineteen-year-old

Sandy Stayaert. Sandy was involved in a car crash, just a few streets away from the house where she lived and spent weeks in hospital in a coma before she passed away. Ilse remembers being taken to the hospital on the day that Sandy died.

'It was my fourteenth birthday. In the weeks before that I hadn't been able to see Sandy. I had quite bad asthma, so I wasn't allowed to see her in her coma in intensive care. I just had to look at her through the glass. We went as a family to say goodbye to her. It was a strange birthday for me. At that point, I had not experienced death at all. Sandy was like a big sister to me. She was my hero. I kissed her and I hugged her, and we said goodbye. That was the first time I ever thought about organ donation.'

'I remember we had had a conversation about it at school. There were complications with my cousin, so she was unable to donate her organs. The doctors didn't expect her to die when she did, so being a donor hadn't even been discussed. My grandmother was also suffering with cancer at the same time, so all these things were going through my head. I have carried a donor card ever since.'

Ilse remains close to Sandy's parents, Cécile and Eddy. She has seen them go through the full range of emotions: anger, sadness, guilt and everything in between. For years they had to drive past the spot where their daughter had the car crash that led to her death.

'I was always sad for them but, at the time, I never thought I would be able to understand the pain of losing a daughter. When I got pregnant, I asked them if I could use "Sandy" as a tribute to their daughter. When our daughter was born, we called her Georgia Sandy Fieldsend after my cousin.'

That memory of what had happened to Sandy prompted Ilse to have a crucial conversation with her husband while they were in King's College Hospital watching over their daughter.

'There was so much going round my head, but I just turned to James and said, "She's not coming back. I need to talk to you." It was at that point, while we were in the room with our beautiful Georgia, that we spoke about organ donation. It was a surreal conversation to be having. James didn't want to listen. It's just an impossible thing to discuss. There we were, two parents desperate for a miracle, but I was convinced we could still try and do some good. It was really hard for James to even think about it, but we took our time, we cried our hearts out, and we both came to the decision that it was the right thing to try and do.'

As a parent myself, I cannot begin to imagine the emotional torment that Ilse and James were going through. I was interviewing Ilse in a little waiting room on the transplant ward at the Queen Elizabeth Hospital. I was captivated by her every word. I remember looking around at this point in the interview to breathe and to try and gather my thoughts. Georgia's story was just pouring out of her mother and I hadn't spoken for several minutes. I don't think I'd have been able to talk without bursting into tears. I looked around the room at the 5 Live team, Laura, and a few other members of staff and everyone was feeling the emotional strain. I glanced down at my phone and it was constantly buzzing with friends and colleagues who were listening to Ilse's story and had been stopped in their tracks.

She continued to talk us through the decision about what to do with her daughter's organs.

'I couldn't stop thinking about Georgia's little brother Joshua,' said Ilse. 'What if we could stop him from dying by accepting an organ from someone else? Would we even have to think about it?'

Ilse and James spoke to Dr Akash. While his team started looking for those who might be able to benefit from Georgia's organs, Ilse and James were waiting for their families to arrive at the hospital to get a chance to see Georgia before they turned off her life-support system.

'It was the middle of the night,' says Ilse, 'and I had the idea that I wanted to record Georgia's heartbeat on my phone. She might be leaving us, but I wanted to be able to hear her forever. I was crying uncontrollably because the heart was too quiet to be picked up by my phone. One of the nurses heard my tears and said she would bring in an ultrasound machine to help. Then I could hear her heart, loud and clear. I recorded it on my phone. I cannot put into words what the kindness of that nurse meant to us as a family. I know it's a small thing, but the small things become so important. I knew Georgia's heart wasn't going to beat for much longer. I knew she was leaving us soon.'

The thing I have always found so hard to come to terms with when I think about Ilse and her family is, how do you think clearly when you feel like your world is falling down around you? There are so many practical and logistical decisions to make when it comes to organ donation. They are big enough decisions to think through in the cold light of day, so imagine the extra intensity and emotion of the crushing situation Ilse and James found them-selves in that night. While they were trying to work out how to say goodbye to their precious three-and-a-half-year-old daughter, the transplant team were frantically trying to save lives.

'They brought us in a form,' recalls Ilse. 'They are as sensitive and caring as it is possible for a human to be, but there is still something vile about deciding which of your dying daughter's organs you are going to allow them to use. We just had to keep thinking about how much good Georgia could do . . . but it was so hard.'

As they were going through the list, James broke down . . . 'Not her eyes, Ilse. Not her beautiful eyes.' Ilse was sick in the hospital bin by the side of their daughter's bed before pleading again with her husband.

'What if Josh was blind?' she said. 'What if a child can see again because of Georgia?'

They talked and cried and cried and talked. They ticked many of the boxes on the list . . . including the eyes.

It was New Year's Eve 2013 and Ilse and James were spending the final few minutes with their daughter. Dr Akash came into the room and calmly talked the couple through what would happen when they turned off the life-support machine. He answered all their questions.

Ilse is in tears as she recalls that night. 'I told him I had to do it. I had to do it myself. We were told that, once the machine was off, we would have five minutes with her before she had to go through the doors and into the operating theatre. If the organ removal was to be successful, there was no other way to do it. They prepared us for what we would see: Georgia would turn from pink to blue once her heart stopped and then it would be over.'

Ilse was shaking as she pulled out the tube which was keeping Georgia alive. She put her hand on her daughter's chest. 'I wanted to feel her last heartbeat. There is still a part of you that hopes it will keep beating, that it will never stop, but . . .' Ilse can't go on, she struggles to catch her breath. '. . . it just goes silent,' she continues, heartbroken again. 'I watched her change colour. We hugged her one last time. It was actually beautiful to cuddle her without tubes for the first time in days. We held each other – James and I – and even though our lives would never be the same again, we both knew we were doing the right thing. I kissed my baby girl and whispered, "Go, Georgia . . . go and do your thing." The doors opened and she was gone.'

If you speak to Ilse, she will tell you how important that moment was. As impossible as it was to let Georgia go, they felt there was a purpose and that gave them hope that they could get through this. The essential operation next door didn't take too long.

'She came back into the room,' says Ilse. 'She still looked like my Georgia. There was a white piece of tape up her body and there were artificial eyeballs . . . but it was still her. I put her favourite pretty dress on her from our luggage and her little dancing shoes. She was lying back in the bed as if nothing had happened . . . she was cold for the first time.'

Georgia saved four lives. Her kidney and her liver went to

a baby and a young girl. At her funeral, a few weeks later, Ilse read out a thank-you letter from one of the families.

The family received another letter later that month to say that two other transplant patients were alive and well because they had Georgia's heart valves.

Two young men can now see because Ilse and James decided to donate their daughter's eyes. Georgia's death was unexpected, painful, brutal and heart breaking but, in dying, she had changed the lives of six other people she never met.

Thankfully, Ilse was our final interview of that show. I am not sure any of us could have done much after that. I thanked everybody for taking part and then walked to the car park in a sort of daze. I rang my wife to check our children were okay. The rush-hour drive along the M42 and M1 back to Sheffield was punctuated by several phone calls from people who had listened to the interview. One fellow parent, whose daughter had benefited from a liver transplant, just wept down the phone for ten minutes.

Over the years I have often thought about Ilse, James and their son Joshua. I have kept across fundraising efforts and read articles about their attempts to come to terms with loss.

Unsurprisingly, the vast majority of parents who lose a child struggle to maintain their relationship. Ilse and James are still together but the years without Georgia have been tough ... almost impossible.

When I called Ilse to catch up, I had to wait on the phone for a couple of minutes because she was making pancakes for the children she was babysitting for friends. 'Sorry, Dan, we have a bit of a full house at the moment,' she says, having run straight from the kitchen. 'There are children and dogs everywhere. I am looking after pets too. It's a madhouse.'

We ask about each other's families and school. Joshua is the same age as our son, Joe. I ask her how she is getting on. There is a long pause.

'I'm tired of faking it,' says Ilse. 'I know that no one wants to be surrounded by misery, so I have learned to smile, or at least I pretend to. Life is lonely a lot of the time.'

It is now seven years since Georgia's death. Joshua, who was two years old at the time, is nine. He only has vague memories of his sister.

'Joshua knows her through us, and I want to remember everything. The problem is I remember the good and the bad. I remember the times that I wasn't the best mum, when I shouted at her, when I told her she couldn't play at the playground for those extra five minutes. I don't want to escape, but I also can't escape. I still have to go to birthday parties for other children who would be Georgia's age. I used to hate it, but I have learned to control myself. You get very good at biting your tongue even though inside your whole body is screaming, "DON'T YOU KNOW MY DAUGHTER DIED?" I'm not sure that would go down well at any party.' Ilse can laugh, but the tears are never far away.

When Ilse, James and Joshua first came back from hospital, they were allowed to bring Georgia's body back with them before the funeral. The funeral company came to check that the room was cold enough and that her body would be okay, but those days were precious for her mother.

'I know people think it's mad. There are probably people reading this now thinking, "What was she doing?" but you never know how you will grieve until you find yourself in that situation.

'I remember bringing her home and I was still in my summer dress and flip flops and it was minus three. I put Georgia in her bed, and I slept in the room with her. I moisturised her hands and feet to stop them getting dry and . . . ' Ilse has to stop to compose herself, '. . . I brushed her hair. It was so blonde and beautiful,' she sobs.

'It was hard for us all. Joshua would sometimes bang on the door and say, "My sister! My sister!" and cry to come in. I explained to him that his sister was asleep. He sat next to her, on my lap, and I would read Georgia a bedtime story.'

Ilse has come under fierce criticism for the way she dealt with her son at the time. 'People shouted at me and wrote horrible things about what we were doing. "How can a parent do this?" "How can you show a child a corpse?" I don't care what they say. If he was older, we would have done things differently. Dealing with the loss of a loved one is intensely personal and that time having Georgia's body at home, before the funeral, was so important to us.'

Georgia's body is now long gone but there are reminders of her everywhere. When they first came home from the hospital after her death, the doll's house they had bought her for

Christmas was still half played with in the living room. That now has a home in Georgia's bedroom.

Next to the doll's house is the little bag of Magic Reindeer Dust which Georgia brought back from her last day at nursery before Christmas in 2013. Georgia asked her mum if they could sprinkle it in the garden. Ilse said they would, but they never got round to it before they left for Egypt.

'It was one of the things we did when we brought her back to the house. I had made her a promise. I held her in my arms, I put some of the dust in her hand and we sprinkled it together.' There was a note on the bag which read: 'Sprinkle on the lawn at night; the moon will make it sparkle bright; as Santa's reindeer fly and roam; this will guide them to your home.' The note is still attached to the bag with the rest of the dust in it. That also has a home in Georgia's bedroom.

Two months before Georgia passed away, Pepper – the family dog – also died. They buried him in the garden together.

'We buried him with a toy and a photograph and a blanket to keep him warm. As we were covering him, I started to cry quite badly, and Georgia came up and grabbed my hand and said, "Don't cry, Mama, it's to keep him warm." We went to buy some daffodils and tulips and we covered his grave with the seeds. Georgia was gone so she never saw those flowers come up. When they did grow, at first, I wanted to rip them out and throw them away but I didn't have the strength. Now I have tried to make it a memorial to them both.'

I consider Ilse to be an incredibly strong woman and yet

she is so willing to talk about her frailties and struggles with breathtaking honesty.

'I still go to school with Joshua and sometimes, particularly in the years immediately after her death, I just wanted to sit in my car at the gates. I still find it hard to listen to parents tell me that they are desperate to get their kids back to school after the holiday. The fake smile comes out again, but it just eats away at you. I have cried at those gates many times, but I have never lost it with anyone. There are times when I just walk into the garden in the middle of the night and scream at the top of my voice. My mouth is so wide open I can almost feel it cutting at the sides. I talk a lot, but we haven't turned to therapy or drink. I know many people can cover the darkness with that, but we have chosen to take on that darkness . . . to take on that grief. That is how we deal with it. A good friend from Holland sent me a punchbag. I take my anger out on that.'

At the moment, every day remains a battle for Ilse. Some days are better than others, but it's hard to feel normal, when nothing feels normal. I am very thankful to have never gone through a grief like hers. I have no idea how I would react to the death of one of our children. I don't know how I would treat my other children if they lost a brother or a sister.

'I want Joshua to be a child,' says Ilse. 'You might think we would be over-protective, but we let him climb trees and run and play and do all the things his friends do. You don't want to scare your children, but at the same time I am always here to talk when he needs me. Sometimes he asks me where she is. Sometimes he wants to know if he has what Georgia had.

Sometimes he wants to talk about death and other times he says, "that's enough talking now". At Georgia's funeral, I told him that Georgia had gone now but that she was in his heart. He looked up at me and said, "With Pepper too?" and tapped his chest. I couldn't tell him that Georgia was in heaven because I talk about heaven being a nice place to be and I couldn't cope with him saying, "If she is in such a good place, why can't we be there too?"'

It was also at the funeral that two friends of the family performed a song about Georgia. Ellie, who was fourteen at the time, and sixteen-year-old Sophie wrote *Georgia's Song* which, even today, is still raising money for charity. Ilse was desperately looking for ways to still be Georgia's mother, even though she was gone.

'The song was all about saying goodbye to Georgia and I asked the girls if I could release it on her birthday. I had some crazy idea to try and get it to number one. It never happened which, at the time, made me feel like a failure but I know people are still buying it and listening to it even now . . . I know Georgia is still having an impact.'

You won't be surprised to hear that Ilse still doesn't sleep well at night. It's the images she can't get out of her head. Images from the beach: of Georgia crying 'Mama!' and then collapsing; Georgia saying, 'my head hurts' and the memory of looking into her daughter's eyes at the hospital, not seeing any response and then turning off the life support.

It's not a case of moving on for Ilse, it's learning to deal with the pain of the past. She knows she still needs help. She knows there is a long road ahead and she knows there are some things she needs to learn to let go. She's trying to let go.

'The heart beat I recorded at the hospital . . . I put that in a teddy bear and gave it to James for Father's Day. He can't listen to it. I still sleep with some of her cuddly toys. Part of me wishes I put them in the coffin with her but, at the time, I couldn't. There are two elephants, a little doll and Peppa Pig from her first birthday.

'I know this is mad,' says Ilse sobbing, 'and I know this has to stop, but I still have her pyjamas and sometimes I sleep in her bed.' She apologises for crying. I tell her it's okay and that she has nothing to say 'sorry' for.

'My husband is very tolerant. I don't care what people think. I have had enough of the judgement. I will make an effort this year to try and make the changes I know I need to make.'

Ilse asks me about some of the other people in the book. I talk to her about Gary Speed and John Sutherland. We talk about Tony Foulds and Ilse remembers hearing about the flypast in the park. Somehow the conversation turns to music.

'Do you like Abba, Dan?' she asks.

'Of course,' I say, 'who doesn't?'

'Well, we've managed to ruin "Dancing Queen" in our house,' says Ilse with a sigh. 'We decided to play it on the way to the funeral for our little dancing queen. You can imagine what happens when it comes on at weddings and every party we ever go to. I wish I had thought it through. That was one of my worst decisions.' Ilse has a similar reaction every time she hears that festive classic 'All I Want For Christmas Is You' by Mariah Carey.

'We played it twice in the hotel room on the day she died,' says Ilse. 'The pair of us sang along and danced like fools.'

I ask her if she is getting any professional help. In 2018, Ilse had an altercation with an angry truck driver on a street near her house. Her car was damaged, and she was left shaken and bruised.

'I don't know why that incident made such a difference to me, but I was in a bad way for a few days. For the first time, I felt that it was okay to go and ask someone for help. It was as if someone blew out a candle on the energy which had been keeping me going and I knew I couldn't survive without help. I am now on some anti-depressants which have helped, but I think it was also important to know that I didn't have to do things on my own.'

Ilse and James' house is full of children. Joshua is always having his friends around and his mum is trying to live her life. She has started listening to music again.

'I try not to moan about things that aren't important,' she says with a knowing smile. 'I have got a lot of things wrong but, if anyone wants to listen, then I would say: put your phone down, play with your child, read that story, give them that extra kiss, stay the extra ten minutes in the playground. Appreciate all that you have and all that they are, because it can be gone so quickly.'

The looks and the comments don't hurt Ilse anymore, but she knows she will never be the person she was before the death of her daughter.

'Some people find it difficult to be around grief. Some

people avoid me. I understand why, but some friends are no longer friends because people cannot cope. That is life. On the other side of things, some people who weren't the best friends before, have been amazing. If I look back on myself a few years ago I was boring and miserable, and I took people down with me. I don't blame anyone. I am much better at pretending. I try and fit in, and if I never fit in . . . that's okay. I am the mother of a dead child.'

Ilse talks to Georgia when she walks her dogs. She tells her what she's been cooking or what Joshua has been up to at school. She picks bluebells for her because Georgia used to pick them for her. She tells her she misses her and that she loves her. She tells her she's sorry that she couldn't save her. Ilse says she feels her in the trees, in the grass and the flowers. Sometimes she goes to the school plays that Georgia would have been in or watches the school sport's day to see what she would have been wearing. She knows she needs to let go, but she still feels like the mother of two children.

Hopefully, you can see why that conversation with Ilse, back in 2015, is still something that I often come back to. I wonder how I would act in that situation. I marvel at the clarity of thought when your heart is breaking and the determination to make a difference when you can't see through the grief. I worry about how Ilse is doing, and I want her to know that, even though she feels weak, she has made a huge impact on the lives of so many other people.

There was a surge in people signing up to the donor register after her interview that day. There were thousands of messages and emails that came into 5 Live from people who were awe-struck by Georgia's story and the impact her death had on so many people.

'I'm happy but angry at the same time,' says her mum. 'I'm angry that it had to be my little girl . . . but happy that she has achieved so much. I'm coping better with it these days. I still don't sleep. I find it hard to rest but I take great solace from knowing that my little girl has touched so many people. I could be the angry, bitter mother, and some days I feel like that, but who does that help? I talk about organ donation because I have to let the anger go and direct it somewhere else.'

There are four people alive today, and two young men who can see, because of the decisions that Ilse and James made that night sitting next to their dying daughter. One of those families still sends cards and pictures to Ilse to let them know how they are getting on.

How does Ilse look back on that choice now?

'James and I had to have an impossible conversation when it was all happening around us. I feel very strongly that people should think about being a donor before they are near a hospital bed. We were both given strength because of the way we were able to say goodbye. We knew that other children were waiting that night, we knew that lives would be saved. Three people die every day because of a lack of available organs. I can't bring my daughter back, but I can strive to make a difference.'

When I was first asked to consider writing this book, Ilse was the first person who sprang to mind. Over the years, whenever I am asked about the most amazing people I have interviewed, she is always prominent in my thoughts. I presented that afternoon show on 5 Live for eighteen months. During that time, we spoke to some incredible people. They all had stories to tell but none of them stayed with me like Ilse has. It is strange but that one twenty-minute interview, from more than five years ago, is still so clear in my mind.

When I caught up with her again, I felt that same connection with her story. Maybe it's being a parent but, even though her pain is so personal, it still affects me deeply.

I find her strength remarkable. As a Christian, who lent heavily on my faith when our child was ill, I am fascinated by how she survives without that personal relationship with God.

Most importantly, I want her to be okay. I want her to know that she can be at peace with the decisions she made and still face a lifelong struggle with grief. I am aware it sounds simplistic, but I desperately want her to know that you can be broken and brilliant at the same time. She may feel weak, but she gives strength to so many around her.

Ilse Steyaert-Fieldsend has an incredible story to tell. She may have lost a life, a life so dear to her . . . but she is inspiring others to change theirs. She is a remarkable person.

'DO YOU WANT WEIGHTLIFTING OR MARIA?'

'So, we can essentially do what we want then?' I asked Ron Chakraborty, the man in charge of the Olympics at the BBC.

'Within reason, yes. The main sport will be on BBC One, so you'll have loads of time to fill on BBC Four.'

Music to my ears. I have always loved the Olympics. I can remember bits and pieces from Seoul in 1988: Ben Johnson in the 100m final and Barry Davies with his 'Where were the Germans?' magic from the hockey. I once met Sean Curly at a corporate event a few years ago and went into full fan-boy mode. I was thirty-two!

By 1992 and Barcelona, I was all over it. Singing along with Freddie Mercury and Montserrat Caballé, I was fully immersed in the sport. I don't think I was alone wandering around the house doing my best David Coleman impression: 'It's Linford Christie . . .' or 'Gunnell goes for gold . . . and Gunnell gets the gold'. I spent much of that summer in an ill-fitting pair of Great Britain shorts.

Fast forward to 2016 and I got the opportunity to cover my third Olympic Games for the BBC. I was working for *Sports News* during Beijing, had a highlights show on BBC One in 2012 and – this time around – I would be on Copacabana beach in Rio for BBC Four.

Four years earlier, London 2012 Olympics had been a truly amazing experience. Our show started at midnight and was essentially a round-up of everything that had happened during the day. We were the ones who turned out the lights in the Olympic studio and it did feel a little lonely in the Olympic Park in the early hours of the morning. Everyone else had gone home before we started and it was just our little team left in the huge televisual temple that was the International Broadcast Centre.

Despite the late nights, it was a wonderful show to work on. The only frustration was that, by the time we had finished, everything was shut. That meant that, even though the salubrious Stratford Ibis hotel was just the other side of one of the main gates, we had to wander all the way over to the far side – around the entire perimeter – to get back to watch the staff putting out the muesli for the following morning's breakfast.

Things were a little different four years later. Half of the BBC team were staying in a hotel near the International Broadcast Centre; just a few javelin throws from the main stadium. I was part of the 'beach' team who were based at the Copacabana studio. Our hotel was about 800 yards back from the famous strip, at the beach-volleyball stadium end of things.

We were on every night throughout the games for seven hours on BBC Four. Our studio was inside one of the little beach huts at the far end of Copacabana – about a twenty-minute walk from the hotel.

Our pre-games plan was always to make the show as inter-active as possible, involve as many locals as we could, and try and turn Copacabana into the world's largest living room so that, after a few days, viewers felt like they could find the light switch in the dark. Our editor was a good friend from the BBC, Matt Roberts.

'We had a remit to move away from the sport,' says Matt, 'and try to show the impact of the games and see what an event like that is like when you are in the thick of it. Our show was never going to be just about the sport. We wanted to pack it with people, with culture . . . with as much as possible. Volun-teers were a huge slice of the 2012 experience and the beach, and the people who lived, worked and hung out there were a big part of 2016. That was our focal point.'

When you are trying to produce a more relaxed magazine show you have to be willing to take a few risks. It always takes a bit of time for the audience to get used to things too.

'Dan, I'm afraid you're going to have to get rid of the golden coconuts,' was the top line of an email that arrived on Day 2 of the games from one of the head honchos at BBC Sport.

One of the ideas we had was to have a part of the set which showed how many gold medals Team GB had won over the course of the games. We had constructed a metal tree and the plan was to a spray a coconut gold, put the face of the medallist on the front of it, and hang it on the tree each time we won one. The coconut would be processed into the studio – accompanied by some appropriately daft music. The hope was that, by the end of the games, we'd have a giant tree of shimmering golden coconuts in the corner of our little beach hut.

Apparently, then somebody at the *Daily Telegraph* listed 'Dan Walker's Golden Coconuts' as one of the '5 Most Annoying Things About The Olympics So Far'. One day in and, unbelievably, the coconuts were already under pressure.

I don't know exactly how these things work, but I think there was a high-level discussion about whether the coconuts would survive. I wasn't in on these discussions but, if you've ever seen the comedy series *W1A* on BBC Two, I don't imagine it was far off that sort of thing – just without Hugh Bonneville.

I made a strong case on email and fought hard, but it was decided that the coconuts would no longer be with us. The gold spray paint went back in the box.

There was one positive that came out of the death of that idea: by the end of the games a tree bursting with 27 golden coconuts would have significantly obscured our view of the beach and that, and the people on it, were to become the stars of the show.

Each night our live coverage on BBC Four became a combination of Olympic sport intercut with slices of Copacabana life and social media interaction from around the world. Matt was determined to get the balance right.

'The key thing we tried to remember was that the Olympics is about the whole country. Alongside the sport, you have to make space for the engaging characters. We also benefited from not having an advert break on the BBC so, instead of that, we could show our audience five minutes of a bloke climbing a lamp post while juggling a football. If you can't make good TV out of that, you're not doing a good job.'

The other element which came to the fore in our coverage was the magic of social media. It's not the sort of thing you can plan, you just sort of hope and trust it will work out. Every night we would get instant feedback. It was a sign of audience engagement and also a good indication of what people liked. We saw really early on that people loved our ten-minute stroll along the beach, where we took the camera and a microphone and just chatted to whoever we came across.

'It was totally unplanned,' says Matt, 'and at times totally terrifying, but the audience loved it and it was completely different to what we were showing on BBC One. Every night we were able to bring our UK audience a large portion of life in Rio and they loved it.'

After a few days my phone would start exploding each night with requests to see 'Antony Worrall Thompson' – or at least his lookalike – who trained every night behind us on the beach. Each evening, at the same time, he would sprint up and down the sand just outside our studio. There would be intense bicep curling, squat-thrusting and some serious burpee-based fun. He was completely unaware that millions of people were mildly obsessed with him back in the UK.

It seems daft, but we would interrupt the archery to bring our viewers live footage of 'AWT', as he affectionately became known, attempting the one-minute press-up challenge. We discovered that our Brazilian look-a-like never trained on a Saturday – which was a huge disappointment to his army of fans – who started a 'No AWT No Party' hashtag, which quickly started trending on Twitter every weekend. Just to complete the magic, in the final few days of the Olympics, we actually had some footage of the real Antony Worrall Thompson from the kitchen in England to prove that the guy on the beach was a different bloke.

We strolled down the beach chatting to those who would come out to fish at night, even though they spoke no English whatsoever. The linguistically awkward 'Fisherman's Corner' became a big hit back home. We regularly discussed the colour of the moon, but nothing got more airtime than the nightly emptying of the Copacabana bins. Over the course of the fortnight we got very friendly with the #Copacabinmen and they became a strangely huge part of the show. They were even getting talked up as we came on air . . .

'Good evening, welcome to Copacabana beach . . . it's Day 5 of the Olympic games. We have news of a Team GB gold in the canoeing, we'll be live at the men's synchronised 3-metre diving – where Chris Mears and Jack Laugher have a chance of a medal – and we'll be catching up on our beach binmen who are due to be with us in about three hours time.'

'I think that was the beauty of it all,' laughs Matt. 'When you are on one of the main channels it can be hard to find your flow. You are constrained by having to go to the news with Huw Edwards and everything you show comes under intense scrutiny. If we were delaying the handball final for five minutes on BBC Four we wouldn't get anywhere near the same number of complaints. I think, during one of the matches, we had a forty-minute break at half-time to stroll around the beach and have some live music. We recorded the second half and put it out later and no one even batted an eyelid. After a few days, the audience got used to the way we were trying to do things.'

Those same columnists who were critical of our coconuts were starting to enjoy the slightly different coverage on BBC Four. 'I know there is live hockey on BBC One, but is anyone else waiting for the binmen to arrive on BBC Four?' wrote one of them on Twitter. We were getting unprecedented viewing figures – up to four million people were tuning in on the bigger nights to watch our live coverage from the beach.

Obviously, the vast majority of the marquee gold medal moments were over on BBC One, but we didn't want to let them have all the fun. I reminded Matt of the time we decided to hand out some fake gold medals to the binmen. 'I can't believe we got away with that really. I have a vague memory of us interrupting them halfway through their shift and having a fully-blown ceremony on the beach! Did that really happen?' Yes it did, and it didn't go down well with everyone . . .

'I can't believe it,' said Mrs Angry on Twitter. 'Dan Walker has just delayed going back to the live coverage of the men's water polo final to hand out plastic gold medals to some Brazilian binmen.'

Rafael, Alejandro, Flavio, Pedro and Luis had become a huge part of the coverage and, whenever they drove their bin lorry down the beach, whatever we were doing on TV would stop. The nation demanded it.

Throughout the games, we invited questions and comments on social media and every night Twitter was awash with related hashtags, most of which derived from the original #Copaca-banter.

Given the incredible success of the focus on the Rio refuse collectors, #Copacabinmen trended most nights but #Copaca-barber went down very well when we had Rio's top hairdresser on, and #CopacaNoodle was perhaps the most controversial hashtag of the games.

One night, as the legend goes, there was a couple directly behind us who decided to, how can I say this, become a little overly amorous on a populated beach. 'There was a lot of flesh on show that night,' remembers Matt. I am pretty sure the couple were aware they were on telly, as they had carefully positioned themselves in shot. They were trying to disguise things by the fella nonchalantly reading a book over his partner at the same time. I remember our crew laughing and pointing while I was talking to camera and I referenced it on air but, despite our camera team offering a close-up (on camera two), our editor wisely decided not to take it.

'Don't you dare take camera two,' giggled Matt to our vision mixer (the person in charge of which camera gets put live during a broadcast).

I attempted to continue the show but it can be difficult while everyone else on talkback (which is what you can hear in your ear while you're trying to talk) is either laughing or passing unhelpful comments. This is what you'll have heard me say on the TV, interspersed with what I was hearing in my ear at the same time. Matt was the editor, who you've met already, our director was a lovely fella called Chris Treece, another Dan was the floor manager and Cath was operating the camera.

ME: 'And for those asking what is going on in the background right now . . .'

EDITOR: 'We all know what's happening Dan!' [Laughter.]

ME: '. . . we are not going to zoom in . . .'

EDITOR: 'Don't you dare take camera two.' [Serious.]

DIRECTOR: 'Oh my word!'

ME: '. . . but, rest assured . . .'

EDITOR: 'What are they doing? Is it . . .?' [Confused.]

DIRECTOR: 'I think it might be!'

BACKGROUND: [Laughter.]

ME: '. . . it's not that . . .'

FLOOR MANAGER DAN: [Points at the couple and hugs himself.]

ME: '. . . it's a hug . . .'

EDITOR: 'That's NOT a hug.' [Laughter.]

DIRECTOR: 'I think you might be right.'

ME: 'It's just a hug. There's a bit of . . .'

FLOOR MANAGER & CAMERA OPERATOR: [More charades – this time opening their hands in classic fashion and laughing.]

ME: 'They are reading a book.'

EDITOR: 'What?' roaring with laughter along with the rest of the gallery.

DIRECTOR: 'Funny looking book.'

ME: 'Apparently . . . they are reading a book.'

EDITOR: 'This is hilarious.'

BEACH CREW: [Half of them pointing . . . the others bent double.]

ME: 'They are reading a book . . . in very strange pose!'

EDITOR: 'You can say that again.' [Laughter.]

DIRECTOR: 'This might break the internet.' [More laughter.]

ME: 'Okay. We'll find out what the book is maybe . . . a little later on.'

EDITOR: 'I hope the Director General isn't watching.' [Serious.]

DIRECTOR: 'Well, that went well.'

As you might expect, social media erupted, and the story got loads of coverage back in the UK. That was our second most dramatic night of the games. Nothing compared to the column inches devoted to the real star of Rio 2016. It's time to introduce you to Maria.

I remember the Saturday night vividly. There was a lot of activity up and down Copacabana throughout that show – more so than a normal night of the week, as you might expect. We had already declined our fair share of drunk Brits ambling past demanding to come on the telly. We had relatives of athletes strolling along saying they were following the coverage back in the UK before coming out. We had a few demands from people who wanted to see Antony Worral Thompson, or the binmen, in the flesh after watching them on TV.

It was a huge night of athletics on BBC One so we weren't really sure how many people would be watching our show on BBC Four. I was in the process of summarising what viewers would be able to catch on the other channel when I heard a commotion behind me. There were about a dozen women singing and dancing their way down the path that ran along the length of the beach.

'Let's see what's going on over here,' I said nodding to Cath, who was behind the camera. She swung around to see what was happening. 'Looks like some sort of hen-do, shall we have a look? There they go. A Brazilian hen-party. They are clearly enjoying themselves. They seem to be all tied together as well. Magnificent scenes. Maybe that's how you do it in Brazil.'

In the middle of that excitable crowd was a Rio resident by the name of Maria De Cezar. 'We had been at my grandmother's house for my party,' she recalls. 'We had had a great night and, after two or three drinks there, we decided to go to the streets and go to some bars to continue things. As soon as we got on the street, the atmosphere was amazing so we just decided we would stay outside, make our way to the beach, and take the party with us. We were already having a great night when we made our way to Copacabana.'

With our cameras now firmly on them, Maria loosened the bonds holding them all together and wandered over. 'There's the bride. Can we see the bride?' I motioned back to Cath to swing the camera back to see a beautiful woman singing into her bouquet of flowers.

'Where are you from?' she shouted over the security barrier in near perfect English. It was one of those moments in broadcasting where you have to make a snap decision.

'I think we had a little bit of time to fill before going back to the clean and jerk,' remembers Matt. 'It was late at night in the UK and I remember thinking that this hen-do looked like a better class of party than you'd get, with respect, in somewhere like Blackpool.'

I beckoned her over. She was allowed past our very alert security guard, Jose, and came smiling to the desk in the studio and announced to the world that her name was 'Maria'.

At the time Maria was working for Fiat Chrysler in their purchasing team in Rio. She was getting married the following month just a few hundred yards away from our studio. 'You have to understand that this all came at an incredibly stressful time for me,' says the now happily married Maria. 'I was thinking about the wedding all the time, but I was also incredibly proud of our city, our country, for hosting the games. We all knew it was a big moment for all Brazilians and we were excited that the rest of the world would be watching and learning about Brazil. When I came over to sit next to you that night, I didn't even know we were live on TV. I thought at first you might be from Brazil. My friends all started chanting my name so I thought I would just enjoy it and see what happened.'

'Can I give a message to my husband?' asked Maria smiling down the camera that night.

Everaldo, the man in question, was living in the city of Belo Horizonte, about 275 miles north of Rio.

'I hope he's watching BBC Four,' I commented. He wasn't, but that didn't stop Maria declaring her love for him, for her football team – Fluminese – and telling us about her tattoos'.

As I watched it back with our editor Matt he couldn't stop laughing. 'We just caught them at the perfect time didn't we? She could still speak, you could make sense of everything she said but all her inhibitions had gone. A few more caipirinhas, and it could have been dangerous. She also had that live crowd to cheer her on. Throw all that together, and you were well on your way to some TV gold. At that point, I didn't really care what they were showing on the other channel, we had the Usain Bolt of hen-dos.'

As Maria was pouring her heart out to the British public, I turned to the camera.

'People are waiting for weightlifting,' I said with a huge smile on my face. 'Do you want weightlifting or Maria?' knowing full well we wouldn't be returning to the live action at Pavilion 2 of Riocentro any time soon. 'MARIA!' came the resounding cry from the BBC Four gallery.

We showed her delirious hen-do crowd once more and Maria asked where we were from. 'BBC,' I said. She looked surprised and repeated 'BBC' back at me rubbing her thumb and fingers together to show what that meant to her before laughing, turning to camera, and saying, 'Guys . . . watch BBC' and then motioning to her friends to start chanting. They delivered. 'BBC! BBC! BBC!'

'Do you know why I rubbed by fingers together, Dan?' asks Maria as we chat four years on. 'About halfway through I realised that we were live. One week before we came down to the beach, I had been to the handball with Everaldo. When we came out of the Future Arena that night, we had seen a huge truck and buildings with "BBC" on the side. It looked so much bigger than all the others and we were all impressed by the facilities. That's why I made the gesture. When you said "BBC" I remembered how nice all that looked, and I knew it was important.'

Eventually, I wrapped up the wonderful conversation with Maria but not before she turned to camera again, put her hand to the side of her head and said 'Call Me' down the lens, flashing her eyes, provocatively. 'You can't ask people to call you,' I interjected, 'you're getting married!'. Maria threw her head back in laughter, thanked us all for having her and returned to her party of admirers.

'You don't get that on BBC One, do you?' I said, giggling down Cath's camera. 'I think we got away with that!' I'll be honest; the clean and jerk seemed a little dull after all that. There was no way the weightlifting could compete with Maria.

I am so happy we took the risk on that Saturday night and invited her over. It was, as Matt said the 'Usain Bolt of hen-dos'. We all knew it was a great bit of TV and our viewers loved it, but it was really late back home in the UK and, even though we all walked back to the hotel that night buzzing, we had no idea what was going to happen the next day.

I was woken up by the combined forces of a loud text message alert and the sun bursting through the largely pointless curtains in my hotel room. There were over 200 messages on my phone. I lifted it up to see what all the fuss was about, and it started ringing. A BBC press officer wanted to know if I was available to do a round of interviews.

The most recent text message was from a friend who analysed web traffic for his job back in the UK. 'What have you done?' it read, followed by a laughing emoji. He included a little graph which showed our interview with Maria had already been viewed over fifteen million times – just in the UK. She was even bigger news in Brazil.

Maria and Everaldo were married on 17 September on Copacabana Beach just as they had planned. They now live in Braga in Northern Portugal and I spoke to them both together about the morning after the night before.

'I was in Belo Horizonte,' recounts Everaldo. 'The next morning Maria called me to tell me she was okay after her big night. She told me she had been out on the streets with friends and had a great time and even went on the TV. She told me she would go off to have breakfast and that she'd ring me again in a few hours.'

Maria, as she often does, was laughing in the background as her husband was talking before interjecting. 'I had a text message from a friend who lived in England. She told me that I was the top trend on Twitter in the UK. I didn't really understand what she was on about. I hadn't even seen the video.'

'And while that was happening,' explains Everaldo, 'my friends were telling me about Maria's video with you, Dan. I rang her back and she explained to me a little bit more about what happened but we both could not really get our heads around it.'

Maria had become an overnight star. She was being talked about and interviewed on Brazilian TV and radio and the following Monday morning, she was on the front page of the local newspaper. *Good Morning America* were playing the clip on their show live from Brazil.

The next few days down at our beach studio were completely bonkers. Each night hundreds, and sometimes thousands of people, would flock down to take pictures and talk to us about Maria. It was a beautiful atmosphere every evening. The mayor of Rio came down to thank us for reflecting his city in a positive light and Maria's mum, Hercilia De Cezar, came on the TV to invite us back to the wedding a month later!

'My entire family are a bit like me,' laughs Maria. 'We are all very spontaneous. They all realised that this was an amazing moment, so they decided to jump in the boat with me and enjoy it. They all wanted to share in that energy. It was lovely. My mum came up with the idea of inviting you to the wedding. She didn't even tell us about it. She just came down to the beach to meet you because everyone was talking about it and she wanted you to be there too. It actually caused quite a stir in the family. A few of our relatives got in contact to say, "Why are you inviting Dan but not us?"'

A few nights after Maria's starring performance, we were

back at the beach, and I noticed a kind looking fella who had cycled past our studio when we went on air. Two hours later, he was still there, sat on his bike and leaning on the railings, quietly listening in and occasionally smiling and waving. I had a little break while the live sport was on, so I walked over to say 'hello'.

'I'm Maria's dad', he said, bursting with pride. We hugged and I asked him why he didn't mention it before. I invited him to come in and take a seat. 'No, No', he insisted through laughter. 'TV is not for me. I will leave that to the ladies of the family. I was just coming past on my way home from work and I wanted to watch you and wait to say "thank you" for all you have done for my daughter. Maria has had the most amazing week and we hope you can come back for the wedding.'

'I think you really helped to calm things down, Dan,' explains Everaldo. 'It sounds crazy, but all the attention was a really good distraction from the stress of the wedding. Maria stopped being worried and started enjoying it. She was trying to fit in all these interviews at the same time as trying to sort out the wedding.'

I think there are two incidents which show you the impact of this story. On the first day I arrived in Brazil I got in a car at the airport and went to the hotel. As I got out of the taxi a young fella bounded up to me with great excitement. 'He wants your autograph,' said our driver, Luis. 'Who does he think I am?' I asked. The pair chatted in Portuguese and, after the lad walked off disappointed, Luis explained. 'He saw the cameras and thought you were one of the presenters from Globo TV [a very popular station in Brazil]. Apparently, you look like him. Don't worry,' said Luis, 'I told him you were just from the BBC and he wasn't interested anymore.'

This happened about three of four times over the course of the week before the games actually started. I became quite skilled at saying 'I'm sorry, that's not me. I work for the BBC' in Portuguese.

On the Monday night after the Maria interview, I was walking back from our beach studio to the main BBC compound on Copacabana. I can tell you exactly where I was standing because it was the point at which my phone pinged to ask me if I wanted to join 'Ryan Seacrest's Personal WiFi'. The US TV star was hosting NBC's night-time Olympic coverage from a beach-front studio and the NBC team were staying in the nearby Copacabana Palace. That was the super-fancy five-star hotel just a few hundred yards away. I used to giggle every time I walked past wondering how big a star you need to be before you are able to demand your own personal WiFi.

Anyway, my phone was pinging, just as I saw a group of six girls waiting patiently outside the door that led to the BBC and NBC compound. They saw me arriving. 'There he is! There he is! Can we have a picture, please?' they screamed politely. They spoke good English, so I started explaining that my name was Dan and that I was not the guy from Globo TV. They interrupted, 'We know who you are. We come for you. You're the Maria Man!'

The second incident came from a phone call on my first day back in the UK. The whole thing was amazing. The guy on passport control at Heathrow smiled as I walked up to him. 'Are you going back for the wedding then?' Maria was all the taxi driver wanted to talk about and while I was in the car my phone rang with one of those 'no number' calls.

It was the Brazilian ambassador to the UK. He wanted to thank me for the coverage he and 'many thousands of proud Brazilians' had been watching from Rio and he invited me to come and join him for the annual celebration of 'Brazil Day' in Trafalgar Square on Saturday, 10 September.

As soon as I returned to the UK I was back into 'normal' life. I arrived on the Sunday, was back on the *BBC Breakfast* sofa on the Monday morning and returned to the full swing of the football season the following weekend. On 10 September, we were due to be filming *Football Focus* live from West Ham's new ground, the 2012 Olympic Stadium. I called the Brazilian embassy back and told them I would love to attend but that I wouldn't be able to be there from the start. I said I would make my way there after *Football Focus* and hopefully be with them about 4 pm. 'That will be too late, Dan. Can we send you a car? What time do you finish?' I explained that the show finished at 1 pm and there was a pause at the other end of the line followed by a brief whispered conversation with someone in the background in Portuguese. 'The ambassador's official diplomatic car will be waiting outside the stadium for you at 1 pm.'

'How will I know which one it is?' I asked rather stupidly. There was kind laughter at the other end. 'You won't miss it, Dan. It'll be the big black one with two Brazilian flags on either side of the bonnet.'

As I sat in the back of the very plush, wide, bulletproof car on my way to Trafalgar Square that day, I will freely admit that I didn't really know what to expect. The moment I stepped out of the vehicle things got a little crazy. I was whisked into a VIP tent outside the National Gallery and introduced to a string of dignitaries including Eduardo dos Santos, the Brazilian ambassador to the UK.

There were hugs, questions about Maria, meat, more questions about Maria, more meat, questions about what I thought of Brazil, followed by even more meat, questions about how I found Rio and about whether I was going back for the wedding. After all that, more meat, and several interviews, I was taken out on to the balcony to see the crowd. There were fifty-thousand people packed into Trafalgar Square. 'What are you going to say to them?' asked the reporter from the *Evening Standard*. 'Pardon?' I spluttered, almost choking on my fourteenth meat kebab. 'It says on the running order you are down to address the crowd at three thirty.' It was 3.21.

I was whisked down the stairs, around the back of the heaving sea of green and yellow, to the back of the huge stage.

The production manager gave me the most enormous hug over the loudest samba music I had ever heard. He shouted in my ear about how important it was for Brazilians to see their country fairly represented on the BBC. 'You talked to real people. You showed the real Brazil. These people want to say, "thank you". I hope you're ready.' I wasn't.

I was standing in the wings with Thiago Braz da Silva, the pole-vaulter who had won one of Brazil's seven golds in Rio. He was introduced to the crowd and they went wild. The presenter started my build up. A minute later he was still going. I was getting increasingly uncomfortable and embarrassed. I don't think I will ever get the opportunity to play Glastonbury in my life but walking out onto that stage was as close as it will ever get. Fifty-thousand people went mad and cheered everything I said. Just when I thought it couldn't get any more bonkers, they brought out a fake bride and we re-enacted the hen-party, and then the wedding on stage. You'll be pleased to hear there was nobody reading a book in the background! It was a truly ridiculous but wonderful experience.

As I got on the train back to Sheffield from Brazil Day, a family ran over and said how much they had enjoyed BBC Four at the Olympics. Another fella shouted 'No AWT, No Party!' and gave me a thumbs up as he wandered off towards the Thameslink platform.

Maria's life was just as crazy. 'I was getting messages of love and support from all over the world,' she admits. 'People in Australia, Dubai, China, America – all over the place – were wishing me the best for my life and telling me how much they had enjoyed the video. There was so much good energy and love.'

The build up to the wedding was filled with the normal worries about guests and flowers but it was interspersed with daily requests for interviews from media outlets all over Brazil. Her husband and family found it hilarious that Maria had a new army of fans who were desperate to know all about her wedding. 'It changed all the focus but in a really good way,' says her husband, Everaldo. 'We both look back at it as such a special time.'

The whole team on BBC Four were truly humbled by how well Maria, and the rest of the coverage, went down with viewers. People have written and said really nice things about what we did on the beach in Rio so just allow me to drop a few names. These are the people who made it all happen.

Matt Roberts, who you've heard a lot from, was our editor and Chris Treece directed the whole thing. They had a top team working with them at the International Broadcast Centre: Lowri, Adam, Caroline, Cameron, Howard and Julie all did a magnificent job in the gallery as did Tim, Steve and Caroline in VT (where we edit our Olympic films and play stuff out from).

Down at the beach we had floor manager Dan and then Cath, Rob, Marco, Gary, Jose, Mauricio, Carlos, Alison in the Kiosk of Dreams and Suzanne, Sam and Becky in the main office where the BBC One studio was. Becky had the job of spray painting the only golden coconut ever used on the BBC coverage.

Sadly, I wasn't able to make it back to Brazil for Maria's wedding. That summer of 2016 had been a crazy one. I had started presenting *BBC Breakfast* in February and then spent six weeks in Paris working on the European Football Championships. Once that had finished, I spent five days at home before going straight to Rio for a month working on the Olympics. I am not asking you to feel sorry for me, because I loved every minute of it, but I desperately needed to spend some time at home with my family.

I sent Maria a message which she played at the wedding but she and Everaldo took things even further on their big day.

'It was all my mum's idea again,' laughs Maria. 'She said, "We can't have Dan at the wedding, but we need to have Dan at the wedding." That's where the face masks came in.'

This is where it gets really weird but, at a wedding nearly 6,000 miles away from my home in Sheffield, every guest had my face cut out on a piece of A4 paper. It didn't all go smoothly though.

'My dad, Ivan, called to tell people that we were ready to arrive for the wedding,' remembers Maria. 'I think I was ready early. The master of ceremonies told my dad that it was lovely that the bride was going to be on time but that we had to wait. The BBC film crew was not there yet so we could not start! So, Dan . . . you delayed my wedding by fifteen minutes and you weren't even there!' Maria giggles as she remembers what was 'the best party ever'.

'Dan, you missed a great night. We were dancing and drinking right by where we first met on Copacabana. You would have loved it.'

I have stayed in contact with Maria ever since that chance meeting in 2016. We talk, we text, we tweet each other. I still get asked about her all the time and she still has her 'fans' checking in on her.

When I look back at the whole incident with Maria, I always think about the importance of taking risks in broadcasting and trying things that have the potential to be terrible.

It was one of those wonderful moments where there is no

script or plan. It just feels right, and it flows. Someone more recently described it to me like this. 'It's like one of those great online videos. Like that professor who was conducting an interview on TV when his child burst in and started dancing up to the camera. No matter how many times you watch it, it still feels fresh the next time.' I don't think it's quite up there with the professor, but it was wonderful to be part of something that brought a smile to the face of a lot of people.

I used to work in a bookshop in my hometown of Crawley, to earn a little extra money at school. I worked there with a friend from school called Paul Stone. During busy periods, it was his job to restock and tidy the right side of the store while I took care of the left. The 'Philosophy' section was in my half and on the top shelf was a book of Chinese proverbs. No one ever bought the book but it was one of those that I always displayed prominently because I liked the quote on the front cover: 'If you're afraid of making a mistake, you'll never make a discovery.'

That's how I feel about Maria. We took a chance on an interview that could have gone wobbly-bob very quickly but, thankfully, it worked out perfectly. We stumbled upon an enthusiastic, fun-loving, kind, friendly bride-to-be who encapsulated the spirit of Brazil and the positive image that the country was desperate to show to a watching world. Before the games there had been so much talk about the violence that plagued parts of the country. Those few minutes of spontaneous television helped to put the focus back on the real Brazil and the joy and vibrancy of the people.

All those Brazilians in Trafalgar Square saw a country they

recognised in Maria's moment. She was happy, proud and full of life. She also appealed to the huge TV audience. We all wanted more of her. The Olympics is about sport and people and sometimes the people are more important than the sport.

Millions, all over the world, watched Maria on television and thousands have followed her life ever since. There is still so much interest whenever I post an update about what she and her beautiful family are up to. She and Everaldo now have a lovely young daughter, Joana.

'She is a copy of her mum,' beams Everaldo. 'She wakes up smiling, she is very spontaneous. No problems sleeping and, just like her mum, she only cries when she is hungry.'

'Everaldo!' shouts Maria, laughing. 'I wish he was wrong.'

'If you want to see Maria mad,' explains Everaldo, 'you need to keep her away from food. But they are both wonderful. Joana, just like her mum, is a gift from the skies.'

'Dan,' says Maria, 'we look back on that day a lot. The day that we met. They love it, my friends, you know. One of my best friends though, her boyfriend, doesn't like you because after that hen-party he didn't see her for a week!'

'You know what is funny?' says Everaldo. 'The newspapers in Rio, on the day we got married, they printed a story saying I was the luckiest man in Brazil. They said I was the only fiancé who didn't need to worry about what happened at the hen-party because everybody in the whole world knows where she was and what she was doing.'

Maria gets a little emotional. 'It was special though, Dan. It is a coincidence, here we all are, exactly four years on from Rio and this time, there will be no games in Tokyo because of the virus. But four years after the best summer of my life, I have another beautiful moment. The birth of Joana.'

The experience of Maria and Brazil has reinforced my opinion that when I am broadcasting from a foreign country there is a responsibility to not just reflect the event I am covering, but to balance that with a significant slice of the culture, history and people who call that place home.

There is so much to learn and to try and understand from different cultures and I feel very privileged to have travelled so much of the world and met some amazing people along the way. My two great regrets from school were that I messed about in every language class, and I never took music seriously. I worked hard, but I was far more interested in kicking a ball about and making people laugh. There is nothing wrong with that, but I would love to be able to play the piano and, whenever I travel to a foreign land, I feel entirely ignorant that I can't speak the lingo. Maybe I am trying to make up for some of that now. If you can understand a different culture, it makes it so much easier to connect with people.

One of the best nights out I have ever had was in a karaoke bar in Shenyang in China. I went there a few years back to make a documentary for ITV with Stockport County who, at the time, were a forward-thinking Championship side. In a bid to 'open up lines of finance and support', they had taken over a Chinese Second Division side and renamed them Stockport Tiger Star.

County had also recruited former Chelsea player John Hollins to manage the team in the northern industrial city of Shenyang.

I was travelling with a cameraman called Bob. Bob was a biker. A hairy biker. A smaller, thinner version of Si King and Dave Myers but with none of their culinary skills. Thankfully, Bob was an excellent cameraman.

Bob was about 5 ft 6 in and had a beard down to his sternum; I was 6 ft 6 in and largely hairless. Together we looked a little bit like a freak show, and anywhere we went in China we attracted a crowd. People stroked Bob's beard and wanted their picture taken with the freakily tall pasty bloke.

We had a few scrapes in China. Our camera kit was confiscated at Chinese customs, despite having all the correct paperwork. We had to grease a few palms to get it released. A little later in the trip, Bob and I were also chased down a moving train by a bunch of Chinese police officers. I think they thought we were filming illegally. When they eventually caught up with us at the far end of the train, the only thing that prevented our arrest was a temporary BBC pass I had at the bottom of my rucksack. I showed it to them and they repeated 'BBC' back to me and pointed at Bob and me. My Mandarin wasn't up to explaining that I did occasionally work for the BBC and was moving there soon, but I was currently working for ITV, so I just nodded. Those three letters were enough to persuade them that our motives weren't dodgy, and we were free to go about our business.

The best night of the trip involved a visit to a huge restaurant with the chairman of the team Stockport were doing business with. There were two rooms laid aside for us. Bob and I were in room two, the head honchos were next door and we were sat around a table with twelve seats. We were the only two who spoke a word of English. When I say 'a word' I really mean it. There was no understanding of 'okay' or 'thank you' or any of the basics. We were flying blind.

For about two hours it was like an elaborate game of charades. Despite being able to communicate only via a combination of pointing, smiling, random hand gestures and rudimentary noises, we were all getting along rather well. At about 11 pm, the fella who was hosting the table uttered a word that everybody understood: 'karaoke'!

He circled his finger around everyone at the table intimating that no one would escape the rather battered microphone that was pulled out of an ornate box in the corner of the room. Bob turned to me, looking rather terrified. 'I can't sing a note. You'll have to take one for the team here, Dan.'

Our Chinese hosts were rattling through their favourite numbers. Bob and I clapped along, but none of them sounded familiar. Eventually, the book made its way round to me. I flicked through several pages of Mandarin text searching for something familiar. At the bottom of the penultimate page I saw 'Thomas Jones – Delilah'. Not exactly the greatest choice, but I pointed it out to the fella who was in charge of the machine and he looked at me with deep confusion. I was handed the micro-phone and, after several minutes of CD sifting, the words 'I saw the light on the night that I passed by her window' appeared on the screen and I was off.

At times like this, I feel it's important to give it your all. My effort levels were slightly higher than the levels of appreciation. On the rare occasions that I opened my eyes, I saw ten blank faces staring at me and one heavily bearded clown giggling away in the corner. No one joined in at the chorus, not even Bob. At the end there was an awkwardly sparse round of applause and I was quickly followed by the next singer who went down like Elvis Presley on a comeback tour. This incident has severely dented my karaoke confidence but it was another example of how it is possible to cross cultural boundaries if you are willing to take a few risks, not take yourself too seriously, and will sing Tom Jones to a crowd of strangers.

I am sure Maria has slayed a few karaoke bars in her time. At the moment, she is focused on Joana and working on setting up an Instagram business called 'Braga For You' with a friend in Portugal. 'You must come and see us, Dan. Joana needs to meet you,' says Maria.

'You know we share something, you and I, Dan,' claims Everaldo, lowering his voice.

'What's that?' I ask.

'We both met Maria the same way. We both met her on the streets of Rio de Janeiro. I met Maria at the carnival party in Rio in 2013. I had the same feelings as you when I met her. I saw the spontaneity, the smile, the fun, the laughter. I fell in love with her that night, just like you fell in love with her, and I will love her forever.'

I asked them if they would ever move back to Brazil.

'I love my country,' says Maria. 'I love Brazil. It is in my heart and soul. But, living away, I can also see things from outside. I am a spectator. We have a lot of problems but the best thing about Brazil is Brazilians. We are funny, happy, smart and you meet Brazilians everywhere. Everaldo, Joana and I . . . we are citizens of the world. Who knows where we will go next.'

'We just want to grow old with each other,' says Everaldo.

There is so much to learn from Maria and her husband. 'Her friends say she sees the love in everything,' beams her husband. For Maria it's just a way of life. 'I always received love. That is the way I was raised. My parents loved me, supported my decisions and, most importantly, there was always laughter in the house.'

'I also have two grandparents, both in their nineties. They are both very kind and full of advice and love. I have so many loving members of my family. Most of them came to the wedding, Dan,' she laughs 'We are just trying to continue that tradition with Joana. Passing it on to our daughter. That is all we can do.'

The day after I met Maria on the beach this appeared in one of the main UK newspapers under the headline 'The BBC's Biggest Olympic Fails.'

'Poor Dan Walker. While Clare Balding got to roam around the sanitised Olympic Park last night, Walker found himself shoved out on a beach where anyone could accost him. And they did. When a Brazilian hen-party intruded on a live link, chanting "BBC! BBC!", you could see Walker's entire career flash before his eyes.'

I'm not sure the author of that piece could have misjudged my mood any more spectacularly. The hen-party incident sums up all the reasons why I love live TV: unpredictable, seat-of-your-pants fun. It could have been horrendous, but it was brilliant. I, and the rest of the watching public, got to meet an incredible young woman.

With her warmth, friendliness and wonderfully relaxed attitude, Maria was the embodiment of all the amazing things we had experienced in Rio. That's not her home anymore but as she says, she is a citizen of the world now, seeing the love in everything, wherever she goes.

'THEY ARE LIKE FAMILY TO ME, EVEN THOUGH I NEVER KNEW THEM'

'Will you make sure you walk the dog before you go to work? She didn't get one yesterday.'

I assured my wife that I would walk Winnie, our little Cockapoo, but I was already running late. I had to get to work in Manchester by midday but before that I had to finish off an article I was writing for a newspaper and I also wanted to squeeze in a little exercise.

Time disappeared very quickly that morning. My dad rang, then I was distracted by a YouTube video of Nick Faldo's Ryder Cup win over Curtis Strange from 1995 at Oak Hill. I was left with only thirty minutes to walk the dog, do some exercise and get ready to leave for work.

I threw on some shorts, grabbed the dog and headed off down the road to Endcliffe Park in Sheffield. It was the sort or morning where you catch your breath as soon as you step outside. There was a noticeable chill in the air, especially if you were stupid enough to be wearing shorts. One half of the street was still covered in a light dusting of frost, the other was tickled by the sunlight.

Endcliffe Park is a beautiful spot in the middle of Sheffield, originally opened in 1887 to mark the jubilee of Queen Victoria. I have walked Winnie through the park hundreds of times and usually follow a well-trodden path. In through one of the side gates, up behind the flats, past the large single tree, into the woods – where Winnie would normally wander off – and then through to the far end near Hunters Bar roundabout, before turning around 'the loop' (as our children call it), past the park café and back home.

On that first Wednesday of 2019, I had to change plan. Speed was essential so we stuck to the paths and, instead of going up through the woods, we took the path that runs along-side the Porter Brook river, behind the café. As usual, Winnie had no interest in running alongside me. She darted left and right across the path, sometimes ahead, sometimes behind, occasionally stopping to spread a little fragrance here and there or sniff another dog's produce.

She spotted an old man about a hundred yards ahead of us and – as usual with strangers – sprinted off to show him just how excited she was to see him. He looked cold. I recognised him from his coat. Occasionally we had seen him from a dis-tance when we walked through the woods on the far side of the path. This was the first time we had come this way.

I could tell from some way away that his hands were shaking as he swept leaves off the path in front of the memorial. I did not know much about the stones next to the path – only that they were there to commemorate a plane crash, something that had been briefly mentioned to me when I was a student in Sheffield studying history in the 1990s.

A lot of people have asked me why I stopped to talk that day and I still can't answer that. But I did. It was a conservation which started with a simple, 'Are you okay?' Five minutes later I had this man's phone number, his address and perhaps the best story I have ever heard. Within a few hours his tale was travelling around the world – retweeted, shared and liked thousands and thousands of times. His name was Tony Foulds.

Tony was an eight-year-old boy playing in Endcliffe Park on 22 February 1944. Just before 5 pm that day, a twenty-three-year-old American pilot found himself in a dangerous situation. Lt John Kriegshauser's B-17 Flying Fortress bomber had been badly damaged during a mission over Nazi-occupied Denmark. The plane, nicknamed *Mi Amigo*, was limping back to base in Northamptonshire. Lt Kriegshauser and the nine other men on board were in serious trouble. They urgently needed somewhere to land.

Below *Mi Amigo* was the city of Sheffield. With the aircraft's engines fading fast, Kriegshauser realised he would have to force the plane down. The only available piece of green land was Endcliffe Park, where a group of children happened to be playing after school that afternoon. One of those children was Tony.

There are all sorts of first-hand accounts about what happened in the park that day. People talk of their parents running from the houses on neighbouring Rustlings Road and the noise of the bomber overhead. Tony distinctly remembers looking up at the plane and seeing the pilot waving. 'I can remember it as clear as if it happened today,' he says in his wonderful broad Yorkshire accent. 'I tell people we were in the park to play football, but we were really there for a fight after school. I was there with my best mate, Tom. We looked up and saw the pilot waving his arm at us. I waved back. I know now that he was trying to get us out of the way.'

Paul Allonby describes the incident in detail in his excellent book *Courage Above The Clouds: The True Heroic Story of the Crew of B-17 'Mi Amigo'*. He explains that the US bomber had been part of a daylight operation from the 305th Bombardment Group, US 8th Army Air Force. They were based at Chelveston airfield in Northamptonshire and their plan had been to bomb the Luftwaffe military air base in Nazi-occupied Denmark – a place called Aalborg.

On 20 February 1944, the 305 was selected to take part in a raid involving 700 aircraft to Leipzig in Germany as part of a week-long joint campaign codenamed Operation Argument. As Allonby explains, 'it involved US bombers attacking by day, and Royal Air Force bombers striking by night. The aim was to attack the Nazi aviation industry, and Luftwaffe bases.'

The planned raid went horribly wrong. Fog in Denmark made visibility a huge issue and German fighters shot down three B-17s. *Mi Amigo* was one of the planes which turned back to England, dumping its four-hundred-pound bomb load in the North Sea on the way. The plane had been badly damaged in the raid and Allonby picks up the story as the engines were fading fast over South Yorkshire.

'He began to descend cautiously, and suddenly came out through the clouds low over a major city – Sheffield, in South Yorkshire. Ahead were houses, roads, trees and a splash of green: Endcliffe Park, a public play area, complete with a river, woods and a bandstand.

'As Lt Kriegshauser used every bit of his skill and experience, at least one engine began to cut out. Seeing only the grassed area of the park ahead, a split-second decision was needed.'

Tony relives that day regularly. 'He avoided us in the park and went up, over the top of the café, and then *BANG* . . . into that hill covered in trees.'

Local residents and firemen hurried to the scene to find trees uprooted and crushed beneath the destroyed bomber, with wreckage strewn across the hillside. The aircraft had split into two and the front section was on fire. Around twenty firefighters fought for more than an hour to put out the blaze.

Lt John Kriegshauser and the other nine men had saved Tony and the other children in the park, but sacrificed their own lives. Tony has been wracked with guilt ever since because of what happened to the men of *Mi Amigo*. They were:

Lt John Kriegshauser, pilot from Missouri.
Second Lt Lyle Curtis, co-pilot from Idaho.
Second Lt John Humphrey, navigator from Illinois.
Melchor Hernandez, bombardier from California.
Harry Estabrooks, engineer and gunner from Kansas.
Charles Tuttle, gunner from Kentucky.
Robert Mayfield, radio operator from Illinois.

Vito Ambrosio, gunner from New York.
Malcolm Williams, gunner from Oklahoma.
Maurice Robbins, gunner from Texas.

Tony says that it wasn't until the 1950s that he started to go through in his mind what happened that day and what their sacrifice meant to him and the others enjoying themselves in the park. Then, in his late teens, he started to lay flowers at the site and when a memorial was built in the late 1960s, Tony took it upon himself to visit it regularly. For many years he has been quietly tending to it and cleaning it.

When I met him on that chilly January day sweeping the leaves, he was eighty-two years old. Most weeks he explained he was there for twelve hours or more looking after the stones which mark the death of ten men he never met. Ten men who gave their life for his. Ten men who he says he loves just as much as his own family. If you stop and speak to him for long enough at the memorial, he will point to the spot where he wants his ashes to be laid when he is no longer around to watch over it.

'I talk to them every time,' he told me that morning.

. 'What do you say to them?'

'I just ask them how they are. Tell them what I've had for breakfast and what I'm up to.'

I asked Tony if anyone had covered his story before and he said he thought he'd spoken to the local paper, the *Sheffield Star*. He had told them about being in the park that day many years ago. As I left Tony, the first thing I did was call the *Match of the Day* office to tell them I was going to be late. I sat on a park bench and Googled everything I could about *Mi Amigo*, the crash, Tony and the park.

I went back to speak to Tony again and asked him loads more questions. I explained to him that I was a presenter on the television and that I worked for the BBC.

'What is it you want, Tony?' I asked him at the end of our long conversation.

'Well . . . what I would love is something to mark the anniversary. Next month it's seventy-five years and I would love to remember these lads with a flypast, you know, over the park. I know that's a stupid thing to ask for. I've written to the Red Arrows but heard nowt back. I asked the police if they could fly their helicopter over, but they said they couldn't say if it would be free. I even called a lad who had one of them hang gliders, but he fobbed me off saying February were too cold.'

By this point I was fully engaged with the emotion of the story. 'Leave it with me,' I blurted out. Tony and I laugh about this now. At that point in my life, I had a grand total of *zero* contacts in the aviation industry. I didn't even know a bloke with a glider.

Tony remembers that initial meeting well. He remembers everything well. 'I enjoyed talking to you, but I did wonder why you were wearing shorts. I remember it were bitterly cold and you kept jogging on the spot. You asked me if I minded if you put the story on . . .' he pauses, '. . . Twitter? I said yes but I had no idea what it was. I still don't really, but people keep telling me about it. I laugh about it now, but that day was the start of the best few weeks of my life. When you left, I remember you saying you hoped to be back the next day with a camera. I thought you were going to come back with a little thing to take a picture. People still say to me now, "did you really not know he was the fella off the telly?" and I say, "Of course not. I watch him now, but I didn't then. I thought he were just a bloke wit dog.'"

Twitter is a powerful tool which can sometimes be abused, but it was time to show it can also be a force for good. When I read back through those first few tweets now, they seem a little ridiculous. Did I really think it would be possible to organise a flypast in less than six weeks?

2 January 2019. Just met an amazing man in Endcliffe Park, Sheffield. Tony Foulds was an eight-year-old playing in the park when a US plane crashed in Feb 1944. He has diligently maintained the memorial ever since. He was planting new flowers. Almost 75 yrs of service. What a man. I'm in bits.

He's been sweeping the leaves away all morning and has replanted and cleaned the whole thing. He re-told the story of the day so vividly and knew the names of all 10 who died. 'They are like family to me even though I never knew them.'

Right. . . I've been back to talk to Tony. He doesn't want a medal. All he wants is a flypast on the 75th anniversary on 22 Feb 2019. Can anyone help? Who has contacts in the Royal Air Force or Red Arrows?

Does anyone know how much a flypast by the @rafredarrows costs? I know I'm asking the impossible here but. . . how much money do we need to raise? Who do I need to get in contact with? @RAFRed1 @RAFRed10.

By this time, I was getting dangerously late for *Match of the Day*. As I strode purposefully back home with Winnie, I sent an email to the editor of *BBC Breakfast*, Adam Bullimore.

Boss,
Have you seen my tweets?
I've just met an amazing man in the park called Tony Foulds.
We have to do something with him tomorrow!
I'm working until midnight tonight on MOTD, but I'll drive home afterwards and be ready to go first thing in the morning if we can get a crew.
Let me know.

Adam was in a meeting at the time but as soon as he came back, he passed the email on to producer Claire Ryan. You'll hear a lot about Claire. She is amazing and was on the case straightaway. She also, thankfully, never deletes an email.

Happy New Year, Mr Walker. Hope you a lovely time with your family. Just seen your tweet about Tony Foulds, do you think we should make a little piece about the anniversary with the two of you?

I responded immediately.

YES ... YES ... and YES! I feel a real burden to get this man a flypast. Do we have any contacts for the Red Arrows or anyone like that? Just a bomber or something!

At the same time, another producer at *BBC Breakfast* – Josh Parry – was looking through social media. 'I was checking through mentions of "breakfast" and saw hundreds of people responding to your tweet,' recalls Josh. 'I thought, "Oh my word, we need to get this man on the programme." Then I stood up and proclaimed to the office, "Has Dan called anyone? Why hasn't he called us about this?" I went straight over to Claire and she said, "Don't worry, I'm on it. I've got an email from Adam that Dan has sent through and we are sorting out a camera for tomorrow."'

Claire is like a dog with a bone when she sniffs a good story, but she also remembers feeling a bit concerned. 'I got your email and the first thing I did was check what was happening on social media. It was going mad and I thought, "Oh no! He's gone in all guns blazing and is already asking for a flypast."'

I drove to Manchester for *Match of the Day* but I only had one thing on my mind. My Twitter, Instagram and Facebook feeds were going crazy. I called Tony to keep him updated.

Just spoken to Tony again. Going to see him tomorrow to talk about the crazy response. The wheels are in motion. Thank you for all your support #GetTonyAFlypast

If you are following this ... I'm now in contact with the RAF and the US embassy in the UK. Hopefully we can make something happen #GetTonyAFlypast

That 'contact' from the US Air Force came from someone else who would become integral to the story: Major Sybil Taunton. Sybil (she says I can call her that) was minding her own business, getting on with her work as the Chief of Public Affairs for the US Air Force based at RAF Lakenheath in Suffolk. She was in her office on 2 January, the morning Tony and I met in the park.

'I can still remember it quite vividly,' says Sybil. 'One of my office administrators, Suzanne Harper, came in and said, "Have you seen this?" pointing at your tweets. "I think it's something really special." I read through Twitter and saw the hundreds of comments underneath with lots of people tagging us in @48FighterWing. I'll be honest with you, right from that first moment there was a sort of schoolgirl excitement about the story. I told Suzanne it was something that we could definitely help with. I could see the hysteria on social media so I thought it would be wise to send you a direct message asking you to contact me rather than make it public.'

I rang Sybil as soon as I could and asked if I could give her Claire's contact details so I could try and get my head around *Match of the Day*. Sybil was just as keen as Claire and me to get the ball rolling.

'Er, Claire . . . it's the US Air Force on the phone for you,' said Josh holding one hand over the receiver in the *BBC Breakfast* office. Within just a few hours of meeting Tony, things were starting to get serious.

* * *

The next morning, I woke up to thousands of messages about Tony on social media and hundreds of emails.

'You're phone was pinging all night,' said my wife. 'Is it all about that bloke in the park?'

'Yes love. It's all gone bonkers!'

'Well, you promised that flypast, so you're going to have to sort it now.'

She was right, of course.

I was meeting Claire, the camera crew, and Tony back in the park again at 10 am. This time I was wearing trousers, but the second day was just as mad as the first.

Met up with Tony again who is genuinely staggered by the response. You'll be able to see his story on #BBCBreakfast tomorrow.

The to-do list has increased... 1 #GetTonyAFlypast 2 He'd love to get some tarmac on the memorial steps so #GetTonySomeNewSteps Determined to sort 4 him.

Tony said he still feels guilty because if he hadn't been in the park that February day in 1944, the plane could have landed safely. Instead, the pilot avoided the children and crashed into the hill. 'I owe them my life. Their sacrifice gave me everything. I love them as much as my own children.'

As the story was getting picked up by the national press, Tony was getting inundated with calls from other media outlets, but he really wasn't interested in the publicity. Claire offered to deal with the requests, and he jumped at the offer. This was going to take up much of Claire's life for the next few weeks.

'Tony doesn't really watch television, isn't on social media and – because of his shaking – can't text. Every phone call he got he referred to me,' remembers Claire. 'It seemed like the right thing to do as a duty of care to this man in his eighties who had no idea what was happening in the world around him.'

'People kept asking me about Twitter,' recalls Tony. 'On t' bus, in t' market and even at local shop. I had no idea what they were on about. I don't have a clue about all that. I'm hopeless with me phone. Even if I wasn't shaking, I wouldn't know what buttons to press.'

We put out our film with Tony the following (Friday) morning and the story hit the mainstream media. #GetTonyA Flypast was the number one trend on Twitter for hours.

Lots of people are asking how they can help. The thing that would mean the most to Tony would be to come to the 75th anniversary on 22 Feb. That would mean the world to him. He genuinely doesn't want recognition. He just wants the men who saved him to be remembered #GetTonyAFlypast.

I'm going to call Tony later and tell him that #Get TonyAFlypast is trending. He'll have no idea what that means but we are moving in the right direction.

Have spoken to Tony who got a round of applause when he went for his breakfast in Sheffield market today.

I've just told him the good news that @Ameyplc have agreed to redo the memorial steps and tarmac the path. THIS IS AMAZING #GetTonySomeNewSteps.

I rang Tony after the show. It always takes him about twenty seconds to answer because he has to find the phone in his deep pockets and then control his hand enough to press the right button. As the call started, I could hear him laughing.

'What have you done, Dan?' he cackled.

'What do you mean, Tony?'

'Well, I walked into market for me breakfast and . . . everyone stood up.' I could hear he was getting emotional re-telling the story. He took a deep breath and gathered himself. 'An ovation, Dan . . . a standing ovation. They were all clapping!'

Tony had not seen his interview go out on *BBC Breakfast* but everyone else had and they were immensely proud of him.

'They were all shaking me hand,' he continued. 'I didn't know what to say. I felt like Danny DeVito.' (I have never got to the bottom of Tony's obsession with the diminutive US film star, but he mentions him a lot.)

My aviation contacts were improving fast. I was in constant touch with Sybil and, that same morning, I had spoken to Air Vice Marshall Harvey Smyth from the RAF. He was another one who played a crucial role in making everything happen. While the US Air Force, largely because of Sybil, were opening doors and fully on board, the RAF needed some gentle encouragement and Harvey was happy to open up his incredible contacts book and rattle his considerable silverware.

'I think the RAF are a bit like the BBC,' ruminates Adam Bullimore our *BBC Breakfast* Editor – the man in charge of the programme. 'When faced with something like this, the British tend to form a committee and make a list of all the reasons why it isn't a good idea to push ahead. The Americans just fully embraced it from the start. I think they fell in love with the story, with Tony and – most importantly – they had the press awareness and the logistical mechanisms to make things happen. It was impressive to watch. It was understandable, with the strong US connection, that they led on this and the RAF followed.'

It was over the course of that first weekend in January that everyone realised this was going to be big. 'My to-do list was growing by the minute,' remembers Claire. 'I was speaking to local councils and Dan kept forwarding me names and numbers of everyone from brass bands who wanted to play at the anniversary, to WWII re-enactment groups who were offering to bring a replica Flying Fortress to the park and re-assemble it for the big day.'

I don't think I have ever received so many emails and messages. It was becoming impossible to wade through them all. I asked my sister to help and, at the end of the first day, she sent a text: 'This is ridiculous. It's a full-time job. I demand a pay rise.'

I had seen one lovely message from an old lady called Beryl who had sent an email offering to bake a 'job-lot of flapjacks' if the flypast happened. I was also waiting for the US Ambassador to the UK, Woody Johnson, to return my call. I kid you not.

'I think the real magic in the story came in that transition,' says Adam. 'The simplicity was the appeal at first; a lovely story about an old man doing something lovely in a park. It was during those few days after the initial film on *Breakfast* that we all came to the conclusion that it was going to be so much bigger than we imagined. If it came off, this was going to be a major public event. The story had captured our hearts in the office, and we thought it could capture the hearts of the nation.'

With all this going on behind the scenes, Tony had become something of a celebrity. 'You've got to understand that, at my age, stuff like this just doesn't happen,' he says now. 'It were like a new life from that first day I met you. I was speechless when you turned up with the cameras and, for the first time ever, people started asking me about what life was like during the war. I was getting whole classes of kids coming down to the memorial. I think when the teachers fancied a bit of time off, they came for a free history lesson,' Tony says impishly.

'I have really vivid memories of that whole time. My brother and I were both evacuees. I was a four-year-old in 1939 when one day, there was a knock on the door. Someone put a label on my coat, and we were off. We were taken to Shireoaks near Worksop. We didn't see Mum and Dad for about eighteen months. We stayed with this old lady – Mrs Stevenson – she were lovely. She had just lost her two sons and I think her husband too but made us feel so special. Every day she would sit us down and say, "Make yourself at home. I am and I wish you were." She just wanted us to be as comfortable as possible. I will never forget that.

'Every day my brother, Brian, and I would sit on a humpback

bridge over the Chesterfield canal and we'd wave to the Spitfires as they went off. We used to count them back in and we were always sad when they weren't all there. To think that little lad who loved planes would be having a flypast in the park [all these years later], well . . . that would be special.'

Amazingly, less than a fortnight after our meeting in the park, it looked like Tony was going to get his dream and we would be able to honour the men of *Mi Amigo*. I'd had a bizarre call and then email exchange with the US Ambassador's office. Things were looking positive. Woody Johnson confirmed that a flypast should be possible, and that it would have their full support. The ambassador was also liaising with Sybil at RAF Lakenheath who was weaving her magic.

'I was having meeting, after meeting, after meeting trying to make it happen,' says Sybil. 'The complicating factor was that it wasn't just us involved. We were trying to organise a joint effort with RAF Lakenheath, RAF Mildenhall and RAF Coningsby. That means three times the bureaucracy. I was also having meetings with Sheffield City Council because the official flypast request had to come from a council or government employee. There was an endless list of hoops to jump through but, along with Claire, I was enjoying making my way through them.'

The other red-tape issue was that a flypast like this required two levels of confirmation from the US Air Force bigwigs. Every American who I spoke to loved the idea and was keen to make it happen, but they had to get the thumbs-up, first from their

European HQ in Germany and finally, and most importantly, from Washington DC.

While all that was happening, Claire and I were trying to organise a way of getting Tony and the ambassador to the *BBC Breakfast* studio on the same day – without Tony knowing. There was also the drama of organising things at Lakenheath where the excited Americans could tell Tony the good news.

The all-important email confirming the flypast came through on 14 January. 'I vividly remember receiving the email,' says Claire. 'I stood up at my desk, looked at Adam and said, in disbelief, "WE'VE GOT THE FLYPAST!"'

The US Air Force would be able to provide the aircraft. They would make their way to Sheffield on the 75th anniversary and aim to arrive over Endcliffe Park at 8.45 am, weather permitting. There would be ten planes to commemorate the ten men who had lost their lives on *Mi Amigo* in 1944.

Tony might have suspected we had something planned for the anniversary, but he didn't know what a lovely surprise we had in store for him and we wanted it to be really special. So Tony and the US Ambassador, Woody Johnson, were invited to the BBC studios in Salford on Tuesday 22 January, a month away from the anniversary, and the flypast would be announced by the commander of 48th Fighter Wing at Lakenheath, Colonel Will Marshall, live on air.

The Colonel was just as excited as the rest of us. 'Right from the start it was wonderful to be involved. We wanted to be part of it after hearing the story, but I don't think any of us expected it to get so big so quickly. I think it is really important to remember people like Tony. There are so many memorials to US forces all over the UK and it was also an opportunity for us to highlight Tony's work and the men of *Mi Amigo* but also show our appreciation to all those who keep those memories safe.'

While Colonel Marshall was preparing to go live at RAF Lakenheath, Tony was in the green room at *BBC Breakfast* sat next to the US Ambassador, who took an instant shine to him. 'I could hardly understand a word he said at first,' says Woody Johnson, 'but I was captivated by his story. I saw, and still see, Tony as a symbol of the union and relationship between our nations. His hard work and care was finally being recognised in the most amazing way.'

At this point, Tony still hadn't twigged what was happening. 'I were in this room with Woody and we were talking about Brexit, Margaret Thatcher and all sorts. I didn't know why he was there. I didn't really know why I was there. He didn't tell me anything. I assumed he was there to talk politics. I thought something wonky was happening when we both went into the studio together.'

Louise Minchin and I were sat on the other side of the famous *BBC Breakfast* red sofa. We introduced Tony, and the ambassador, and they talked together about the story. We all then turned to the screen in the corner of the studio and handed to our reporter, Jayne McCubbin, who was live at RAF Lakenheath alongside a beaming Colonel Will Marshall. He told Tony to 'look to the skies on 22 February because . . . you've got your flypast!'

The servicemen and women behind Will whooped and hol-
lered and I turned back to Tony who, for a split second, gave
me a withering look. I could tell he was annoyed that I hadn't
told him the flypast was confirmed but then the emotion got the
better of him. I always think hugs look a little uncomfortable on
live telly – especially when you're sat down – but I couldn't just
leave him there sobbing on his own, so I got involved.

'Those lads at Lakenheath,' remembers Tony. 'What a day
that was. On live TV . . . I lost it, didn't I? I didn't know what to
do. It doesn't happen. It certainly doesn't happen to me. When
I heard him say "look to the sky" I realised what was going to
happen and the rollercoaster of those few weeks just hit me. It
were like I was living in this dream. I looked at Woody and he
had this giant grin and then I looked at you and thought, "Ya
little bugger! I can't believe you didn't tell me!" but I couldn't
be cross because I was just so happy for the lads. This whole
thing was for them, and their memory, and now it was going
to happen.'

Tony wasn't the only one who was feeling the emotion that
day. 'Having the opportunity to make that announcement about
the flypast is one of the moments I will treasure forever,' said
Colonel Marshall.

Major Sybil Taunton was overjoyed at how it had all gone
down. 'The day we announced the flypast I was incredibly
nervous. I was watching so carefully from the sidelines making
sure it was all going according to the careful plan. It didn't really
sink in until much later. I was so worried because I had never
been involved in something so big. I waited until later in the

day before I watched it back in the office. I just sat there and cried. It all caught up with me.'

Tony had taken over social media again. We had somehow managed to sort a flypast in 12 days. We had announced it was going to happen live to millions of people and now we had one month to pull off the biggest event that *BBC Breakfast* had ever been involved in.

As the days went by, the story just kept growing in size. Our initial plans, in the early days, had been to have a BBC reporter in the park on the day. I had been pushing for an all-singing-all-dancing full outside broadcast, but Adam wasn't sure. Two things made him change his mind: one was a conversation we had and the other was the return of the *BBC Breakfast* planning editor, Lisa Kelly.

Lisa is a force of nature. She has boundless enthusiasm and always sees the possibility for magic in every opportunity. She strolled into the office and instantly told Adam that we had to throw everything at it.

'Lisa cannot do half-arsed,' says Adam. 'As soon as she arrived it was like "why have you been dithering?" She seemed to think there was no way that anything could go wrong. I am a natural pessimist; she is a natural overpowering optimist and Claire is a practical genius. Together we made a formidable team.'

It was on the same day Lisa arrived back in the office that Adam called me. 'Dan, I need to talk to you about Friday.' He was mildly frantic. 'Be honest with me, how many people do you think are going to turn up?'

I had been making a case for the whole of the show to come from Endcliffe Park for a couple of weeks but that had become complicated by the fact that I couldn't be there for the event itself, for reasons to be explained.

'Adam,' I said, aware that this was an important conversation, 'this is going to be HUGE.'

The day before I had done some basic calculations based on the number of people who had either told me they were coming or had asked questions about where the park was. There were hundreds of emails, and thousands of messages on Facebook, Instagram and Twitter. My basic assumption was that if one hundred people said they were coming, ten might turn up. In addition to that I factored in all the residents of Sheffield I had seen over the past month. In the few weeks before the flypast, I was getting stopped thirty to forty times a day by the good people of Sheffield asking what time they needed to be there. They told me that their aunties, uncles, mums, dads, grandparents and long-lost cousins were coming from all over the place to make sure they were there to mark the *Mi Amigo* anniversary.

'I can guarantee you at least two thousand people, boss, and I wouldn't be surprised if we got five or six thousand,' I claimed confidently to Adam.

'Really? Are you sure?'

I was. 'People in Sheffield really care about their city. They care about the fact that this fella has been quietly doing this job for a long time. Some of them feel guilty that they've either forgotten about *Mi Amigo* or neglected to tell their kids or grandkids about it. This is the opportunity to put that right. This is the chance to shout about Sheffield on national TV and, most importantly, we have a real "I was there" moment and so many people feel that they want to be part of it.'

There was a long and uncomfortable pause at the other end of the line. 'Well, that settles it. If you're sure, we'll do the whole programme from down there. I'll speak to Claire at this end. Steph [McGovern] and Charlie [Stayt] will be in the park. We'll send a truck, the whole crew, and we'll be live from 6 am, building up to the flypast at 8.45 am. Let's hope the crowds do what you can't do, and turn up!'

Adam was referring to something which had become a real source of tension over the previous few weeks; while I had been carefully planning the flypast there was something else bubbling away in the background.

Back in November of the previous year I had a meeting with a BBC TV executive called David Brindley. David was putting together a team to take part in a Comic Relief challenge in 2019 and wanted to know if I was interested in taking part. I told him I would love to be involved but was well aware that there was very little chance of me going. David was honest enough to tell me there was a long list and, in addition to that, the balance of the group had to be right.

In the middle of January, I was told that, if I was still interested, I was on the shortlist and was asked if I would be available for the last few days of February and first week of March. The challenge would be to climb Mount Kilimanjaro in Tanzania.

The 'Return to Kili' would see nine 'celebrities' retrace the steps of the original climbers – led by Gary Barlow – a decade before.

I told David I would love to take part and – as long as I was free on Friday 22 February – I would be all over it. One week later I got an email. I remember staring at it in silence for about ten minutes. The dates had changed for the Comic Relief Challenge. I had made the final nine but we all had to fly out on Thursday 21 February (the day before the flypast), and we'd start climbing the mountain on Saturday 23 February.

There was a period of a few days where I was desperately trying to find a way around this shambolic clash of dates. Obviously, the flypast was immovable, but I spent hours scouring airline websites looking for an alternative way of getting to Tanzania at the right time. It simply wasn't possible.

I'll be honest with you, I don't think I have ever agonised over a decision like this before. There were four people I needed to speak to: my wife, my agent, my boss and my friend, Tony. My wife is always great on occasions like these. Sarah was calm and measured and said that both were once-in-a-lifetime events and that both could go ahead with or without me. She also wisely pointed out that not being in Sheffield on the day would remove the temptation from others to make the story about me and Tony. That could easily detract from the anniversary and the memory of those ten lost Americans.

My agent, Jonny, was keen for me to climb Kilimanjaro, but fully understood my attachment to Tony and the story, which would come to a conclusion with the flypast.

The most difficult conversations were with my boss, Adam,

Winnie Mabaso and Lisa Ashton. Lisa first met Winnie in 2004 and she had a huge impact on her life.

Palesa, Lerato and Maki on the day their family was reunited at Ilamula House.

Gary Speed with his sons Tommy (left) and Eddie (right).

John Sutherland during his time with the Metropolitan Police. John spent twenty-five years as a police officer.

John Hartson giving a birthday message to a soldier's family in Camp Bastion, Afghanistan.

The *Football Focus* team alongside troops from the British Army and representatives from the English and Afghan Football Associations. This was taken just after our match.

A lovely handwritten invitation for us to go and visit Blue Watch.

The items that Ilse Steyaert-Fieldsend said she felt guilty about keeping after she lost her daughter, Georgia. The teddies, photos and Georgia's favourite pyjamas.

The family: Ilse and her husband, James, with Georgia and her brother, Joshua. Joshua was two when his sister died.

The magical night on Copacabana when I got to meet Maria live on TV.
She was in the middle of her hen-do.

I got an invitation to the wedding but couldn't make it. Maria's mum
came up with an interesting way of making sure I was there.

Maria and her wonderful husband, Everaldo.
They now have a beautiful daughter called Joana.

This was the picture I took on my phone on the first day I met Tony in Endcliffe Park, Sheffield. He was sweeping leaves at the *Mi Amigo* memorial.

While millions were watching the flypast in the UK, I was in Tanzania about to climb Kilimanjaro for Comic Relief. I was watching the *BBC Breakfast* coverage on the hotel's dodgy WiFi.

Back in Sheffield, there were an estimated 15,000 people in a packed Endcliffe Park, and thousands more gathered across the city.

This was the final picture taken of
Martyn Hett and his family before Martyn was
killed at the Manchester Arena in May 2017.

Figen Murray with her son.
Martyn was planning to go on a
once-in-a-lifetime trip to America the
same week he died in the bomb blast.

Terrence with his mum, who he looked after for many years. It was after her death that he started to struggle with loneliness.

The moment Terrence opened his front door to hear the students from the Oldham College choir singing his favourite carol, 'Silent Night'. Sophie is fourth from the left on the front row.

Terrence and Laurie Boult from Age UK on the *BBC Breakfast* sofa with Louise and myself. Behind us is the Christmas tree which started it all.

Ken and Kia. There are eight decades between them but they have formed a great friendship. Kia's gesture of giving Ken a cushion with his beloved wife's photo on it was watched by millions of people around the world.

The incredible Tony Hudgell. Tony wasn't given much of a chance of survival after being abused by his birth parents but, inspired by Captain Tom, he ended up raising over £1.5 million for the hospital which saved his life.

and Tony. Adam was understandably furious and felt I was in danger of scuppering the entire operation. I told him I felt that wasn't the case, and that it would be possible to speak to me live from Tanzania on the day. I assured him that I would continue to work relentlessly on the flypast and would make sure that everything would be in place on the day. He was angry but I think, eventually, he understood.

I told him about an incident that happened a few years ago which I always use when I talk to journalism students as a reminder that you have to always be aware that the story can sometimes be better without you in it. When Mario Balotelli was playing for Manchester City, he was headline news virtually every week. If he wasn't setting off fireworks in his house, or handing out bundles of money on the streets of the city, he was scoring huge goals. Nobody could get an interview with him.

The club were understandably careful around him and he just turned everything down. I came up with a suggestion of getting Noel Gallagher to be part of the interview. Noel used to dedicate a song to Mario at every gig and I knew Balotelli knew Oasis and was a big music fan. I pitched it to the club and, after two months of negotiations, they said yes. The next job was to persuade Noel to adjust his world tour to fit in a trip back to England. Another few weeks of negotiations led to a rearranged tour, and a date in the diary. The plan was for me to sit down with the pair of them and talk about their love of football and music.

On the day of the shoot, Noel and I were waiting at the training ground and Balotelli came charging around the little road that led to the complex gates in his camouflage Bentley convertible. He left it running, jumped out of the car and came over to say 'hi'. Noel broke off from telling Sergio Aguero about an amazing night out he had with fellow Argentine Diego Maradona to hug Mario and tell him what a fan he was.

From those first few moments of seeing them together, I could tell I was going to get in the way. When they eventually sat down for the interview, we quickly rearranged the room to have them sitting together on a sofa and I was off to the side – out of shot – just chipping in with the occasional conversation starter. It turned out to be one of the best and most popular pieces we've ever made for *Football Focus* and, despite planning it for months, I took myself out of it, and it was better for it.

There was a similar feeling now about the flypast. I had poured my heart and soul into it, and it had taken up most of my life for the past month, but it would still be brilliant without me.

I rang Tony and asked if I could meet him in the park. He was already there so I popped down to tell him face to face. He was his usual bullish self. 'Don't be daft, Dan. You've got to go. I'll look after the lads at this end, you get up that mountain and raise some money for those kids.' We were both gutted. I told him I was feeling I couldn't say 'no' to Comic Relief.

'You got the steps. You sorted the flypast. You've changed my life,' he said, without hesitation. We embraced. We both shed a tear, but Tony's reassurance made the decision a much easier one.

*   *   *

The final few weeks before the big event were frantic. Claire was making hundreds of phone calls a day, Lisa was an organisational machine and Sybil was playing a blinder; travelling up and down motorways meeting with Sheffield City Council to organise every little detail.

We know how to make telly, but we don't know how to manage a huge event with thousands of people. There was a whole team at the council who were incredibly accommodating and walked us through the process step by step. Laurie Harvey, the council's PR man, was fielding an unprecedented number of press requests but dealt with each one with a smile.

We had managed to track down some family members of the crew of *Mi Amigo* and, thanks to Boeing, the plan was to fly them over for the anniversary. Jim Kriegshauser was the nephew of the pilot John and was a doctor based in St Louis. I called Jim about two weeks before the flypast to introduce myself and tell him about the plans for the day. He was incredibly excited about being part of the anniversary and said he couldn't wait to meet Tony to thank him personally for tending to the memorial. His family were all coming to the event. So was Megan Leo, the great niece of bomber Melchor 'Rey' Hernandez, who was a student in London.

As the weeks went by, the story just kept growing in size. It was regularly updated on the national BBC bulletins and was featured in national and international publications. Meanwhile Tony was noticing a different crowd at the memorial each week. 'I had forty people come through today [Sunday]. Some lads from Newcastle had driven down, a bunch from London, army,

US army . . . and a couple from Ukraine. They read about it, came for a holiday, and wanted to come and see the memorial to the lads.'

Throughout the final few days there was no let-up. I was either packing for Kilimanjaro, seeing or talking to Tony, or spending hours on the phone to everyone from local schools who wanted to bring their whole year to the park and Sheffield City Council who were spinning hundreds of logistical plates. We both had interviews and press requests coming out of our ears. Tony was a regular on American television, while we also appeared together on *The One Show* in London on the week of the flypast.

'The last time I went to London I were eighteen. My granddad worked in one of those hostels at Colnbrook, right next to the runway at Heathrow. We used to watch these big Russian planes take off and I remember the cutlery in the hostel would shake as they went over. The only other thing I remember about London is Marble Arch. Don't know why! It was back in the 1950s, so that's a good excuse,' Tony says laughing.

It didn't stop at *The One Show*. One evening a large black Mercedes was parked outside Tony's house. There was a knock at the door. Tony's re-telling of the conversation makes me laugh every time I think about it. A 'big lad' got out of the car and came to the door. This is what happened next.

'Hello, is it Tony?'

'Yes.'

'I've driven up from London.'

'That there, London? Why?'

'I'm here from *This Morning* with Holly and Phil.'

'Who?'

'Holly and Phil – from *This Morning* on ITV.'

'The television?'

'Yes, they'd love to have you on the show tomorrow. I'm here to take you and someone from your family down to London. They'll put you up in a hotel and then you'll be on the show in the morning.'

'I can't.'

'Oh . . . are you busy?

'Aye, I've got fried breakfast at the market in the morning with Wayne and a few pals.'

And that was that. Huge TV show appearance verses his usual fried breakfast. No contest. The reason I love that conversation so much is because it is the perfect example of Tony's motivation. It has never been about him.

Pat Davey, who is chairperson of the local arm of the Royal British Legion, remembers hearing about Tony and meeting him, at the memorial, in the early 1990s. 'My husband had done his national service in the RAF. He was also a former vicar in the Anglican church so, once the local branch in Sheffield heard about his old job, they asked him to be their padre. One of his jobs was to take the annual service at the memorial every year. The first one he did was in 1991 and that is where we met Tony for the first time. It was just a muddy slope and the stones back then. There were no steps and no flagpole. Every time we went back, Tony was there and had been for some time before that too.'

I told Pat I wouldn't divulge her age but she's been around almost as long as Tony, and she sees him every other week in the park. 'He always has a crowd around him now,' says Pat. 'It's lovely to see that people are interested in him, in the history, but all he talks about is those ten men.'

'You have to understand that I have felt a deep sense of guilt my whole life,' says Tony. 'I never wanted to be seen. I would drop a pot of flowers off or watch from a distance. I never told anyone about it because it was between me and them lads. It were personal. Once I retired it became more regular, and then I started coming down when I could. I just wanted it to be the best-looking memorial in the country. Nobody would ever have known about it unless we had met.'

The day of the flypast was a bit of a crazy one. I had just arrived in Nairobi and was on my way to Tanzania, so I'll let Claire pick up the story.

'We had finished really late the night before. It was freezing cold in the park and pitch black. There were WWII re-enactment enthusiasts trying to bring all sorts of vehicles into the park, but the police and council said we had to limit it to two or they would get stuck in the mud. The whole BBC team were running around with a few torches trying desperately to get things ready.'

One of those frantically running around was the man leading the technical side of the operation, director Gareth Knowles. 'I remember when I first checked the date I was on holiday. I was desperate to be part of it so cancelled my leave immediately. I called my dad and thankfully he agreed with the decision. "You've got to do it," he said. "When they make the movie in ten years' time, you'll never get over the regret of missing out on the chance of a lifetime." The one thing that sticks in my memory was that it was a massive park and we needed to create a TV set from a jeep and an old fire engine. We were working in the pitch black to try and set things up for the morning. The fuel pipe on the fire engine burst, so the whole crew had to push this enormous thing into place. The fella who drove it to the park said he'd sleep in it overnight to make sure it didn't go anywhere. The following morning all the glass was steamed up, so we had to clean it. It's little details like that which stick in your head. We built a whole platform so guests could be raised off the mud and the crowd could see them. At the other end of the park we had to erect a giant screen. This wasn't a TV show, it was a huge mass participation event and I'd been going through every detail in my head for weeks.'

It was a massive operation for *BBC Breakfast* but, as Adam Bullimore says, it was a show that everyone wanted to be part of. 'On one level it wasn't a headache at all. Everyone was so up for it. Nobody minded the hard work, and everyone knew about the story. I remember every single person we spoke to was engaged from the start. The only thing that worried me was that it might get too big for us and we'd lose control of it all. We could make great TV, but we didn't know anything about putting on an air show. We had to rely on the specialists. We leant heavily on the council for things like insurance and public liability because our main concern was not letting Tony or the story down. So many people were invested in this, and we had to do it justice.'

Steph McGovern and Charlie Stayt would be the presenters in the park and, like the rest of the team, arrived in Sheffield the day before. 'I first saw it on the telly on that Friday in January,' remembers Steph. 'I was a viewer like everyone else and fell in love with the story. I love the way it all came about. *Breakfast* has always been good at meeting people and learning about their lives and this was a story which hit every button. It was so ordinary and so extraordinary at the same time. To see all of that come from a little meeting in a park . . . well, that sounds like the start of a movie.'

While Steph and Charlie were reading through all the information about their guests the night before, Tony was off having dinner with the relatives of the men of *Mi Amigo*. 'I sat there with the pilot's nephew Jim, and he said he wanted to give me something which had been passed on to the family. He gave me a handle from a door on *Mi Amigo*. I didn't know what to say. Jim told me he said he thought it would mean more to me than it ever could to them, and he wanted me have it as a token of their appreciation. That will always be one of my most treasured possessions. I went to bed that night dreaming that it was going to be a day to remember. Jim asked me about the weather in Sheffield. I laughed and reminded him it was February, and anything could happen.'

The next morning, Claire was one of the first on the scene. 'I was in the park at 3.45 am but the news was bad. Although everything was in place in Sheffield, there was thick fog in Suf-folk at RAF Lakenheath. We were told it was near impossible to fly. This was the worst possible start to the day. The rest of the *Breakfast* team arrived over the next hour and everyone was stressed. By the time we went on air at 6 am we were told it was 50:50 at best.'

Adam was pacing around in the broadcast truck in the park, unable to sit down. 'I couldn't believe that we'd got this far, and we were about to be undone by the weather. Dan and Claire had managed to pull this thing off in six weeks and it was all unravelling because of fog. We were getting minute by minute updates from the military. I have never experienced such a tense atmosphere on a broadcast. The crowds were building in the park from first light and we went on air with no flypast.'

Then, suddenly, there was word from Lakenheath that the fog was clearing. After a discussion between the US Air Force officers in the park, the magical words came back . . . 'We are good to go.' The planes from RAF Lakenheath, RAF Mildenhall and RAF Coningsby were on their way to Sheffield.

Steph was ready to make the announcement on air with Charlie. 'I was absolutely delighted when I knew I was going to be on air that day. I was actually just filling a shift for Naga [Munchetty], but it was such a special day. Each part of the broadcast was taking my breath away. I was stood in the park at 4.30 in the morning thinking, "What if no one turns up?" Dan had assured us all that Sheffield wouldn't let us down, but it's so rare to get a crowd for anything these days.'

One of the voices Steph could hear in her ear was that of

Gareth, the director. His weeks of careful planning were coming together. 'Going to bed the night before I had a good feeling it was going to be big because the people love the big red sofa. I had no idea it was going to be so significant and so emotional for so many people. I had been blathering on about boring things like safety and protocols for weeks. I had planned every camera angle in my head and rehearsed them in the car on my way to work for a month. We were also looking after the big screen on the other side of the park. This was a huge public event and a TV show going out to millions at the same time. I felt enormous pressure to get it right. This was a huge moment for Tony. I had tried to prepare for every eventuality and we'd even successfully managed to book the BBC helicopter for the day. We had every possible toy at our disposal and by 8 am, forty-five minutes away from the flypast, the weather was perfect and we were ready. Every single one of the team knew their job. This was it.'

Tony was in the middle of the growing crowd trying his best to take it all in. 'I had to be there very early. Claire had given me clear instructions, so I wrapped up warm and I was ready. When I got there the BBC gave me a bodyguard. I couldn't even go to the toilet without being watched. I was excited but I was worried. I told Claire I didn't think many people would come. Dan had told me for weeks the park was going to be packed but I just thought, who is going to turn up for this, in February?'

My wife was one of those making her way to Endcliffe Park that Friday morning. She sent me a video of packed streets. There were thousands of people flocking to the park. The atmosphere was incredible. The council had been warning

Sheffielders for weeks about parking restrictions but that hadn't put anyone off. They were still finding their way there. By 8.30, South Yorkshire Police estimated there were fifteen thousand people in Endcliffe Park. There were six thousand people in the Botanical Gardens, less than half a mile away, the same number in Meersbrook Park and even more waiting for the planes on the Bole Hills, one of the best vantage points in the city. The good people of Sheffield had come out in their thousands.

The enormity of the occasion was starting to hit Tony. 'Every time I looked around the crowds kept growing. I couldn't believe all these people were turning up. I felt proud as punch. People were calling my name, asking for pictures. I've never had anything like that. When you think there were fifteen thousand in the park. I was there, in the middle of it all, holding the hand of the great niece of one of the lads. What a day.' Tony didn't let go of Megan Leo's hand for most of the morning.

Meanwhile, I was watching all this from a hotel in Tanzania, about a thirty-minute drive from where we due to start our climb of Kilimanjaro. I had set up an iPad at the back of the hotel and was sat at a small table, on my own, watching the footage from Endcliffe Park. Every ten minutes I lost the signal, as the hotel WiFi threw a wobbly, and I had to start the whole login process again.

BBC Breakfast had spoken to the Comic Relief team and the technical wizards Nick Robertson and Lance O'Meara were setting up a camera on the veranda which would allow me to speak to Tony in the park. Unfortunately, they were relying in the same WiFi signal that was proving a little patchy for me.

I was determined not to cry on TV. I know that sounds stupid, but I wanted the day to be a celebration and I wanted all the attention to be on honouring the memory of those ten men. The problem was I could feel myself getting increasingly emotional. I was receiving texts and pictures from family and friends in the park who were amazed by the number of people who were there. I watched the video my wife had sent me. The whole thing looked incredible.

After the first hour, some of the other Comic Relief team started coming down for food. I had only met Jade Thirlwall and her fellow Little Mix band member Leigh-Anne Pinnock about ten hours before at Nairobi airport. As they walked across to say 'good morning' I was gently sobbing into an iPad. I'm not sure I made the best impression.

Back in Sheffield the emotion of the occasion was getting to everyone, especially when the first of the planes was seen in the sky.

'I was trying to hold it together,' remembers Steph, 'but I couldn't stop thinking about all those years of dedication. It was all so raw and so real. You could see on people's faces how important it was to them. I watched Tony's lip tremble and I was a goner. It was about relationships, people, friendship, community, history, reality and there wasn't a celebrity in sight. It was beautiful.'

Adam was still stalking back and forth in the *Breakfast*

gallery. 'I've had some incredible moments working on this programme; life-changing moments. I was there for 9/11, the Gulf War, the death of Diana, elections . . . but this topped the lot. So much of what we cover is based on division, argument and conflict. This was pure. This was different. Everyone was in the same emotional space and it was incredible to watch. I was so emotional. As the planes approached everyone in the gallery was either crying or trying not to cry.'

Standing close to Tony was Colonel Will Marshall from the US Air Force, the man who had announced the flypast. His job on the day was to describe what was happening to the viewers at home and talk the audience through the flypast. 'What stood out for me was the nobility of what happened. I have to be honest and say I was dubious it was going to be so big and so popular. It was a freezing cold February morning. An event like this would never have happened back home.

'I was watching the planes but also looking at Tony. I was transfixed. I saw in the face of that eighty-two-year-old man the face of the eight-year-old boy who had been in the same park seventy-five years before.

'He had seen so much and suffered a deep loss at such a formative age. It's easy to see why he would carry that for such a long time. He held no responsibility because there had been so many events which led to *Mi Amigo* coming down. The planes flew over in what we call the "missing man" formation. There is a gap in the planes. We fly it on very rare occurrences to mark someone who didn't make it home. It conveys instantly what we are trying to communicate. It is always a humbling experience. I think we all felt we were witnessing history. There was a combination of cheering and sombre remembrance. Everyone did what they felt was appropriate. There are very few of that great generation who still live among us. It's essential that we continue to tell that story. It was my honour and privilege to be a part of it.'

Josh Parry, the BBC producer who had seen my tweets and gone crazy in the office back in January, was in New York. He'd just come in from a night out to celebrate his birthday. The party was continuing in the early hours, but Josh was hunched over a laptop watching the footage. 'It was amazing. I am not emotional. I had just come in from a huge night out and it was all too much. I cried . . . and I don't cry.'

There were so many people who did an amazing job that day. The technical team were unbelievable. Our sound legend, Paul Cutler, ran an incredibly complicated operation from the back of an Enterprise van. At the centre of the televisual hive of activity was Claire.

She had been focusing on doing her job in the middle of the park. 'I was running around all over the place, organising guests and making sure everyone was where they needed to be. I was in my own little world and I remember someone tapping me on the shoulder and saying "look behind you". I turned to see this enormous crowd. I had been so engrossed in getting things done, I hadn't stopped to see what was happening around me. My brother doesn't watch the news at all. He refuses. My phone was buzzing all morning. One message was from him. "Bloody hell, sis . . . it looks like Glastonbury!" It did feel a bit like that in that it was all a blur. I can't honestly remember all the details of the day, but I know it was amazing.'

Claire wasn't the only one experiencing the blur. Gareth was in the truck. 'I was so stressed at the point of the flypast, I felt I was on a higher plane. It sounds stupid but it was like I was thinking clearly but wasn't thinking at all. At that point I was beyond crying. It was only when I watched it back that I felt that sense of euphoria. I then understood and was able to take in the magic of that moment. The crowning glory was the day after, seeing still frames of our pictures in the national press – my heart was bursting with pride.'

Steph was similarly mesmerised by the spectacle. 'I forgot I was on TV. I had no idea where the camera was. I think I accidentally stepped into shot at one point because I was wandering around like an idiot. It sounds daft but it wasn't about the cameras, it was about sharing a moment. I had no idea what I was due to say next – none of it was really scripted. We were just trying to react to what we saw. It's a good job Dan was a few thousand miles away . . . he'd have been a complete mess.'

Steph was right. I had received a phone call from my then eleven-year-old daughter Susie halfway through the morning. 'Dad, you came on the big screen in the park,' she blurted out with pride, 'and all the people cheered. They cheered you, Dad.'

Just like Colonel Marshall, it was Tony's face that had sent me over the edge. After all the hours of work, all the emails, texts, tweets, messages, phone calls, badgering, pleading and questions, there was something magical about watching Tony wave at those planes as they flew over his head. I may have been thousands of miles away, but I felt as though we were side by side.

The magnificent Major Sybil Taunton had been stood with Tony that day. Sybil's official role had been to read out the ten names of the crew members of *Mi Amigo*. 'I had no idea it was going to be so difficult to get their names out. I was concentrating so hard and trying not to let the occasion get to me. The way the event had grown was remarkable. When we first discussed it, I was told it would be a maximum of thirty minutes of TV. It turned out to be a three-hour extravaganza. It is, without doubt, the highlight of my career so far. I have never worked on an event like that, and I never will. It was a special privilege to be so near to Tony on the day. I was watching him all morning. He had an eye on everything and everyone around him, soaking it all up. I can't remember how people reacted because I wasn't listening. I was transfixed by Tony. I think we all were.'

Megan Leo was stood next to Tony as the planes went overhead. 'What happened that day was not the fault of the children in the park. Everyone did the best that they could. Tony has been amazing and loved this park and loved the crew in ways we didn't even know about.'

Next to Megan was Jim Kriegshauser. He felt the day had changed everything. 'Things are different now. It's not just a memorial to men but to the human spirit – to the men of *Mi Amigo* but as much to Tony as to them.'

It was a day that had changed a lot. The crash in 1944 was one tragedy among thousands at a time when the world was consumed by catastrophe. Without Tony, and the dog walk, it would not even have survived as the smallest footnote in the history of World War II. Now, seventy-five years on, thousands of people were paying tribute in a park and millions more were watching at home and around the world. The whole city came to a standstill for a few moments. My friend Mark was in his car on the parkway in Sheffield, the main road which joins the city centre to the M1. 'It was like a scene from *Independence Day*. People had just pulled over and they were out of their cars looking up at the sky.'

There was a message from a family member on my phone. They were in the park that morning and it felt a bit like Christmas Day. 'Everyone knew they were there for the same reason. We were all saying "hello" to each other and shaking hands and being friendly. Everyone knew about the flypast, and about Tony, so it was just one huge, wonderful shared experience. There was laughter and tears, but we all talked and took care of each other. I have never known anything like it.'

Claire celebrated with a giant hot chocolate. She spent hours thanking everybody and watching Tony have picture after picture taken. Steph became his minder for a few hours. Adam turned to his colleague, Lisa Kelly and said, 'It's a good time to leave. What a way to go out.' This was to be his final major event before leaving *BBC Breakfast*.

Colonel Marshall, along with the other US dignitaries, made their way back to their hotel. 'We met people there who had travelled from all over the country to be in Sheffield. When the team eventually returned to base, they all walked a little taller with their chest out a little further. Many of them are still friends with Tony now. That day will remain the highlight of my time in the UK. It was a special privilege. It will stay with me forever.'

I won't bore you with all the interviews, questions and requests which followed – just to say, it was incredible. Seven of the top ten trends online in the UK for the whole of the day were related to Tony, *Mi Amigo* or the flypast. Everyone in the country was talking about it.

When I arrived back in Sheffield ten days later, the first thing I did was head to the park. I was walking Winnie, just as I had been in the first week of the year. As I crossed the bridge over the Porter Brook and turned right, down behind the café, there was Tony, still sweeping the leaves.

We laughed, we cried, we shared a brew and a flapjack, and we decided it had really happened.

It had been a mad few weeks which changed both of us. I don't think I will ever be involved in anything like that ever again. It was a once-in-a-lifetime-experience. Within six weeks of meeting Tony, we had put together a huge national event. The beautiful thing for me was that it was as much planned as it was unplanned. None of it could have happened without the effort of so many people and yet, despite that, it felt spontaneous. It just all came together and, nobody knew quite what to do, but everyone knew they wanted to be there. It wasn't at lunchtime or after work. It was early, on a frozen morning. You had to make an effort to be there and thousands upon thousands kept their promises, and did just that. It was the people's event and it was unforgettable.

Sybil says she still gets asked about it. 'I tell people about where I work and they say, "oh, you did that event in the park in Sheffield, didn't you?" I am reminded of it all the time.'

The same is true for Tony. 'There isn't a day that goes by that I don't get asked about it. I will never stop. I can never stop now. People don't realise how close I feel to these lads. They took some persuading but my family have agreed to put my ashes behind the memorial when it's all over. I think I thought the flypast might help, but I still feel the guilt. I don't know how to deal with it. Dan has talked to me about dealing with it. I know he knows Jesus. I went to church with him at Christmas. Maybe one day I'll get to that point. I can't believe the life I have now. It's like a new life in my eighties. A new life from the day I met Dan. He won't put this in the book but it's all down to him. [I tried to take this bit out, but I got told I wasn't allowed to.] He is like family to me. He didn't need to keep coming back. He spoke to me, it went on the telly and everyone said he was lovely, but he made me a promise and he kept coming back. I'll never forget that. He doesn't like me talking about that but it's the truth.

'I get invited all over the place. I can't believe it but I was named Yorkshireman of the Year and Englishman of the Year, and so many people have been touched by it. Even lifers at Leicester Prison. I went to see them, and they made me and Dan a plaque to say "thank you". That's on the wall in my living room. There isn't much space anymore. It's wall-to-wall *Mi Amigo*.

'I'm good friends with Woody (Johnson) now. He invited me to the American Cemetery near Cambridge where three of the lads are buried. What a day that was. One of the boys, Andy, from Lakenheath, he comes up to Sheffield every now and again and we pop out for food. When I'm waiting for the bus, the amount of cars that beep me. It's crazy. On my estate, any shop I go in, they're on to me.'

Tony is always quick to thank me for what I did but he has had a much bigger impact on me than I had on him. Wherever I go I get asked about Tony. How he is? What he is up to? The truth is, he's normally in the park these days. I see him, or speak to him, most weeks. We go for coffee, he comes round for tea, we have become real friends.

When I was given an honorary doctorate from Sheffield University in 2019, most of my speech to the graduating journalists was about Tony and the story of the flypast.

People don't like journalists much. Only politicians are seen as less trustworthy. Even estate agents are more desirable characters according to the surveys. Tony reminded me of the importance of listening to people. Giving them time to tell their stories. I told the new crop of students that they were the sword for the unarmed and a shield for the defenceless. That they could shout for those without a voice and ask questions for those who had no words, seek the truth and defend it.

All you have read about in this chapter, came from one five-minute conversation which started with a simple, 'Are you okay?' Tony reminded me to be interested in the people around me, to be a functioning part of the community. I don't know about you, but I spend far too much time on my dog walks, and my life, staring at my phone and not looking at the world and people around me. Tony has taught me to talk less and to listen more.

The final lesson I learned from the whole saga was the power of collaboration. Next to the memorial in Endcliffe Park, by the side of the beautifully tarmacked steps, stands a flagpole. At the foot of the flagpole is a plaque which tells you who raised the money to pay for it. Two very different organisations, which shows you how far a great story can spread. Half of it was paid for by Boeing, the world's largest aerospace company, and organised by a wonderful lady called Claire MacAleese. The rest of the money came from a fundraising event organised by the children of Birkdale School, just around the corner from the park.

I know it won't last forever, Dan,' said Tony in a recent conversation. I was asking him about his latest school visit where he goes in and talks about his life in the war. 'I know it won't be long before people walk on by and the horns don't hoot. I hope the kids remember the lads. I hope they don't forget what happened in the park. Whatever happens, we'll always have that day, with the planes, for the lads. That was special.'

'YOU SENT ALL THIS TO KILL MY SON . . . AND I WILL TURN IT INTO LOVE'

One of the things I love about my job is that much of it is live. There is so much that can go wrong but it also keeps you permanently on your toes. The mind is always spinning, trying to work out what is happening now and what is coming next.

Back in 2001, I was the Sport's Editor at Key 103 – a radio station in Manchester. It was formerly Piccadilly Radio and had a long history of covering Manchester United, Manchester City and the rest of the local sport, but music was the bread and butter. Even though it was a commercial radio station, we took news incredibly seriously.

On 11 September 2001, I could tell you exactly where I was stood in the office as we watched the twin towers of the World Trade Centre collapse to the ground following a terrorist attack. I had been up those towers the previous year when I went to New York to pick up an award for our coverage of the Harold Shipman Trial.

Key 103 normally played music for most of the day. James Stannage had a phone-in show every evening and there was a sport show when there was a big game on but, predominantly, it was all about the music.

At about 2 pm our Head of News, John Pickford, asked me to go and sit in the live studio and update the listeners with the very latest from New York. I didn't leave until 9 o'clock that evening. The head of the station decided to stop playing music. He pulled all the adverts and, for about eight hours, we became a talk station.

It went by in a flash, but it was one of those moments when your senses are heightened, and you operate on pure adrenaline.

Everyone at Key 103 played a part that day. We had our station engineer, Dave Crookston, running in with technical data about the aircraft used in the attack. Tony Edwards, the legend of the post room, was manning the phones at one point and the whole newsroom pulled a double shift to make sure we were accurate and up to date with the information we were giving out on air.

Other than one inexplicably ludicrous moment when I referred to the Pentagon as 'an octagonal shaped building in Washington', our coverage went down incredibly well with the audience. I remember walking out of the studio physically and mentally shattered.

About two years before that, I had graduated from Sheffield University. I did a degree in history first before adding an MA in Journalism. During my time there, I had helped to set up the student radio station at the university. All of it was invaluable experience but nothing prepared me for the test on that day at Key 103. There is nothing like learning on the job and that was one of the most important professional experiences of my life.

You might have the biggest story of the decade to tell. You might have a lot of information to give . . . but you have to get things across clearly, carefully, accurately and in a way that doesn't feel like a verbal assault.

There have been a number of occasions like that, throughout my career, where you walk away having learned so much. I remember sitting in the tunnel waiting for an interview at Wembley on FA Cup final day and hearing our brilliant editor, Richard Hughes, coming across the TV talkback. 'Dan,' he said in a mildly raised tone (which for Rich means it's serious), 'we've lost the studio and we can't play anything out from the truck. Can we come to you now?'

'Yes,' I said jumping to my feet and grabbing a microphone. I stood in front of the camera and heard Ian Finch (the match director) say 'take the tunnel camera . . . cue Dan,' the red light went on and we were off.

We were about thirty seconds in when Richard said, 'Just keep it going as long as you can. Have you got the team sheets yet?' We hadn't.

It felt like a lot longer but in the end, it was somewhere between three and four minutes. That feels like an eternity in telly. Earlier experiences in my career had taught to never, ever, go into a live broadcast unprepared. It is still something I won't do to this day. I never sit in a studio, or on location, without having something I can comfortably talk about for between one and two minutes up my sleeve. Ninety-nine times out of a hundred you will never need it but, without it, a broadcasting disaster is never far away. That day, I wandered off down the tunnel, showed our viewers around, explained where I was, what was happening and, eventually, ran through the team which was handed to me live on air. I loved it.

One of my first experiences of live TV came in the tennis at Wimbledon. It was a quarter-final in the men's singles. Andy Murray had come back from two sets down and it looked like he was about to force a decider with Frenchman Richard Gasquet. I was despatched to Henman Hill at top speed to find someone to speak to. 'We'll come to you and you'll have a minute . . . DO NOT GO OVER,' said the editor as I legged it out of the office by Court 18 and down to the chunk of tennis-loving humanity assembled on the Hill.

At the time, I was a sports presenter of News 24, and had very little experience of live network television. I had covered some games in the Six Nations, reported for *Match of the Day* and worked on the Grand National, but this was taking things up a notch.

We arrived at the bottom of the Hill just as the set finished. There was a huge roar from the crowd. On our way there I was desperately trying to scour the huge human sea for potential interviewees. I had spotted a table of middle-aged ladies. They were about three picnic tables deep and, just behind them, was a fella with a giant inflatable parrot. Perfect.

'Get ready . . . we're coming to you in fifteen seconds.' We clambered into position. If you've ever seen the end of the film *Crocodile Dundee*, where Mick Dundee climbs across the crowd to get to Sue, it was a bit like that.

'Dan,' came the shrill voice of editor Carl Hicks over talk back. One of the things I loved about Carl was his brutal honesty. He wasn't a man for beating about the bush. 'There are thirteen-and-a-half million people watching . . . don't eff it up.'

Thankfully, I didn't. I love that rush. Even though that story wasn't a matter of life and death, I love it when you can feel your heart beating, everything slows down a bit, your mind is in overdrive and you get that empty feeling in your stomach. It is a sink or swim moment.

It's at moments like that where experience is vital. In the technologically obsessed world we live in today, live TV is a brutal place to exist. Presenters, interviewers, commentators – and even guests – aren't really allowed to make or learn from their mistakes without an element of public shaming.

A lot of that criticism is uncalled for and unfair, but there are occasions where you do feel the pressure to get every detail right. I had only been at *BBC Breakfast* for about six weeks when the inquest into the Hillsborough Disaster published its findings. The panel decided that the 96 football fans who lost their lives at Sheffield Wednesday's ground in 1989 were unlawfully killed. It was a huge moment for the families of the victims who had tirelessly campaigned for justice for over twenty-five years. The next morning our show was coming from the Anglican Cathedral in Liverpool. I remember watching that fateful FA cup semi-final between Liverpool and Nottingham

Forest with my dad. I had covered various stages of the fight for justice and had regularly interviewed campaigners and family members over the years.

That night I arrived in Liverpool at a hotel about five minutes from the cathedral. It was already late. My alarm was set for 3.15 am and it was 9.30 pm. On my bed was a huge file of information to go through. We had about fifteen guests lined up to be interviewed in the cathedral, live on *BBC Breakfast*. I felt it was my responsibility to know their stories, their families and lost loved ones inside out. It was one of those days when accuracy was even more important than normal.

Mistakes about dates, names, timings would be unacceptable on such an emotional morning, so I stayed up all night making notes and working out how to do the best job possible. I am not a coffee drinker. I can't bear the smell of it, but I did drain the hotel's supply of tea that night. Thankfully, the combination of a brilliant team, some wonderful guests and a truck load of adrenaline led to a successful programme the following morning. As well as getting the information right, we also hit the right tone, which is just as important.

That is one of those shows that always stays with me. The same can be said for the morning of 23 May 2017, when I was woken up by a text from my *BBC Breakfast* boss at the time, Adam Bullimore, at about 2 am.

'Dan. BIG breaking story in Manchester. Not many details yet. You might want to get in early.'

Fortunately, I was staying in the hotel just around the corner from work that night. I had been filming something the night before and hadn't gone home. I was able to get ready quickly and make my way in.

My fellow *Breakfast* presenter, Louise Minchin, had received the same message at home. 'This is why I always leave my phone on. For moments like that,' says Louise, who remembers it vividly. 'I called Adam straight away and he told me what he knew. There had been an explosion in Manchester at an Ariana Grande concert. We knew that many people had been injured but other details were really sketchy. At about the same time I got a text from my best friend, who was in America. She was watching the breaking news over there and asked if I was on my way to the studio. I got in my car and drove straight to work.'

During that trip, Louise listened to Radio 5 Live to try and pick up as many details as she could about the police operation. It was a story that felt very close to home.

'I just kept thinking that my daughter could have been at that concert. She had asked me to go, but my husband and I had said "no" because she was in the middle of her GCSEs. Dave (her husband) would have gone to pick her up. I knew the type of people that would be there. I kept thinking about that. It would have been packed with teenage girls, like my daughter. It was going to be an awful morning for a lot of desperate parents.'

Louise was right. The eventual death toll from the Manchester Arena bomb would be 23, including the bomber. A further 139 people were injured and more than half of them were children.

Louise went to the office to make sure she was across all the facts. The plan was for her to go to the scene and for me to be back in the studio in Salford. She jumped in a cab and they quickly made their way down to the steps at the side of the Manchester Arena where some of the concert-goers would have run from the venue. It was 5.15 am and we were on air at 6 am.

'I remember how light it was,' says Louise. 'The streets were eerily quiet. The whole area was cordoned off and it was packed with police officers. On a morning like that, tone is everything. I think we were both conscious that the nation was waking up to a shocking story. It was right at the heart of a big city that I love. It felt so personal and we needed to tell our viewers in a way that was factual but without shocking them.'

This is one of Louise's great talents. If you watch her on mornings like that, she never rushes headlong into anything. She carefully walks you to the bad news. She never starts with the number of people who have died or a gruesome fact. That is her many years of experience and an understanding that there is no need to scaremonger when the truth is painful enough.

'I was presenting the BBC News Channel on the day of the 7/7 bombs in London,' says Louise. 'It's strange how your brain works on days like that. I tend to prepare mind maps in my head so I can access the information I need. I try and make sure that every single thing I say is grounded in fact. People need a moment to process news and, every morning, a lot of our viewers are watching as a family, with their children. Sometimes our job is to prepare them for bad news. Unfortunately, that was one of those mornings.'

I can still remember sitting alone in the studio that day. There are six cameras in our studio and the one we use the

241

most is camera 3. It is the one that sits in front of the desk and provides the two-shot of the presenters. Beneath that camera is a large digital clock. The brilliant *Breakfast* team were incredibly calm that morning. Louise was in position for the headlines at the scene; our director was checking the camera shot and the editor was reminding us all that there would be precious little on the autocue because news was changing all the time.

I looked at the clock beneath camera 3. It read 5.59 and 30 seconds. I can still see it ticking over. In half a minute, the *Breakfast* titles would run, and we'd be live to the nation. Sitting on that sofa is a peculiar privilege. You are inside people's homes, their bedrooms and front rooms. You are sharing an important moment, having breakfast with them and preparing them for the day ahead. Just as Louise said, 'I am always aware that we are talking to families; to children getting ready for school.'

It was one of those moments when all that time in the saddle becomes invaluable. The experience of covering 9/11, the morning after the Hillsborough inquest, the tennis, the mistakes, the triumphs, the hours and hours of broadcasting all boil down to one morning when you have to get it right.

The tone, your words, the sentiment, the accuracy ... everything has got to be perfect. There is no script on a morning like that. You are simply reacting to what you see around you. Things are changing all the time.

I love working with Louise. We have sat on that sofa together for many years, and, right from the first week, I think we began to develop an understanding. In all those hours we have sat next to each other, I think we have spoken over one another about two or three times. We understand each other's body language. I know that when she shuffles, she has something to say, and my peripheral vision is so finely tuned, I can see her raised finger (to indicate she has a question for a guest) from anywhere. She is an incredibly generous broadcaster and I think we both enjoy sharing a studio because it is never a competition for who gets to speak.

Essentially, it comes down to trust. We trust each other to do a good job. We know that we have one another's best interests at heart. We both care deeply about the programme and the people who work on it and we trust each other at those crucial, tense, emotional moments when every word is so important.

'Trust is the key,' says Louise. 'We have worked together long enough. I know you won't interrupt me, or cut me off, and that is so important. We have both learned to cope with that adrenaline rush. When the brain is in overdrive, you have to learn to slow everything down. There is that sweet spot of extreme focus and extreme calm. It you can get there, and report with humanity at the same time, that is when you can do the best job . . . even in a horrible situation.'

Louise can't remember much about that day. She has almost no memory of being in Manchester that morning. When I ask her, she can't recall much about the show other than listening intently to the guests we had on. She remembers walking back through Manchester afterwards and the stunned look on people's faces.

'That was the thing that really struck me on the way home.

Ever since we moved to the northwest, Manchester has felt like a big part of my life, like part of the family. For the four hours we were on air that morning, I was in a broadcasting bubble. It was only when I left, that I could see the true depth of the pain caused by what had happened at the Arena. The city was stunned. There are so many stories we cover that feel very far away; we observe from a distance. This was different. It was personal, it was close. The whole city was in shock.'

Throughout that morning we were giving out vital pieces of information. On a day like that, our audience can be two, three or four times larger than normal. There were families desperately trying to find loved ones. One of those glued to the TV that day was Figen Murray. She was the mother of Martyn Hett who had been to see Ariana Grande the night before.

Figen had five children and Martyn was always the one she was worried about the most. He was the sort of child who would call his mum a lot. There was always a crisis in his life, always something happening. His mum was permanently tidying up his metaphorical mess.

'There was one time when he was studying in London,' recalls Figen. 'He called me and told me he urgently needed some money. His landlord was chasing him. He promised he would pay me back,' she laughs, '. . . of course I never saw it again.'

'He would call in the middle of the night. "Mum, I'm in Nottingham and I don't know what to do." There was some long excuse about how he had got to Nottingham and why he was stuck there. It was always that way. From an early age Martyn needed my help. He got stuck in a set of decorating ladders when he was only four years old.' Figen giggles as she recalls having to ring the fire brigade to get him out. 'It was my job to look after him. I was his mum.'

After studying in London, Martyn worked in public relations in Stockport. He was likeable and always surrounded by friends and new people. He was happy, full of life and full of energy.

'If I tell you about his flat,' says Figen, 'it will give you the perfect picture of what Martyn was like. He had what he called a "Diva toilet" with golden baubles, a golden toilet seat, a golden toilet roll holder . . . you get the idea . . . and there were LP covers all over the walls. He was a huge fan of *Coronation Street* and his flat was like a museum to the show. If I was an estate agent trying to sell it, I would definitely describe it as "quirky".'

What does she remember about the Monday night of the concert in Manchester?

'I had seen Martyn on the Sunday morning. I told you about his *Corrie* themed flat . . . so you won't be surprised to hear his cat was called "Emily Bishop" [Emily was played by Eileen Derbyshire, the longest-serving character on the show]. He rang me to ask me if I could run him to Asda to get some food and cat litter. On the way we had a long chat about his trip to America. He was leaving on the Wednesday morning for the trip of a lifetime. He had saved up for two years and was going to spend two months travelling the States and would finish off with two weeks in Florida. We owned the flat he was in at the time, but he said that, when he came back, he was getting a promotion and he wanted to buy the flat. He told me it was

245

"time to grow up and own a property". We laughed about it because, well, that was Martyn through and through . . . full of promises. I dropped him off and told him I'd pick him up on Wednesday to take him to the airport.'

At the time of the Arena bomb, Figen Murray was a highly respected counsellor and therapist. That Monday had been a particularly difficult day with clients. There had been a number of tough sessions, so she went to bed early. Her husband, Stuart, was doing paperwork downstairs. Two of her three daughters – Louise and Nikita (aged nineteen and sixteen at the time) – were living at home. Nikita was in the middle of her GCSEs and Louise was doing an art foundation course at college. After a long, tough day, Figen feel asleep instantly.

'The next thing I remember,' she says, 'Louise was in my bedroom. I looked at the clock and it was 10.40 at night. Louise apologised for waking me but wanted to know if I'd had a message from Martyn. His friends were texting her because they had been out to a gig with him and they had lost him. She told me there had been an incident and some sort of explosion. Before she had even finished her sentence, I was running downstairs. Stuart was watching the news and I told him that Martyn was there.'

Stuart tried to reassure his wife. He reminded her about what Martyn was like and told her that he'd probably left early and was off buying a friend some drinks somewhere. His mum was starting to worry. He still wasn't answering his phone. His friends kept texting to find out where he was. Figen was glued to the news but she knew that something was wrong.

'I don't know why but I can remember the time exactly when I turned to Louise and said, "I think he's dead." It was 11.16. There was a really strange feeling that came over me. I felt, for the first time in my life, that I had no connection to him. It actually felt like some scissors had cut something inside me. Don't ask me how, but I knew he wasn't on the planet anymore.'

Figen spoke to one of Martyn's friends on the phone and told him to prepare for the worst news. She stayed watching the coverage all night and through to *Breakfast* the following morning. One of the messages we gave out that day was an update from police asking anyone who was looking for a missing person to go to the Etihad Stadium in Manchester.

'I knew I needed to go and ordered a taxi. Stuart was a doctor and called work to cancel his surgery for the day. I told him I could go on my own but, months later, he told me he imagined a stadium filled with dead bodies and I would have to try and identify my son.'

They stayed at the stadium all day. More and more families arrived and each one was assigned a family liaison officer. Figen was ringing home all the time trying to arrange for her children to be looked after, but she felt like the whole family needed to be together, and the police sent a car to collect them. In total, including Martyn's friends, there were thirty people waiting for news on his whereabouts at the stadium. They were told at 6 o'clock that they would start the process of identifying the bodies. Figen picks up the story.

'One after another, families kept being taken into a side room. They would all come out in tears. Everyone was expecting the worst. Our time didn't come. Just after 9 o'clock, we were told that it was best if we went home. We were about to get in the car when a police officer asked us to come back inside. It was the news that we were all dreading. I had known for hours. Martyn was one of the victims. He was dead.'

Everyone went back to the family home, all thirty of those who had been waiting to hear if Martyn was going to be okay. They all stayed the night. Nobody wanted to leave.

'We all remembered him,' says his mum. 'We laughed, we joked, we cried . . . we drank vodka and Coke. I woke up the following morning about 11 o'clock and Nikita was there in her school uniform. I told her she didn't need to go but she looked me in the eye and told me she was doing it for Martyn.'

Nikita ended up with eleven A*s in her GSCEs. She poured her grief over her brother into her education. School was the only consistent thing in her life. She knew her family needed good news after Martyn's death, and she did her best to provide it. She is now studying maths at Nottingham University. Her mother's professional life changed forever on the night of Martyn's death.

Figen Murray was a gifted therapist and a counsellor. She lectured others at Stockport College but the move into management didn't work for someone who loved helping others one to one. She had clients who had issues with child abuse, rape, domestic violence, depression, anger and everything in between. She loved her job, but all that came to an end on that night in May 2017.

'The day he died I knew I had to stop working. My job is

all about being there emotionally for my clients and I instinctively knew I could never do that again. My whole perspective changed when I lost my son. How could I show empathy to someone who was struggling at work, or had an issue with something which, in comparison to what I'd been through with Martyn, seemed insignificant? I'm not sure it's the best advice to tell someone who needs help to "stop complaining and get on with it."'

Her employers asked her to reconsider. They offered her the chance to take a three-year sabbatical but Figen knew that she couldn't go back.

'Part of me was broken forever. I didn't just lose Martyn. I lost my career and my professional reputation overnight. I have always known my own mind. I would often tell my clients to try and see the bigger picture; to use what we call "helicopter skills". It's about being able to watch a situation from an imaginary helicopter above it. You look down on the scenario; you see yourself, how you are reacting to others and what is happening around you.'

Did Figen use any of the therapists techniques on herself after the death of her son?

'I was like a zombie,' she admits with honesty. 'Our house was filled with friends and relatives for weeks, but I was drifting around in a daze. I just kept thinking about Martyn. He nearly didn't go that night, Dan. He was trying to save money for his trip to America and only decided to join his friends at the last minute. People always tell me that Martyn was in the wrong place at the wrong time, but maybe he was in the right place at the right time. Maybe it was his time. Martyn always said he would die a spectacular death before his thirtieth birthday. He used to say it with a smile on his face, but I could tell there was more to it than that. He was twenty-nine when he died. We found funeral instructions on his laptop. My son lived life at two hundred miles an hour but managed to cram two lifetimes into those twenty-nine years.'

The belief that it was Martyn's 'time' was even reflected at the trial of the bomber's brother in 2020. Figen heard a victim impact statement from a young girl who had stopped and spoken to Martyn moments before the bomb had been detonated. She described how she felt survivor's guilt that the conversation delayed Martyn and, if it hadn't happened, he would still be alive today. Figen's immediate response was a desire to tell her to let it go. She was desperate for the young girl to know that, in her eyes, there is nothing she could have done to change Martyn's destiny.

Figen takes great comfort from the fact that her son died instantly at the Arena. He was talking to people outside the main hall and was standing close to the bomber at the time of the explosion. That night Figen had lost someone so precious to her but, as much as she missed and loved her son, she couldn't stop thinking about the man who killed him, and twenty-one others.

'I wanted to know why he did it. I was riddled with grief but, the more clearly I could think, the more I knew I had to try and understand terrorism.'

I have had the pleasure of interviewing Figen on a number

of occasions. The first time was quite soon after the Arena bombing. It has been incredible to watch her transform from a grieving mother into a powerful campaigner. I admire her clarity of thought. I admire her determination to bring something good out of something so terrible and I think it's inspirational to see her trying to make sure her son didn't die in vain.

Figen is Turkish by birth. Her family emigrated to Germany before she was three and she came to England in 1983. She met her husband in the UK and the pair renewed their vows in November 2019. The family are all trying to deal with Martyn's death in the best way they can. His brother, Daniel, is a software engineer and is producing an educational game about Martyn. Nikita tried to focus on her studies while Louise, who was looking forward to moving out and going to university, decided to stay at home because she felt she needed her mum to be near and her mum needed her. When you speak to Figen, or hear her talk, she looks strong. She seems to be coping. She is coping, but her grief is all consuming and her family will never be the same.

She often finds herself looking at a family photograph which was taken just a few weeks before Martyn died.

'I can't remember why,' says Figen, 'but we were all at the house. It was a final gathering before Martyn left for America, so he suggested that we all get together and have a picture taken outside the front door. That was the last time we were a family. That was the last time we were all with each other. I think about that a lot. I know I will never get over losing him. He is in my thoughts when I get up and when I go to sleep. I speak to him in my head all day long. It has been crushing for me personally, as a mum, but also as an independent woman. I have never relied on someone else. Losing my professional income and standing in the counselling community affected my dignity. It is a long road, but I had to start from scratch and reinvent myself.'

That reinvention started just a few days after Martyn's death. The catalyst was another photograph.

The house was filled with people after the bomb. Family, friends, a constant stream of well-wishers and passers-by and almost endless visits from police officers. The media were camped out on Figen's doorstep. We all remember how the tragedy brought Manchester together and the coverage was front page news for weeks afterwards. Each day, members of the family would buy a pile of newspapers from the shop across the road from the house. Each day they would be left on the dining room table. Each day Figen would walk past them and ignore them until, one day, she was transfixed by an image on the front page.

'It was his face. The bomber's face,' says Figen. 'I froze and just stared at him. He looked so young. I thought, "What have you done? Why did you do it? Why did you waste your life?" I couldn't stop thinking about him. Three weeks after that I saw another photo on the front page of the *Guardian* which had a huge impact on me.

'Do you remember the attack on the mosque in London?' she asks me.

On 19 June 2017, nearly a month after the Manchester Arena

attack, a man called Darren Osbourne drove a van into pedestrians near a mosque in Finsbury Park. He said he wanted to 'kill all Muslims'. One person died and another nine were injured. The picture on the front page of the *Guardian* was of five men linking arms to prevent the crowd from getting to Osbourne.

'It was amazing,' says Figen, 'to see those men protecting him. In all that terror, with all those heightened emotions, they instinctively chose to keep him safe – despite what he had done to people they knew. They wanted him to stand trial for what he had done. This man had tried to kill them, but these men were doing the humane, the decent thing. Protecting him from the mob. I couldn't stop thinking about it and the picture of Martyn's killer.'

When her husband came home from work that night, Figen told him she was going to get in touch with the media. She wanted to publicly forgive Martyn's murderer.

'I had to try and stop the hate. Just like those men linking arms . . . I needed to do something. It just felt like the right thing to do.'

Figen did speak powerfully, but she didn't cry. People expected her to cry. There was an inevitable backlash.

'I got trolled. "How can she not hate him?" . . . "She doesn't care about her son" . . . "Grieving mother? Did anyone see any tears?" I was "irrational", I was "stupid" and I was "unhinged". People asked me how I could do that as Martyn's mum. I was still numb at the time, but my son was kind and caring. He always looked out for the underdog and, if he'd been there, he would have told me it was the right thing to do.'

Figen has never cried in public over Martyn and people confuse that with an absence of emotion.

'There are certain things you learn as a counsellor. Not all of them are helpful. It sounds silly now, but one of the things I used to do was to run workshops for gravediggers. I used to try and explain to them the depths of emotions they would see at the graveside, so they were prepared for their proximity to grief. This was before I lost Martyn. After his death, after experiencing that pain myself, I knew that the theory I was teaching the gravediggers bore no resemblance to the truth. I was living through that emptiness every day. So, when people said, "you don't look like a grieving mother" or "why aren't you crying?" all I knew was that each day was a battlefield. I was able to switch into professional mode when I needed to because that was the only way I could cope. In private, my world is broken. The pain is immense. Try lying in bed too tired to stay awake but unable to sleep because he's not there anymore. That's when it really hits you. The hardest part for me, was not the day he died, but the day we had to go and identify his body in the morgue. I can tell you about that if you like.'

Maybe it's because of her background as a therapist but Figen has a rare ability to observe objectively. You can learn so much from her honesty about her own frailties but also her relentless optimism that things can get better and that she is just one person who is determined to make a difference. She is also a loving mum who lost her son and that will always be what defines her.

'I had never seen a dead body,' says Figen. She didn't want

to see Martyn. 'I know it sounds silly, but he had a tattoo of Deirdre Barlow and it's little things like that which can send you over the edge.'

Figen's voice lowers as she talks about the most difficult few hours of her life. Turkish funerals are very different from those in the UK. Figen's only knowledge of a morgue came from what she had seen on TV. She was expecting to see dead bodies with a name tag hanging off the big toe, but it wasn't anything like that when she went to see Martyn's body. She was immensely thankful for that.

'The bereavement nurses led us every step of the way. We were told we could stay as long as we wanted. There was never any pressure to act in a certain way. I suppose they see a lot of different ways of coping with death. We went in and it was set out like a private hospital. Martyn was in a room on his own. There was a bed and an armchair next to it. He was lying in the bed under a quilt. The sheets were crisp and white. They were perfect. I was so worried about what he would look like, but he just looked asleep. It's not an image I will ever get out of my head, but I'm glad that it doesn't haunt me. Do you know what I mean? No mother wants to see their dead child but, at the same time, we had to see him. It's the coldness of his body that will never leave me. It came as a shock. I hugged him but the coldness stayed with me for the rest of the day.'

There are many mothers out there who had been through the crushing pain of loss. There are many parents who find it hard to see a way forward after the death of a child. I have interviewed many of them during my career. Most recently I have seen it in the face of Charlotte Charles, the mother of Harry Dunn, who was killed outside a US Air Force base in August 2019. It is believed that Harry's motorbike was involved in a collision with a car driven by Anne Sacoolas – the wife of an American diplomat. Ms Sacoolas claimed diplomatic immunity and the international row surrounding that, which even at one stage involved an audience with President Donald Trump (while Anne Sacoolas was apparently waiting in the next room), continues to roll on. Charlotte Charles, just like Figen Murray, will tell you she's exhausted. You can see the pain and the unremitting grief in her eyes every time you talk to her. The tears are never far away. While Charlotte fights for justice, Figen fights for change.

'I couldn't do anything until the first anniversary of his death,' Figen says. 'I had an emotional block until then. The anniversaries don't get any easier, but the first one was impossible. Everything comes back to you so powerfully. I kept telling myself that after that I would start contacting schools and trying to talk to young people about their chance to change the world around them.'

One of the things I really admire about Figen is her ongoing desire to try and understand – even though one of those she is trying to understand killed her son.

'I remember a conversation with a high-ranking police officer,' says Figen. 'I was talking to him about the number of people who had died in the blast. He kept saying 22 and I corrected him and said it was twenty-three; there were twenty-two innocent victims and one terrorist. He told me that I was very noble but, for me, the important thing is that I need to stay human. I can't allow hate to destroy me. That young man was somebody's son.'

Figen fundamentally believes that terrorists are made and not born. She has delivered that message to over seven-and-a-half-thousand school children since Martyn died. One of her talks opened up an even more important door for her. She was speaking at the University of Central Lancashire. She was in the staff room and one of the lecturers showed her the syllabus for the counter terrorism course. Figen is always searching for the bigger picture – the aforementioned helicopter view – and here was her opportunity to learn all about it.

'I often ask myself if I have Martyn's blood on my hands. I have done that from day one. We are all angry at terrorists, but they are angry at something and that is something I feel I have a responsibility to try and understand. I knew I needed to do the course.'

Before Martyn's death, Figen knew nothing about terrorism. She would turn off the news when it came on. When her family talked about it, she would ask if anyone wanted to watch *The Chase* or talk about what they would have for tea that evening. Martyn's death changed everything. The more his mother thought about it, the more she felt the world had something to do with it. She needed to try and understand the anger of the ideology. She needed to understand what caused her son's death.

'I feel we all have blood on our hands. I feel it is a societal problem that we cannot afford to ignore in this country. It is fuelled by inequality and grounded in international politics. I am not saying that terrorism isn't a choice. I know all about the effects, the pain and the ongoing suffering, but we have to try and get a handle on where that anger comes from. Terrorists aren't just at home watching box sets . . . they are ready to strike us again. At the same time as trying to understand, we have to be prepared . . . that is what Martyn's Law is all about.'

Martyn's Law is Figen Murray's attempt to change the law forever; to try and make sure that other families don't have to go through what she has experienced. Figen never set out to be an activist but, as a parent, she knows that no one is immune from violence. In addition to tracking down and stopping the perpetrators, Figen wants us – as a society – to get better at protecting each other. That would mean putting in place basic security procedures so that every venue and public space has a plan. This would not be a one-size-fits-all solution but would depend on the venue and the circumstances. Martyn's Law is all about measures which are relevant to the threat.

Figen's point is that it's absurd that we have legislation that sets out how many toilets a venue must have, and how food must be prepared, but nothing that holds those same venues responsible for having basic security in place. Martyn's Law won't stop terrorism, but the hope is that, if the government makes the changes to the law, improved security and well-thought-out anti-terrorism strategies will make it much harder to inflict mass casualties and fewer people will have to suffer.

Figen was convinced things would be different in Manchester after her son died, but she was given a shock on one of her first trips out after Martyn's death.

'My children bought Stuart and I some tickets to go and see a singer in Manchester. I took a handbag with me. I made sure it was a small one so that it would make the bag search an easy one. I assumed that someone would check what I was taking into a packed public venue. No one looked in my bag at any stage, not even once. I remember sitting in the audience crying. Stuart thought it was because it was a sad song, but I wasn't even listening to the music. I was just sat there thinking "this is why people die".'

It was fascinating for Figen to see how the system of campaigning works.

'I felt that we needed a petition. I can't tell you how frustrating it is to watch something you care about so much struggle to get 25,000 signatures while the campaign to bring back *The Jeremy Kyle Show* was into the hundreds of thousands. We just have this strange apathy to the issue of security. I know I see it with a clear focus because of what I've been through, but I find it amazing that we don't think about it as a society.'

Figen may not have had the most signatures, but she does have a powerful voice. Her plans for Martyn's Law have been held up by the global pandemic but she is in regular contact with government ministers and is confident that change is on the way.

'I like to be straight with people, especially people in power. If someone makes me a promise, it's my job to make sure they follow through on that. I am only a short person,' laughs Figen, 'but I am not going to go away. Every public venue needs a terrorism protocol in place. It's about training, risk assessment, having an action plan and working with the local authority. Simple things like – when a concert ends – why can't we change the timing of the traffic lights to get people away from the venue as quickly as possible? I have told the Securities Minister to his face that I will not let this go . . . and I won't. The media want headlines,' she bemoans. 'I understand that. That's why you get "Mother Of Arena Victim Wants Airport Security For Pubs" but it's not like that. I just think we owe it to each other to make a difference. That is my goal in life now. That will be Martyn's legacy.'

It has been a strange few years for Figen Murray. She has moved from counselling to campaigning; the mother has become a motivator. What is it that still drives her on?

Martyn's death not only changed her life, it also changed her personality. 'Before my son died, I was an introvert. I hated big crowds. I would sometimes have a panic attack before I gave a lecture – that's how much I hated it. But I felt as though something snapped inside me. I felt like it set me free . . . 'You killed my baby. Wait until you see what I'm capable of.'

Figen says her son would laugh his head off if he was able to see how much she has changed since his death. She surprises herself every day and has completely lost her ability to feel embarrassment or shame. The awkwardness and anxiety which could cripple her, has disappeared. The former therapist inside her thinks she knows what is happening.

'We have all heard of post-traumatic stress but there is also something called post-traumatic growth. I think that is what I'm experiencing. I make it sound positive but, the truth is, I don't think I have any control over it. Once we have sorted out Martyn's Law and secured his legacy, I will have to find something else to do.'

There are still dark times for Figen as you would expect. She combats them with the unusual combination of box sets and knitting. The box sets feed the couch potato in her and the knitting allows her to be creative. That would be her advice to anyone who has experienced trauma: to use the other side of the brain; to make something, bake something. Figen began by knitting vintage hearts and then moved on to bears. She knits every day and sells quite a few of them online. Each bear has a name and an individual story. This is her outlet. This is how she fights back when the walls of grief are closing in.

Like many of those featured in this book, Figen Murray makes me think about how I would act in a similar situation. Loss hits almost all of us at some stage in our lives and we all react in different ways. I'm thankful that Figen has found a way to fight the hate that could so easily have consumed her. I find her attitude to those who have torn her life apart inspirational. In hearing her story, it reminds me of the importance of trying to understand those people with whom I fundamentally disagree. It's far more difficult than making a joke, or throwing an insult, but Figen is moving mountains to leave a legacy for her son.

*　　*　　*

There is no clearer indication of Figen's perspective on all this than in her response to the news that, in August 2020, the bomber's brother was sentenced to 55 years in prison for his part in planning one of the deadliest terror attacks on British soil. It was the maximum sentence the judge was able to hand down.

On the day the news was announced, Figen listened to a phone-in on BBC Radio Manchester. 'There were so many angry people ringing in. They wanted the death penalty, they were screaming about the broken justice system, about the need to make sure he would never get parole and that we needed to stop immigration and close the borders. It was all coming out. I know that many people don't agree with me. I know I don't speak for all the victims' families but, for me, what it boils down to is two brothers who got it really badly wrong. One of them is dead and the other has no life. I heard the sentence and I'm happy that the judge had the measure of the man.'

The brother showed no remorse, refused to leave his cell to attend court for the verdict (having dismissed his legal team the previous week) and didn't listen to any of the victim impact statements. Figen was one of those who addressed the court. 'I know some people are furious that he wouldn't listen to what he had done to us all, but I was glad he wasn't there. I feel, when I look at what terrorists' aims are, they want to cause pain and heartache. They have done that. They destroyed so many lives, so why would I want to give this man the chance to listen to my heartache, to see me cry in front of him? Why would I let him see how much he has hurt me and taken from me?'

Figen is aware that there aren't many of the victims' families who feel the same way as she does, but she has to stay true to her instincts.

Has she forgiven her son's killers?

'Yes,' she says, without hesitation. 'I know I may be alone in that, but I have forgiven them both. When I was there with him in court [in the earlier part of the trial], the brother, I caught his eye once or twice. We saw each other. I thought, "You knew what you were doing." I see the stupidity of what he has done. He has thrown his life away and taken my son's life at the same time. Maybe the penny will drop for him one day. Maybe he will come to see the extent of what he has done and, if he doesn't, he's in the right place.'

I ask Figen how she would feel if he ever did say 'sorry' for his actions.

'I would go and give him a hug,' she says. 'No one has ever asked me that before, so I am just responding on instinct. You might think that is stupid. You might think I have lost my mind. You might even hate me for it, but my humanity is what drives me on. That is my focus now. My son had compassion for those around him. How can I not share that with others? Where would we be without it in this world? We would all be killing each other.'

Figen speaks with certainty but she would be the first person to admit that she struggles. She has bad days . . . and then really bad days. She misses Martyn all the time. She describes a physical pain which grows out of a maternal longing to see him again. She would love to hear him moan. She would love him to ring her up in the middle of the night and ask for a lift. She would love him to be a pain in the backside again. The weariness never leaves, but her memories of Martyn are inspiring her to try and make a difference far beyond the boundaries of Manchester.

Just as Louise said earlier, the Arena bomb felt intensively personal for me too. I started working in Manchester in 1999 and walked those streets for years and watched many gigs at the Arena. The idea that so many were injured and killed on that night in 2017 will forever leave a stain on the city.

Figen and I have spoken for well over an hour-and-a-half. The time has flown by.

'Before you go, Dan, can I tell you about the nails?'

'Of course,' I say, intrigued.

'It was the third day after the bomb. My sister, my brother and my brother-in-law were all at the house and they had taken over the cooking. It was one of those situations where I was happy for everyone to be doing the jobs in the house, but I also needed to be busy; to be occupied. The washing basket was full, so I quietly went downstairs into the basement of the house and put a load in. I thought, "I love my family, but I can't ask them to wash my underwear."

'As I was putting the washing in, I saw a brand new screw on top of the dryer. I picked it up. I was about to put it in the bin when my back went cold, and I thought of Martyn. It's hard to explain that feeling. I kept that screw and I started collecting others. Everywhere I go now, I find screws, nuts, bolts and nails. I find them all over the world. I have over five or six hundred of them.

'I know it sounds strange but there is a reason for this. Martyn was very close to the bomber when he detonated his nail bomb that night in Manchester. He was so close that the medical examiner found sixteen separate pieces of metal in my son's body. I have asked the police if I am allowed to have those fragments and they have said I can, but only once the inquiry is over.

'I have an idea. I know what to do with them. Eventually, I will take all those nails, bolts and screws that I have collected over the years and I will melt them all down and make a bear out of them . . . like the ones I have been knitting. I want the bear to be holding a heart made of the sixteen screws that were in my son's body. I want to keep that bear in our house as a permanent reminder that terrorism will not beat me. That is my way of rejecting the hate. That is my way of saying, "you sent all this to kill my son . . . and I will turn it into love". That will be my son's legacy. That is how I will remember him.'

CHRISTMAS CHEER FOR TERRENCE

We have something on *BBC Breakfast* which Louise calls the 'Breakfast cuddle'. We often deal with subjects which are difficult to discuss on national TV and, when we do that, we tend to be joined by a couple of guests: one is normally an expert and the other is a case study.

We always put the case study next to us because they often need to be taken care of and looked after during the interview. It's much easier to do that when they are within touching distance. It is awful to see someone crying when you are too far away to hold their hand or offer them a tissue.

Wednesday 11 December 2019 was one of the days we employed the cuddle.

I woke up at the normal time of 3.11 am on that day, and by about 3.20, I was reading through the briefs for that day's show. We had some great guests lined up and one of the final slots on the programme was about the issue of loneliness at Christmas.

We had two guests booked to talk to us: Laurie Boult, from Age UK, and Terrence, who had spent twenty Christmases on his own after the death of his mother. His life had been turned around after becoming a volunteer for the Oldham branch of

Age UK. He was coming in to try and encourage others who might find themselves on their own over the festive period.

I only have strong memories of one of my grandparents. One of them died before I was born, two died when I was very young, and my mum's mother passed away when I was 14 years old. Thankfully, none of them ever suffered from loneliness, but the statistics I read through that morning were harrowing.

According to an Age UK survey, Christmas is the loneliest time of the year for over 1.5 million older people and, as Terrence had experienced himself, almost 870,000 older people would be eating dinner alone on Christmas Day.

Terrence came into the studio with a stick to try and keep him steady and I remember our floor-manager brought him onto the set a little earlier than normal so he would have the opportunity to get comfortable before the live interview. They arrived while Carol was doing the weather which gave Louise Minchin and I a precious few minutes to talk to them before we were live.

'I remember being extremely nervous that morning,' says Laurie. 'We had this huge campaign to launch and we were doing it on the biggest breakfast show in the UK to a huge audience. I knew the subject inside out but it's really nerve-wracking to talk about something that is so important and has a huge impact on so many people. I was also really sensitive to the fact that I might be describing a situation that someone at home might be experiencing themselves. That was my motivation to get it right.'

Laurie was sat at the end of the couch and Terrence was next to me – in the *Breakfast* cuddle position. This was pre-social distancing days, so we were all quite cosy on the famous red sofa.

'It was quite overwhelming,' recalls Terrence when we meet up to remember what was a crazy few days. 'The lady who looks after Age UK in Oldham is called Maggie and when she told me I was going to be going to the BBC studios I thought "why do they want to talk to me?" I'd just done the Christmas advert for the charity down in London and I thought it might be good fun to come on. So we did. I was a little nervous, so I was glad we got to have a chat before it all started.'

Louise and I introduced ourselves while we were waiting to come back to the studio. I had a little chat with Terrence, asked him if he was okay and what he thought of our tree. He said it looked amazing and I asked him if he had one at home this year. 'No,' he said. 'I haven't had a tree for a while.'

'Fifteen seconds' came the cry from the gallery. 'Would you like one?' I whispered as the countdown continued. He nodded. 'Leave it with me. We'll see what we can do.' We introduced Terrence and Laurie and started the interview.

Laurie was so impressed with how clearly Terrence told his story. 'He was brilliant that morning,' she remembers. 'It made my job so much easier. I just had to mention a few statistics and talk generally about our campaign. Terrence did all the hard work by talking so openly about how he became lonely and how badly it affected him.'

Terrence was certainly a star that morning on the TV. We talked about the fact that he has spent so many Christmases on his own and I mentioned the conversation we'd had off-air about that fact he didn't have a tree.

'Social media can be a horrible place but, we don't often do this . . . if you're out there and you can help Terrence get a Christmas tree, decorate the house . . . then get in touch. We'll try and help you out and make sure that, this Christmas, is a great one.'

I put the appeal on social media and there was a huge response. *BBC Breakfast* producer, Marta Newman, was watching it closely.

'There were loads of offers from Christmas trees and decorations from big companies and supermarkets but there was one tweet which came through from Oldham College, just around the corner from Terrence.'

Hi Dan. Oldham College want to provide a tree, deliver and decorate it for him at his home. Can you call Carl please to discuss and arrange?

'It just looked like the perfect offer,' remembers Marta. 'It was around the corner from Terrence and I have a big thing about young people caring for the elderly, so it was wonderful. I was already fully engaged in the story because my granny had passed away earlier in that year. She [Helena Szczupacka] was an amazing woman who had died in February 2019 at the age of 107. That is one of the reasons why this story about Terrence was so important to me. That is why I do the job. I used to get told a lot that, as a journalist, if you're not into business or don't specialise in politics then you're not really doing the job properly. I fundamentally disagree with that. I am so into social affairs and I want to shine a light on people like this and issues like this. For me, that is just as important as interviewing a top-earning CEO or discussing what happens at Westminster.'

By the time Marta rang me, I was already back in Sheffield as I was filming an interview with Tony Foulds in Endcliffe Park (the flypast man, see his own chapter) which was going to go out on Boxing Day. I asked Marta if she could go back to Carl at Oldham College and ask him if they had a choir. If we were going to do this, I wanted it to be a bit special.

'I sent the reply to your tweet but didn't expect to hear anything back,' says Carl Marsden, the new Head of Communications at Oldham College. 'I had been in the job about two months and I was excited about the college because it had so much potential and so many great students. I can remember that morning quite well. It was freezing cold and I was walking between two of the college buildings. I decided to look at my phone and I saw your tweet on my timeline a few times. Loads of people were talking about it so I watched the clip and instantly thought "who doesn't love this bloke?" Terrence seemed like everyman's neighbour and friend, the sort of bloke who slips through the cracks without anybody really realising it. I just wanted the college to be involved in making a difference if we could.'

Marta called Carl and asked about the choir. Sometimes, things happen for a reason.

'The choir was an inspired idea' says Carl. 'Our choir at the college had actually recorded a Christmas record that year. They all kept asking me if I thought I could get them on the

TV to promote it and I kept telling them how unlikely it was. I remember thinking, "shall I run this by the chief executive at the college or shall we just go for it?" I decided to go for it and check later. I'm glad we did. I rang the guys who ran the choir and asked them how many people they could get together in two hours.'

The rest of the day was a little frantic to say the least. While Terrence went back to his house in Oldham, there were all sorts of things happening to try and make that Wednesday night a memorable one for him. Carl's team at the college raced off to the garden centre to buy a Christmas tree, lights, cards and presents.

They also had to get the choir back together from their Christmas holidays. I like to imagine this as a scene from *The Blues Brothers* with Jake and Elwood driving around in that old police car picking up the team. I think, in all likelihood, it was a little more sophisticated than that. Sophie Jones was one of the members of the Oldham College choir who got the call.

'I were in Bolton and got told that I needed to get back to Oldham as soon as possible. They wouldn't even tell me why . . . it was like this big secret. I raced back on the tram and we all got together at the college. They showed us the video of Terrence on your show and we were all in bits. At the end of it they said, "we are going to sing for him tonight" and it was such an amazing feeling. We all thought "we have deffo got to do this." We were in tears but buzzing at the same time. We sat there on the floor and cuddled each other but then we had to get cracking. We spent most of the rest of the day learning the carols and coming up with some harmonies. We wanted to make sure we got it right when we surprised Terrence.'

While Sophie and the choir were cracking on in Oldham, I was back in Sheffield filming with Tony Foulds in the park. We wrapped things up about three in the afternoon and, on the way home, I got a call from one of our assistant editors at *Breakfast,* Liam Blyth. I had been receiving messages and emails throughout the day and Terrence was all over social media, so I had a feeling I knew what it was about.

'Do you fancy a trip to Oldham tonight?' was Liam's opening gambit. I laughed back at him. 'It's your own fault,' he said, 'you should stop promising to do things on air.' Just a few hours after speaking to Terrence on the telly, everything was coming together. The new man in charge at *BBC Breakfast* was Richard Frediani, the editor. He'd joined from ITV and had been in the job for a few months. 'Fredi' – as he is universally known – is a passionate believer in following a story through. That's what we were trying to do with Terrence.

Liam and Marta had planned everything perfectly and Carl was pulling up trees to make sure it would all work logistically with the choir. We arranged to meet two streets away from Terrence's house at 6.30 pm – we would plan our secret mission from there. I got home, grabbed a sandwich, and drove to Oldham.

Meanwhile, back at the college . . .

'Somehow it looked like it was coming together,' says Carl. 'The students had been brilliant. They were all into it. I spoke to a producer called Ayo [Bakare] from the BBC. He told me where to meet and mentioned that the *Breakfast* cameras would be there to capture it all. I told the students and they were really giddy. This was really important to all of us, but I was feeling the pressure a bit. I hadn't sung a carol for a few years and even I got dragged into learning "Silent Night" as we were a little short on numbers.'

'We had the carol down by the middle of the afternoon,' remembers Sophie, 'so we got told to go home, get changed into something "more suitable". You can imagine what a bunch of performing arts students are like . . . we were all covered in baggy, black sports gear. I were like Wonder Woman . . . changed in a flash and back to college where we all divided into cars and vans to head off to see Terrence. We were all giggling in the back. Sounds daft, but it were properly like Christmas.'

I arrived at 6.30 and saw the little huddle of students on the street corner.

'I think some people thought we were up to no good,' laughs Carl. 'We got a few dodgy looks from passers-by but what we were planning was the opposite of anti-social behaviour.'

Sophie was one of those in the huddle. 'The guys had said the TV cameras were going to be there, but we didn't know you were going to turn up. I don't want to give you a big head or anything, but it was quite a buzz when we saw you get out of the car. We whispered "It's Dan Walker" but tried to act like we weren't bothered. It was like . . . nerve-wracking though, really. None of us knew how it was going to come out and, most annoyingly, it started raining didn't it? Us girls had all straightened our hair for the telly and it started to go frizzy.'

We hatched a plan which would involve me going up to the house, with a camera. I'd go in, if Terrence let me, and – while I was having a little chat with him – the Christmas tree deliverers could get into position outside the door. Once I'd let them in, the choir would then get ready and then I would open the door again and bring Terrence out. 'Only one problem,' said one of the choir leaders, 'we need to plug our speaker in.' I told them to leave that with me and I'd scope things out once I was in the house.

I walked up to Terrence's front door with our cameraman Justin Oliver and knocked.

'I'd had quite an eventful day,' remembers Terrence. 'So many people had made contact with me on Facebook after I went on *BBC Breakfast* and I know that Age UK were really happy with the response. Lots of people were commenting about the plea for a tree, but I was preparing for a quiet night in when there was a knock at the door. I don't know if you remember,' continues Terrence, 'but I actually had the chain on at first and when I saw you, I said, "what the hell are you doing here?"'

I told Terrence that I was 'Dan Walker from the telly' and asked if I could come in. We went inside and, as soon as the door shut, the next phase of 'Operation Christmas' went into action as the tree team got in position.

While all that was going on in the street, inside Terrence made a cup of tea and we sat down to discuss his day and he told us a bit more about how he had ended up spending twenty Christmases on his own. I'll tell you a bit more about Terrence later, but he has a complicated family background.

He always had a strained relationship with his father who walked out on the family in the late 1960s. His brother, Jeffrey, died in 1969. He was only twenty-six years old and their mother, Annie, never recovered from that loss. Terrence's sister, Valerie, didn't really want anything to do with the rest of the family and she passed away in 2019.

Terrence looked after his mum after the death of his brother, right up until she died at the age of eighty-three, in March 2000. 'I used to go out of my way to make sure that Mother had a good Christmas,' says Terrence. 'I used to buy her all sorts. She liked her whiskey and had a soft spot for chocolate and biscuits. I'd wrap them up, put them in a pillowcase, and then I would take them round on Christmas morning. She said something to me once that really struck me . . . she said, "If it wasn't for you Terrence, I'd have no one." In the end, it was me who discovered what that loneliness was really like.'

After the death of his mother, Terrence wanted to spend the first Christmas on his own remembering her and that's just the way it stayed. He would sit alone in his house with no tree, no friends, no phone calls and only a turkey sandwich for company . . . for two decades. 'I didn't like it. I was desperate for company. I cried my eyes out for the first few Christmas days but then, I just got into a routine. You get used to being alone.'

Joining the local group of Age UK transformed things for Terrence. He was planning to share his first Christmas dinner since 2000 with Nancy, the ninety-year-old dementia patient he had befriended as a volunteer, but he still didn't have a tree.

'We have a little surprise for you Terrence,' I told him while we sat on the chairs in his front room. 'We said on air that you didn't have a Christmas tree and we promised we'd sort one out for you ... am I allowed to go and open your front door?' Terrence said 'yes' but did look mildly concerned.

'At that point, I was wondering what on earth was going on,' he recalls.

I opened the door and in came four students from Oldham College. They were carrying a tree, decorations, presents and cards and they told Terrence they were there to put his tree up for him. I could see that Terrence was struggling to hold back the tears as he slowly got to his feet and then came the outpouring of emotion as he wept in his living room.

'When I watch it back now, I look like I completely lost it,' says Terrence with a smile 'and I think I did. It was a big enough shock when you turned up. I just wasn't expecting anything else. What you saw there was just pure joy and happiness. Nothing like that had ever happened to me in my life. I couldn't believe that people cared. I couldn't believe that those lovely students were trying to make a difference to one old man. It's hard to explain but, the whole time my father was around, he would constantly tell me that I was an idiot and that I was worthless. Here were some young people who actually wanted to spend time with me ... it was too much.'

Carl remembers that the next day some people on social media were asking why the four students who came in with the tree were Muslims. 'That was part of the magic of it for me,' says Carl. 'That is what Oldham College is like. Those were our students. That is Oldham. That is what the campus looks like. They were Muslims but, just because you don't celebrate Christmas, doesn't mean you can't enjoy making someone else feel good about theirs. They were just as desperate to be involved.'

While Terrence was talking to the students in his living room and they were deciding where to put his new tree, my phone was buzzing in my back pocket. It was our producer – Ayo – who was outside with the choir. They were in position, but we still needed to sort out some power for the speakers. I went into full Ninja mode and, while Terrence's was distracted by the tinsel, I opened the door and grabbed the power lead. 'I just need to plug in the lights' was all I could come up with. 'Have you got a spare socket somewhere Terrence?' Thankfully, he was so taken with the students who had brought the tree, he didn't notice me dragging a massive cable across his living room and plugging it in behind the telly. My phone buzzed again. 'It works,' said the text from Ayo. 'We are ready when you are.'

'Terrence,' I said, 'we have one more surprise for you. I heard you like a carol. Do you have a favourite?' Now, at this point, it could have all gone horribly wrong seeing as we only had one backing track and the choir had been practising 'Silent Night' for most of the day, but thankfully, our secret squirrel from Age UK Oldham had informed us correctly. Terrence said his favourite carol was 'Silent Night' and we led him to the front

door where the choir from Oldham College were ready to produce the festive goods.

'We were all in position,' says Sophie, 'but so nervous. There
was a TV camera there and I were stood at the front, next to
Amy. We were singing the harmony. We were waiting for our
cue which was you opening the door. I put some tinsel in my
hair at the last minute just to make it extra special.'

Carl was standing just behind the choir with his smartphone
at the ready. 'I know this sounds corny but, being there on the
street that night, was like being in one of those Hollywood
Christmas films. I haven't felt like that since my son, Oliver, was
about nine years old and we snuck downstairs to see if there
was anything under the tree!'

I was standing behind Terrence during 'Silent Night', but I
could see his shoulders shaking.

'I can't tell you how hard it is to keep singing,' says Sophie.
'If you watch the video back, we were all there with tears in our
eyes. It was heart breaking but so uplifting at the same time.
It were the best night of my life. I remember it so well . . . he
took his glasses off and started crying. That was me done at that
point. When he started singing along . . . it were one of them
moments. I felt the hair go on the back of me neck. You don't
get many of them. I think we all grew as people that night. We
were part of something so big and so moving.'

'Did you see the sleigh, Dan?' asks Carl. 'When we stopped
singing it got even more surreal. All the people on the road had
come out from their houses and it started snowing. Just when
you thought it couldn't get any more Christmassy, a sleigh came

round the corner of the street and went straight past Terrence's house. It was crazy. A local charity had a fella dressed up as Father Christmas sat on it. We all just looked at each other and laughed. What are the chances of that happening at just the right time?'

I ask Terrence what he can remember about the singing in the street, and once again, the tears flow.

'I will never forget that night. I looked around and saw all those people. I had spent so many years feeling worthless and it was quite overwhelming to see them all there with big smiles on their faces. The thing is, I love that carol so I needed to pull myself together so I could join in.'

It was quite a privilege to witness it all. I never expected everything to come together like that at such short notice and I don't think any of us expected to feel quite so emotional.

'That is what music can do to you,' says Sophie who has dreams of becoming a professional singer and has released her first song called 'Alive'. 'It was actually inspired by that night. You saw the impact it had on him. It made us feel alive . . . that is what we felt. It were such a buzz. We were all like Wow! What have we just done?'

We finished filming and everyone was invited inside for a cup of tea. They stayed for hours, listening to Terrence's tales, and he treated them all to a 'chippy tea'.

Sophie signed up there and then to be an Age UK volunteer. I told them all to make sure they were watching *BBC Breakfast* the following morning, before I left and drove home to Sheffield. Ayo and Justin took the footage back to the BBC to be edited, and I called the office while I was on the M60. Liam Blyth was still on-shift and asked me how it had gone.

At that point, I had been up for nineteen hours without a break, so I had completely lost all editorial judgment. In the fog of tiredness and hunger, I told him it was either the best telly I had done in ages or the worst. It felt brilliant to be part of, but I was a bit worried it might come over as a bit cheesy. About ten minutes later I pulled in for a sandwich. Ayo had sent me his video from outside the house. I watched it, and immediately called Liam back and told him to ignore our previous conversation . . . it was wonderful.

I didn't watch it go out live the next morning because I was taking the kids to school, but my constantly buzzing phone was a good indication that our follow-up with Terrence had gone down well. When I got home, I started to wade through the messages and emails. I checked social media and it was easy to see the impact Terrence's story was having. These were the top 10 trending topics across the UK.

1) Terrence
2) Terence
3) BBC Breakfast
4) Terrance
5) Christmas
6) Age UK
7) Oldham

8) *Dan Walker*
9) *Tree*
10) *Liam Payne*

We nearly had the full set, but I'm not sure there has ever been a day since 2010 that at least one member of One Direction hasn't been trending on Twitter.

I remember screen-shotting some of the responses we received when the video went online. They are still on my phone under 'favourites'. I read some of them to Terrence when we caught up.

'This has made me want to a) volunteer for Age UK b) have a chippy tea.' Dave Morton

'Just a reminder that not everyone has family around them at this time of year. Pick up the phone and speak to your family and friends and make sure they have someone to go to for Christmas.' Stuart O'Brien

'This is just too much. The general election has drained me of all my energy but Terrence, Dan and that gorgeous choir have reinvigorated me. Time to stop moaning and call Age UK to volunteer.' Alice Kilbane

'Why is Dan Walker trying to break me this morning? I'm so pleased Terrence has had this experience, hopefully we can all work together and make sure even more people don't feel lonely this Christmas.' Katherine Mattock

*'Real Britain. Decent, compassionate, pluralist, con-
nected. The hill worth defending to the last.' Matthew
d'Ancona*

*'Sod the election. It's done and over. Find the "Terrence"
in your area and spread a little love.' Nikki Groom*

There were thousands of them. The video was being watched
by millions of people all around the world.

'I was getting messages from everywhere,' remembers the
man himself. 'It was just wonderful. The most important thing
was the impact it had on Age UK. If the legacy of it all is that
just a few more people get help to deal with loneliness, then I
can die a happy man.'

'The response we had to your visit to his house was . . .'
Laurie Boult from Age UK pauses to find the right word,
'. . . phenomenal. It's hard to overstate the engagement we had as
a charity after that. We had a good pickup after his appearance
on the sofa but the following day – after the tree video – it went
through the roof. We were inundated with people who wanted
to help. It was amazing to see how one man's story of loneliness,
beautifully and sensitively told, could have such a huge impact
on so many people. He touched the hearts of millions.'

'Let me give you an idea,' says Laurie, excitedly. 'Donations
went crazy and volunteering requests went up remarkably. We
had so many inquiries and website traffic was incredible. All of
a sudden there were millions of people sharing the story. When
we came on the show that morning, if you'd said we would get

a tenth of the interest in our campaign, we would have been delighted. We were blown away. It shows that people do care. It shows that people are concerned. Our job now is to keep that issue relevant. This is real life for thousands of people just like Terrence.'

'It were too early for me, Dan.' As expected, most of the students in the choir – including Sophie – didn't make it out of bed in time for Breakfast TV the following morning but they certainly knew about it once their eyes opened.

'It went worldwide. I had fifty messages on my phone when I woke up . . . about 9.30. I was getting directs from Insta and Twitter. Loads of question like "Are you that person who sang for Terrence?" and "Thank you for doing such a good deed." It felt weird but people were looking up to us as an example how to look after people.'

Sophie was now on the volunteer register after signing up in Terrence's living room over that 'chippy tea'. 'It's lovely to know that we made a big impact on him, but I think he had just as big an influence on us. I think this experience is something that he, and we, will never forget. It broke my heart when he was telling us about his life because he said no one had listened to him for so long. I've got grandparents and aunties and uncles the same age. I think my grandparents were even more emotional than me about it, because they know how easy it is to fall through the cracks.'

Sophie watched the film later with her family. 'My brothers were so proud. We were dancing around the house ringing my mum. There are still hundreds of messages I haven't even replied to. What I really loved about it was the fact that we changed a few opinions about what young people are like. We care. We want to help and that were about as special as it gets. We might not all grow up and change the world, but we can make a little difference. What better time to start than right now?'

While Sophie was fast asleep, a very excited Carl Marsden had gathered the troops at Oldham College. 'We watched it at work ... together. It was incredible. The phones were going mental. We had voice messages on reception from all over the place. So many people asking for his address to send presents or cards and it was all generations too. Older people saw something of their own experiences and young people saw someone they could show some love to.'

The following day there were stories of high-fives all over the college campus and their Twitter account was still getting retweets and favourites months later. For so many people it was a timely reminder of how many people we take for granted.

'I showed it to my son, Oliver,' says Carl. 'We watched in on the telly together and he said, "What about our neighbours? We need to help people." Ever since Christmas, Oliver has been taking board games around to some of our elderly neighbours and we always try to stop and talk. It had a big impact on him.'

The office at *BBC Breakfast* was a hive of activity. There were all sorts of people trying to get in contact about Terrence – most of them wanted to send him a Christmas card.

Marta Newman, who had originally seen the tweet from Oldham College, had just finished the night shift. 'I remember when they brought the footage back into the building from

Terrence's house, I snuck into the edit suite to see it coming together. It is so special to be part of a story like that. You do get emotional working nights sometimes and we were all sobbing and then I cried again the next morning when I watched it go out live. We had just finished covering the election and, at that stage, we all needed a story like that. It was lovely to celebrate a small act of kindness and put a smile on someone's face. I love my job for opportunities to give people a voice and it is a privilege when it works like that. That is all the motivation you need.'

It seemed like the end of a wonderful two days for Terrence, but a certain star of the stage and screen had other ideas.

John Barrowman was one of the guests on the *Breakfast* sofa that Thursday morning and when he saw the film with Terrence go out, he felt compelled to act. John sent Terrence an invitation to attend his show in the City Hall in Sheffield that night. What followed was another flurry of phone calls and – to cut a very long, logistical story short – Terrence and I met again for the third time in two days. This time we were going backstage to meet Mr Barrowman.

'I couldn't actually believe it was happening,' says Terrence. 'One of the other things that John had said was that he loved the rainbow rug that I had in my living room. He'd seen that on the telly. I spent that afternoon, before we went to Sheffield, going back to the carpet shop in Oldham to see if they had another one to give him as a gift. I was a bit excited, and I hadn't really given any thought to how I was going to actually get it to Sheffield.'

I can tell you it was quite a sight to behold when Terrence arrived in his taxi outside the City Hall only to tell me there was something in the boot which I had to carry for him. It was the giant rainbow rug! John was a little surprised but delighted by the gift when we met in his dressing room and handed it over.

He introduced Terrence to his husband and Terrence told the pair of them all about his life and John asked him to sign the rug and assured him that he'd find a place for it in his home in America. John told Terrence that he had a special surprise for him and to make sure he didn't leave the show early.

'I thought he might just say "hello" halfway through the show,' laughs Terrence. 'I was already emotional after what had happened the night before and John's kindness really set me off.'

'Who was watching Breakfast television on the BBC this morning?' said John, nearing the end of his Sheffield show. The packed crowd all cheered. John explained about how he had been moved by Terrence's story and that he'd invited him to the show. He then told a delighted audience 'that man, Terrence, is here tonight' and asked him to stand up.

'I didn't do it to start with. I was too embarrassed. Maggie from Age UK Oldham was with me and said, "Stand up then!" and gave me a shove. It took me a while to get to my feet,' said Terrence, 'but I could feel the warmth of their kindness.

'It was incredible,' recalls Terrence. 'The end of the best twenty-four hours of my life. I remember looking at John, and looking around the room, and the tears were pouring down my face'. He laughs. 'You know what my mother would have said, Dan? "I don't know what all the fuss was about!"'

Terrence has pictures of his mother everywhere. They were very much alike – kindred spirits – with a good line in sarcasm and a wicked sense of humour. 'My mother had all three of us during the war,' says Terrence. 'My sister, Valerie, was born in 1940, I was born in 1941 and my brother, Jeffrey in 1943. I loved my mum, but both she and my father were drinkers and we all had a tough life.'

Terrence's dad was called Ernest and he and Terrence never saw eye to eye on anything. Terrence had no idea what happened to his father. He walked out on the family after his wife had a miscarriage in the late 1960s.

'He wasn't much of a father at all,' says Terrence. 'He was like a Northern Del Boy, constantly on the deal and trying to make money. He couldn't read or write but one day he would have £2,000 in his back pocket and the next day he'd be flat broke. He was one of life's gamblers.'

Terrence left school at fourteen with no academic qualifications. His father told him he was useless and that he had to get out of the house and get a job. Terrence started as a van driver's mate on the bread lorries.

'"You're an idiot, Terrence," he would say to me over and over again. "You see that", he would say, pointing at something I had done . . . "only an idiot would do that." Nothing I could do was ever good enough for him. He saw me as a waste of his time and a waste of space. Over the years, that starts to make you think he's right. He got on with my sister and brother, but never with me.'

Terrence is fighting back the tears. 'I fought against that my whole life,' he says, 'being told that I wasn't good enough for him. He found out I had dyslexia and used that against me. I had no bond with him at all.'

Terrence was badly bullied at school. The fact that they moved house so much with his father's job didn't help. The experience of being taunted at school and unloved at home had a deep and lasting effect on him.

'If I'm looking for a positive,' he says, as Terrence often does, 'then I think that is what made me a natural carer. I will give my time to anyone and I think that is because I was very much a loner for so many years, even though I felt like a sociable person. I never wanted anyone to experience the pain that I went through and, for me, the best way to do that was to go into the caring profession.'

Terrence is a firm believer that you don't find a job, the job finds you. His brother was a nurse and Jeffrey encouraged him to follow in his footsteps. He applied, and loved every minute of it. Terrence was a nurse for much of the 1960s and, in the early seventies, started working with the mentally and physically disabled and eventually, despite a lack of academic qualifications, became the manager of a care home.

'I remember thinking about my father when I got that job; an "idiot" couldn't be the manager of a care home, could he? I know it was a long time ago, but his words still ring around my head. On the day I took my driving test he told me that, if I passed, he would give me a Morris 1000. I came home and told him I had failed and off he went again; telling me I would never achieve anything and that I was an idiot. I have tried all my life to prove him wrong.'

After his brother died in 1969, Terrence took on the responsibility of caring for their mother. With that added burden, much of his own private life disappeared, and the end of a relationship one Christmas prompted a deep and severe depression.

'I had no idea what was wrong with me. All I could think about was how many times I had been walked out on. It started with my father and carried on from there. When you spend your life searching for someone to love and settle down with, it's hard when you never find it. My mother had died, and I was on my own. I was lonely. I was unloved and I felt unlovable.'

Terrence would just sit there on the sofa for hours on end – never seeing or speaking to anyone. One night he had a severe shaking attack and a friend said he had to go to the doctors. He was told he had depression and was prescribed Valium. He still couldn't see a way out.

'I have fought for gay rights my whole life,' says Terrence. 'Since I was twenty years old. I heard that our local branch of Age UK had an LGBT group for the over-fifties. I'll be honest, I had no interest in going there at all, but I went for a cup of tea and chat. There were four people there, including me. I didn't really want to go back, and I used to come up with so many reasons for not being involved until Maggie from Age UK told me to stop making excuses. I went to another meeting after that, and I have never looked back.'

Terrence has now been a volunteer for Age UK since 2013. He visits other people and speaks to those who are struggling with loneliness.

'It's like being a carer again,' he says with a huge smile. 'You have the natural instinct inside you, and I had probably lost that over the years in a mixture of loneliness and grief.'

Terrence's story made a huge impact on so many people. He had a wonderful Christmas, received hundreds of cards and has formed a strong bond with so many of those young people who came to sing him carols. His story has a happy ending, but there are so many others still struggling with the issue.

Caroline Abrahams is the director of Age UK: 'Loneliness is a very common experience amongst older people. It sounds basic but, as you get older you start to outlive the people you love. There is a huge experience of loss. Long gone are the days when you get invited to weddings, but funerals are a common occurrence. The loneliest ones are those who have a real attachment to someone – like Terrence with his mother – and then find it hard to function once that special someone disappears. There are also people who have been lonely and have carried it their whole lives. Disability or struggles with transport can all bring their own issues. It's okay feeling like you are the life and soul of the party, but what happens when you stop getting invited to that party?'

Loneliness is also a very common experience for carers, but it is so hard for many people to admit that they are struggling. It is heart breaking to hear that it is routine for volunteers on the Age UK helpline to hear from someone who hasn't spoken to another human for a few days – for others it can be weeks.

'It is amazing to see how company can transform someone's life,' says Caroline. 'For some people, it can give them a reason for living. How you feel makes a big difference to how you are and having a sense of purpose makes an enormous difference. For Terrence, his life changed after becoming a volunteer. For the first time in many years, he became depended upon by someone else, he mattered to someone else. He started to make a difference to others and experienced the thrill of being needed. People wanted him to be there, and that gave him a reason to live.'

2020 was a particularly difficult year for those suffering with loneliness. 'Research has shown that more young people than ever before have felt that pressure of being alone,' argues Caroline. 'Older generations are used to being on their own or being self-sufficient. We have heard from a number of older people who have said, "Welcome to my life. This is what every day is like."'

Laurie Boult was on that sofa alongside Terrence the first time we saw him on the telly. One of the things she has learnt from her time at the charity is that loneliness is not something which only affects people who live on their own.

'You can be in a house with lots of people and still be lonely. It's about being able to participate in meaningful activities. It's about being valued. Physical activity can be a huge factor too. As that deteriorates in later life, it can be an issue just to get out of the house.'

Laurie has worked in the charity sector for much of her career but it's easy to see why Age UK means so much to her. 'Ageism is the last acceptable prejudice,' says Laurie. 'It's everywhere and rarely do we push against it. As a woman this is even more apparent – you can be written-off at forty, with another forty years or more ahead of you. Older people can be judged for how their later life pans out – as if loneliness is some-thing of their own doing and therefore not worthy of support. I've worked for many charities in the last twenty years, and it is far, far harder to get people to understand the injustice, but to also see the incredible value that age, and experience, can bring to others. So, I work for Age UK because I love older people and I want others to see their value. I was lucky to grow up in a northern family with my mother, my grandparents, and my great grandmother. At one time, we were all living under the same roof. I suppose I've never seen anything other than the brilliance of older people.'

And that is what Terrence has enabled many people to see and it's something that has becoming an important part of Sophie's life.

'I like to go shopping for the elderly and it's always nice to deliver it too. I have a list of people to call every other day and I can sometimes be the only person that they speak to. There was one old lady who literally had no one,' explains Sophie.

'All her family had died. I was the only voice she heard. For the first few weeks, we were just talking about her and she was telling me loads of stories, you know, all this stuff about World War II and getting separated from her family. Then, a few weeks into it, she started asking me about my hobbies and we found out that we both love music. Last time I spoke to her she said, "I love talking to you, Sophie." That were one of the best things about meeting Terrence. Opportunities like that.'

Sophie also visits Terrence, as do many of the other students from Oldham College. They have even taught him some of the most popular dances on Tik Tok. Apparently, Terrence is a natural! On their most recent Facetime call, they organised to meet up for a chat in his back garden as soon as it's safe to do so.

Sophie has had a big impact on Terrence, but she is quick to point out that the whole experience has been enormously positive for her and changed her whole outlook on life. 'I cannot recommend volunteering enough – charity shop, befriending, shopping – whatever it is. Don't worry about your background either,' says Sophie passionately.

'I don't mind saying that I've got really bad anxiety. Volunteering has given me a real perspective. I used to think to myself "if I can do this, if I'm to help someone else and make them happy . . . why am I bullying myself?" My social anxiety has improved so much. I can talk to people.

'I struggle speaking to others when I don't know them. I have anxiety and I have been diagnosed with PTSD from something which happened a few years ago. I feel a lot more at ease since talking to people like Terrence. I couldn't even order food in

McDonald's – that's how bad it was. My friends had to do it for me.'

Sophie currently works in a pharmacy but would love for her music career to take off. Whatever happens, she is determined to continue to volunteer for Age UK.

'I know some people worry about Terrence, you know, who is looking after him? We are! He is well taken care of now. He's got loads of cool young friends and all the choir are thinking about getting together and having a big dinner with him . . . maybe a chippy tea! We are all going to phone him and keep sending him cards, so he knows that we are thinking about him. We want to make sure he is never on his own again.'

'We invited Terrence to everything before lockdown,' says Carl from the college. 'Any awards ceremony or big event, he always gets asked to come. We won't forget him now. We all feel a duty of care to him and, the best thing about it is, we don't even have to say "who is talking to Terrence this week?" because the students have just got on with it off their own back. It has been quite inspirational to watch.'

The choir has grown in numbers and they have big plans for the future – maybe even a Christmas single. Terrence says he won't be singing on it . . . even if they ask him.

'It's still hard to get my head around it all,' he says sat back in the same chair he was in when those students came into his front room with the Christmas tree. 'I speak my mind and that rubs some people up the wrong way. I suppose I should be thankful you asked me if I had a Christmas tree that day,' he laughs.

'I couldn't have expected what happened. I just told my story and then sat back, and was amazed at so many people being so kind and so generous. When you've been on your own for so many years, it's easy to remember what a difference just a tiny drop of kindness can make.'

That is one of the things I take away from all this. We have to look out for each other. When I look back on it now, so many people were involved in making this happen. Laurie wanted to help the charity, Terrence wanted to help others, Carl wanted to support an old man, Marta was determined to make it happen, Sophie and the choir brought the magic and so many others went above and beyond to bring a little slice of festive joy to the millions and millions of people who watched it around the world.

'It reminded me of the importance of caring about how someone feels,' Laurie said, as she watched Terrence interacting with those students, 'you could see what a difference it made to him to see that someone cared about him. They wanted to spend time with him.'

There were so many people who got in contact in the weeks after Christmas – people who felt guilty about their parents, or elderly relatives. People who said they had been to see their neighbour for the first time. People who talked about simple, meaningful interactions they had had which had made a difference to someone else.

We are all busy, but surely there is time to have a conversation, offer to help or simply ask if someone is okay?

In listening to Terrence's story, I also see the importance of encouraging my own children and not limiting their horizons or trampling on their dreams. It must be crushing to grow up in harsh and unhappy home where, like Terrence, you then spend the rest of your life trying to please a father for whom his best was never enough.

'I've got big plans for my eightieth birthday you know, Dan,' says Terrence with pride. 'Don't worry, you'll get an invite.'

Terrence knows Christmas will never be as mad as it was in 2019 but, he also knows he will never again spend it on his own with just a turkey sandwich.

'I've been a fighter all my life. I like to think I am going to be around for a while. It's wonderful to think that there are more people out there supporting others after listening to what happened to me. I would say to anyone who is finding loneliness a problem . . . become a volunteer, help someone else. It will give you a new lease of life and . . . if you dedicate your time to helping others, whatever anybody says, you will never be an idiot.'

HOW WILL YOU REMEMBER 2020?

I sat down and interviewed the Prime Minister in the second week of January. It was his first interview since the Conservatives won the election of 2019. We talked about Iranian nuclear weapons and he promised a plan for social care within 'weeks'. He assured voters in Northern England that he would improve their lives and proposed a plan to 'bung a bob for Big Ben bongs' to celebrate Brexit. The Prime Minister said it wasn't the government's place to save struggling companies like Flybe and refused to be drawn on Harry and Meghan's decision to step back from public life. He said there was very little chance of Anne Sacoolas coming back to the UK to face charges over the death of Harry Dunn and he said he wouldn't be a prime minister who 'hides in the shadows' but would be as 'available as he possibly could be'.

He also said he had thought about going vegan but was worried that it required 'too much concentration' and felt the whole thing was a 'crime against cheese lovers'. For some reason, he insisted on pronouncing it ve-GAN which sent a large proportion of the audience around the bend.

I have to confess that at no point during my preparation or

research for the interview with the Prime Minister did I think about asking him whether the UK was prepared for the possibility of a global pandemic. I think, if I had thrown it in as a final question, I would have been laughed out of the room and my boss would have had some serious questions about my future.

Less than three months later, the Prime Minister was being rushed to a London hospital with a deadly virus.

It wasn't long after that interview that all the subjects we talked about – even Brexit – seemed insignificant when compared to the closure of everything from schools to offices and places of worship. Coronavirus has impacted virtually the entire world, killed hundreds of thousands of people at the time of writing, dominated every news bulletin and spawned intense fear and anxiety, alongside the occasional conspiracy theory.

The streets were deserted, the economy started to shut down and the virus was all most of us thought about for months. People were panic-buying toilet roll and parents were tearing their hair out trying to home-school. After spending a week trying to teach our thirteen-year-old mind-numbing algebra, I respect teachers more than ever.

At *BBC Breakfast*, we were making special coronavirus programmes, sitting two metres apart on the sofa and learning about the importance of PPE. We were all washing our hands, clapping our key workers and pointing our fingers at those we felt were to blame for restricted lives and spiralling death rates.

While the chancellor was subsidising wages, we were praying for a vaccine, watching daily briefings and all typing 'Barnard Castle' into Google Maps.

At first, the virus didn't seem as divisive as the Brexit debate, but it wasn't long before the shouting started. People were worried about themselves, their families, their friends, their livelihoods, businesses, finances and futures.

For whatever reason, broadcasters counted as 'key workers' and continued to sit on the sofa throughout the pandemic. Each day we were talking about death tolls to virologists, politicians and broken families. We all needed good news. That is what this chapter is about.

I wanted to go back and speak to some of those people who made a lasting impact on me during the pandemic. There are some that we all remember like the amazing Captain Tom. It was a real privilege for our team at *BBC Breakfast* to play a small part in helping him raise millions of pounds for NHS charities. This wonderful old man came along at just the right time and inspired so many people to follow his footsteps in his garden. I always enjoyed reading out the amount of money he raised on the television because the page also showed you just how many people had donated. There were thousands of people all getting behind Tom and donating an average of £10 a time. It was brilliant to watch.

The *Breakfast* team organised a cake and an RAF flypast for his 100th birthday and showed his local village hall which was filled with thousands of cards. His lovely family, led by his daughter Hannah, became regulars on TV and, amid all the madness, the centurion even had a number one single.

The story behind that is an interesting one. Like everyone else in the UK, our boss at *Breakfast*, Richard Frediani, was mildly obsessed with Captain Tom and what to cover next.

299

One morning in the office, he was pacing around, wondering about how to take the story on when it dawned on him ... MICHAEL BALL. The call to Ball went in, the song was recorded, Captain Tom's singing was edited over the top and, two weeks later they were top of the charts! Mr Frediani probably deserves a producer's credit somewhere.

There has been plenty written and said about Captain Tom and his extraordinary life. I think if you asked the entire population, you'd get a universal acknowledgement that he is a solid gold hero. Whatever your boxes are, he ticks almost all of them.

I often get asked who my heroes are. I had a worrying obsession with Glenn Hoddle as a child – it even got serious enough for me to ask my parents to change my name to Glenn! The Hoddle years were preceded by the era where Garth Crooks adorned my bedroom wall (please don't tell him) and were following by a period of time where Boris Becker and Nick Faldo were vying for top spot.

There was also a time during the early 1990s when I was devoted to the Tour de France. My favourite name in sport belongs to a man known as 'The Tashkent Terror': Djamolidine Mirgarifanovich Abdoujaparov. I would race home from school to watch him take on the likes of Lauren Jalabert. Abdoujaparov was one of the big sprinters of the day with a swaying style that would annoy other cyclists and often cause crashes. I remember a huge one during the final stage on the Champs-Elysées in 1991. He was showboating and hit a giant advertising Coca-Cola can and went over the handlebars. Despite dripping with blood, he managed to regain his composure, cross the line and win the green jersey for being the best sprinter in the race. No bike ride I ever went on as a teenager was complete without a little impression of Mr Abdoujaparov.

I feel the need to also confess a deep love of Des Lynam. I wrote him a letter when I was eleven asking how I could get his job. He wrote back with some fantastic advice which only added to my admiration. He remains the finest example of what broadcasting is all about: a beautiful mixture of approachability, authority, empathy, knowledge, kindness and humour.

The sportsmen (and Des) who took centre stage in my childhood were briefly interrupted by Luke Skywalker and Han Solo, a brilliant teacher called Mr Torr and a fella from Louisville, Kentucky called Jim who stayed at our house for a few months while he was training in the UK. Not only was Jim funny and loud, he was as strong as a bear and could hold both me and my brother above his head. I wanted to be Jim for the entirety of that summer.

A few years ago I was asked to give a speech to some students at St James's Palace in London. The organisers asked me to talk about my heroes. Glenn Hoddle got a mention but there are two individuals who I always come back to.

I love the story of Shun Fujimoto. Mr Torr told me about him at school and I've been engrossed ever since. Fujimoto was a Japanese gymnast at the Montreal Olympic Games of 1976. Japan and Russia were going toe to toe in the team event and Fujimoto was probably the least well-known member of the defending gold medallists.

He broke his knee during the floor exercise but, despite

the crippling pain, managed to continue and scored a 9.5 on the pommel horse and then 9.7 on the rings. It was a personal best. As he landed the triple summersault dismount, he added a dislocated kneecap and torn ligaments to his growing knee problems. After the judges awarded him his huge score, he collapsed in a heap on the floor. Japan won the gold by one of the narrowest margins in Olympic history ... they were just four-tenths of a point ahead of Russia.

Fujimoto was asked afterwards if he would do it again and he said 'no' but, for me, that is what team sport and life is all about: making a sacrifice for others. Going the extra mile, pushing yourself through the pain barrier and taking one for the team.

The other man I mentioned in the palace would be familiar to you if you've ever watched *Chariots of Fire*. You may well know the name Eric Liddell; the Scottish athlete who wouldn't run in the 100m on a Sunday but went on to win the gold in the 400m at the Paris Olympics of 1924. His achievements on the track were one thing but it was what he did after that which always captivated me. Liddell left athletics behind and went to go and be a missionary in China where he eventually became a prisoner of war in the 1940s when China was invaded by Japan. There are all sorts of stories of how he used to share food with his fellow prisoners and teach the children science. Just before the Beijing Olympics in 2008, the Chinese made it known that, back in 1945, a prisoner exchange was organised which would have sent Liddell back to the UK. They said he refused the offer and gave his place to a pregnant woman instead. He died soon after.

That sounds like a hero to me. There is an old proverb which says, 'mark the man who acts with honour when no one is watching'. That sums up Eric Liddell. For me, self-sacrifice is an essential strand of heroism and Liddell had it in spades. His achievements off the track, and his impact on those around him, seem even more impressive than what he achieved on it.

There have been plenty of examples of self-sacrifice during the global virus. We could all sit around a table for hours and discuss some of those who we feel are worthy of that hero status, and it's been a pleasure to have interviewed hundreds of people who have done incredible things for others during the pandemic.

I would love to give just a few of them some attention in this chapter. I think the people included here have shown all the elements of heroism in different forms. Some have just survived, others have transformed lives, provided hope in death, inspired those around them, raised money for a good cause or proved the doubters wrong.

I think we all needed a boost at times. These are some of the people who stole our hearts and lifted our spirits. When I was sat on the *Breakfast* sofa for the first months of the pandemic, there were so many messages from viewers asking either for some 'good news' or saying 'thank you' when we were able to shine a light on someone who was doing their best to make a difference.

I remember being at home on many occasions calling our

children into the room to watch the stories of some of the people detailed here. They gave us a little hope when there didn't seem to be much in supply. Much of that hope was centred around admiration for our key workers. Through their dedication to their jobs, and a desire to improve the lot of others, they provided a much-needed tonic to the rising sense of concern in the wider population and around the world. They kept our heads above water when it would have been so easy to drown in a sea of anxiety.

The first person I want to tell you about is a man who says he wouldn't be here if it wasn't for some of those amazing key workers. He is someone who survived the virus. We spoke to him just after he had come out of having spent five days struggling to breathe in intensive care. He was one of those who had a triumphal exit from hospital, wheeled down a corridor, cheered by those who had overseen his recovery.

Hylton Murray-Philipson is a former investment banker and now a farmer and conservationist. His passion is the protection of the rainforests of the Amazon. In March of 2020, as chairman of Global Canopy (a non-profit organisation which campaigns for a sustainable deforestation-free economy) he was hosting a fundraising dinner in London.

One of the notable speakers at that conference was from Brazil and, after the conference, Hylton heard that he had returned to his home country and had become ill. Hylton was at his parent's home in Leicestershire to be with his dad who was dying from a long-term illness. On 12 March, Hylton started to show early symptoms of the virus.

'I didn't think much of it because I didn't have the cough that everyone was talking about. I did have the high temperature. Eventually, I felt bad enough to call 111 but it slowly dawned on me that, as the world was spinning around me, I needed an ambulance. When the paramedic walked into the house he was dressed like an astronaut – covered head-to-toe in a protective suit. He tested me and, even though I was ill, he told me to stay where I was and to call back if the symptoms worsened. The next day, 19 March, I collapsed in the house and was violently sick. Even the stiff upper lip was wavering. I think if I'd tried to tough it out for one more day, I wouldn't be talking to you now. I called the ambulance again and this time I was straight into hospital. I was actually on day 10 of my infection and within 24 hours, I was in intensive care.'

When Hylton looks back at his text messages, he was sending them for all but two of the days he was in hospital. He was conscious enough to text, but had no idea whether it was night or day and felt very close to the edge of life. What first drew me to his story was that, of all the people I have heard explain the effects of coronavirus, Hylton was able to describe what it felt like to think that your next breath might be your last.

'During my time in intensive care, I permanently had that feeling of fighting for air. If you can imagine coughing . . . and then, all of a sudden you don't know when your next breath is coming. We all know that feeling of being underwater and then, when you run out of air, and try and get to the surface there is that panic that sets in if something gets in your way; like another person or a dingy or something. When you're swimming, you get that adrenaline rush from the panic to breathe and that spurs you on to reach the surface and open your lungs. That panic followed every breath in intensive care . . . but there was no surface. That is when you learn to rely on the incredible NHS staff around you. I cannot begin to describe what it feels like to not have air in your lungs and to reach out your arms for help and to feel the touch of a human hand, squeezing yours and telling you that you are going to be okay.'

At the darkest moments, Hylton said he had a very strong feeling of the love of God as he was lying in that hospital bed. 'There were strong images of Jesus in the bow of the boat on the Sea of Galilee in my mind. You know the story, where Jesus tells the disciples in the middle of the storm "Why are you fearful? You of little faith." I felt very much as though he was calming the storm in my body. It was my moment of greatest need.'

There were harsh reminders of the dangers of coronavirus all around Hylton. When he was released back on to the regular ward, the man opposite him died from the virus. 'I remember watching him for much of the day,' says Hylton. 'He kept pushing the mask away. He seemed to be wanting it to come to an end. He'd had enough. It was heart breaking to watch and very sobering for the rest of us.'

Hylton has a real gift for putting his emotions into words and one of the most powerful elements of his story is his inter-action with the nursing staff who cared for him, the impact they had on him in hospital, and the lasting legacy of their treatment.

'The nurses were amazing. One of them was looking at the notes at the end of my bed and noticed it was my birthday. She asked if I wanted a present. As I lay there, I felt like I needed nothing . . . I was just so thankful that I had just been given my life back. She asked me again and I told her that a shave would be incredible. I know it sounds simple, but I had been in hospital for 10 days at that point and I felt dirty. I never thought that such an everyday act could feel so transformational. She had the cheap, renewable razors, but she shaved me with such determination and such love it was strangely emotional. The feeling of being held . . . being cared for like that is so powerful. It is the best present I have ever had. The ward becomes like your home and you know everybody. It is not only what they are doing for me, it is what they are doing for everyone. You see these people in uniforms . . . people from all over the world . . . here they are caring for everyone. Pulling together and doing their job. I think that's why, when the staff all came back later to sing me "Happy Birthday", I just lay in my bed and wept. I was so thankful to them and I had no other way of expressing it.'

When I first spoke to Hylton on *BBC Breakfast*, I remember him telling his story with a huge smile on his face. We were only meant to do five or six minutes with him but, he was so compelling, it went on for double that. The part which really struck me was when he talked about his father. At the time, my own dad had recently been diagnosed with cancer so it really hit home and I remember having to hold it together in the studio, as my mind was racing about how I would act in a similar situation.

Hylton's dad died the day before his son went into hospital. Hylton's mother and his sister were also receiving treatment at the same time as him. That meant that not a single member of the family was able to be present at his father's funeral.

'I watched it on my phone,' recalls Hylton. 'It was at a time when there were so many restrictions around funerals, so no one could be at the graveside. My two other sisters were able to watch from the side of the church yard but none of us could be there with him. My father was ninety-two and running out of road but these are important markers in our lives. The sacraments are an essential part of my Christian life. My mother had been married to him for sixty-five years. She was a child refugee in the war. She didn't see her own parents from the age of five to eleven and those experiences prepare you for the darker moments in life. She dealt with it amazingly well, and still does, but it must have broken her heart to not be there at the end.'

I ask Hylton how he felt about being so close to death himself. 'I had no fear of letting go,' he says, after a long pause. 'There was no fear of dying. In some senses, I was ready to go. I felt very close to God – almost as though I had journeyed to a place of light and peace – but I was propelled back by a number of thoughts: my sons, my mother and a sense of purpose.'

Hylton's wife had died from cancer in 2016 leaving their two sons – Jim and Luke – without a mother. Hylton couldn't stomach the idea of leaving his boys without a father too. He was also driven by a determination to make sure his mum didn't lose her husband and her only son in the space of a few days.

He feels very strongly that there is a reason for him still

being here, a purpose that now drives him on. 'If you're not a Christian it's hard to understand the power of prayer,' says Hylton. 'I prayed a lot during my time in hospital and I know a lot of people were praying for me. It felt like a hammock underneath me . . . holding me up. It gave me clarity and, when I left hospital, I thought long and hard about something I needed to apply myself to. I am an environmentalist who firmly believes that we can all make a difference.'

Hylton thinks there is a strong link between the battle which took place in his lungs, and the battle for the lungs of this planet. 'If there is to be a blessing from this awful virus, maybe it is to encourage us to be gentle with our world and gentle with each other . . . not to simply go on consuming everything. Change often comes out of suffering. Suffrage came after World War I. There was a feeling that, if you are good enough to die for your country, you're good enough to vote in your country. In the aftermath of the second great war, we saw the birth of the NHS and the welfare state. Is the legacy of this global pandemic going to be a better understanding of our need to protect the future of our planet? Will we go back to business as usual or profoundly think about what we are going to leave for our children? We needed a teenager from Sweden to get the message across, but we cannot have infinite growth on a finite planet. My passion is protecting the rainforest and the promotion of sustainable, renewable energy. I firmly believe we can be part of the solution rather than being part of the problem.'

Does he feel like a different person now after his experience with coronavirus? 'I've never known a year like it,' says the sixty-one-year-old. 'I lost my father, I nearly lost my own life and I put my two boys through the mill. I genuinely look back and it requires quite an effort for me to think of myself as the same person I was at the start of 2020. I think so many people have been through such a deep trauma because of this virus. My overwhelming feeling is one of thankfulness. I am thankful to God for the fact that I am still here, and I am eternally grateful to the amazing team of doctors and nurses at Leicester Royal Infirmary. Without their care and love . . . well, it's obvious . . . there would be no more me.'

We had a huge reaction to Hylton's story on *BBC Breakfast*. It came at a time when we were all worried and we needed to know that people were coming out the other side of the virus.

Hylton talked about us having a better understanding of our fragile planet after coronavirus. I hope he's right, but I also think one of the legacies will be a greater appreciation of our frontline workers. I don't know about you, but I loved the Thursday night street-clapping sessions. Our children drew rainbows and 'thank you' signs for the windows and we chatted to neighbours while waiting for the fella a few streets away to set off his customary firework.

My little sister worked as a nurse on an intensive care ward throughout the height of the pandemic and our family WhatsApp group was filled for a time with pictures of her PPE covered face after another gruelling shift. Every time we interviewed a health care worker on the programme, you could see them getting emotional when they were asked about the show of solidarity on a Thursday night.

One of those health care workers we spoke to was a staff nurse at Fairfield Hospital in Bury. Her name is Leona Harris.

Leona is the sort of person who gets stuff done even after working a fourteen-hour shift on the frontline. 'When we were in the face of it, it was tough for everybody,' says Leona. 'You've got to stay positive and remind yourself why you went into the job in the first place. I love helping people and sometimes a lot of people need that help and support.'

Leona was working on the Covid ward from day one. Many of her colleagues were anxious about supplies of protective equipment and the prospect of taking the virus home to their families. Following procedure was essential and Leona took the decision not to see her own children during the height of the pandemic.

'There was real panic,' she said. 'I could see it in people's eyes. I do think the media played a part in that. Don't get me wrong, people were ill, and people were dying, but we were also discharging a lot of patients from the hospital.'

One of those patients had a significant impact on Leona. She was approached by a palliative care nurse who mentioned that they had just transferred a woman to a hospice. The patient was terminal and had lost her mobile. She had two children and had no way of communicating with them.

'It's one of those things you can't leave at work,' says Leona. 'I couldn't stop thinking about it. That night I spoke to one of our neighbours and they said they had an old iPad with a crack in it. It still worked and they said they would happily donate it. That gave me the idea. There were other patients who needed help. We had a lot of dementia patients on the Covid ward. They couldn't see their family, but they were desperate for a friendly face . . . they needed people they could trust. All they saw, all day, were people in masks.'

Leona started pestering her friends and family. Two friends auctioned off a few pieces of sporting memorabilia and, all of a sudden, she had over £1,000. Her husband, Nick, and his mates got involved and started shaving their heads and doing sponsored walks. By the end of the first week, Leona had raised £30,000.

'It was at that point that we came on your programme,' laughs Leona. One of the things I love about *BBC Breakfast* is that we have a very generous audience. When they see a good cause, they jump on it.

'The generosity blew me away,' remembers Leona. 'After talking to you, the money had doubled in less than a day. Then, because so many people had seen it, the phone went mad. I was getting calls at work but had to tell everyone I would ring them back. Charlie the butcher had seen it and handed me a cheque for £250! I was in work and one of the physios said she had some money for me. It was from a patient who had been saving cash for bingo. There was an envelope with £1,000 in cash! Covid has been really tough,' says Leona, 'but it has brought many people together too. It feels like a lot has changed for all of us, but it would be great if we could combine the best bits of the old world and best bits of the new one from now on.'

Leona's initial plan was to use the iPads for patients to Face-time their families. She has now been able to buy hundreds of them and distribute them all over the UK. 'At the start, I was just thinking about patients talking to their families, but it's been amazing to see how far it has gone. They are being used as educational tools in maternity units and motor neurone patients are playing the piano on them. I've just sent some to children at a hospital in Scotland where they are using them instead of an old flipchart. We've sent loads to care homes because we all know they've had a tough time. They are being used to stimulate memories in dementia patients, at hospices where children haven't got time to make memories and to help with everything from sign language to interpreting. Sometimes, it's just nice for a chemotherapy patient to be able to watch a film on one. The uses have been endless.'

Leona made a massive difference to so many people and has received hundreds of messages of thanks and support from people all over the UK. I love the fact that she saw a need and got on with it. She knew she could help people and she dragged thousands of others along with her. When you speak to her, it's quite clear that her motivation is grounded in that basic desire to help others.

'It has been one of the best things that has ever happened to me,' says Leona. 'I think it has been the busiest time of my life, but it has been so rewarding. When I wasn't working fourteen-hour days, I was out visiting hospitals, answering emails, phone calls or going on the telly to try and raise more money. Don't get me wrong, I love being busy. I get up at 5.15 am every morning; sometimes just to clean the house!'

Leona has been nominated for a whole string of awards and was one of the 'Coronavirus Heroes' asked to turn on the illuminations in Blackpool. Despite the media attention, the truly special moments have come from the lives she has managed to change.

'There was a lady who had a stroke and her family were all in America. She was disorientated and feeling low, so it was wonderful to see her face light up when we connected them. I was just watching her watching her family. I had another patient with dementia who spent two days shouting and throwing everything she could at me every time I went near her. I asked her sister if we could contact her and that interaction totally turned her around. She went from throwing her cups at me, to smiling and asking me if I could brush her hair. The family were so grateful.'

Some of the most emotional responses to Leona's #StayTogether campaign have come from people who were able to use the iPads to say goodbye to dying family members who they couldn't visit because of Covid-19 restrictions.

There was a young girl called Summer Rogers from Norfolk who wasn't able to say goodbye to her granny in hospital before she died. Summer, aged eleven, had written to her local newspaper to raise money for an iPad so that no one would have to go through that again and would be able to connect with their family. Leona saw the article and donated two tablets straightaway. Summer wrote her this poem as a thank you.

In a world full of uncertainty, with many people facing
  fear;
It's such a special time right now, to know an angel's
  near.
Leona fundraised to help so many, people who are in
  need;
And lots of people joined her, in fundraising for this
  good deed.
Covid's taken the world by storm, and separated so
  many people;
But with the help of #staytogether, she's helped us up
  that steep hill.
Leona supported our little girl, and made her wish
  come true;
Our family is so thankful, and hundreds of others
  too.

Leona is still raising money. 'I have learned that we have got some amazing people in this country. I love my job. I love being a nurse. It's hard. It's tough. The greatest thing for me is to look after someone and to see them go home.' She laughs. 'Maybe I'm a bit soft.' She isn't. Leona is amazing.

Thankfully, Leona stayed fit and healthy throughout the most dangerous part of the pandemic, but the same can't be said for all frontline workers. There were many families torn apart by coronavirus and a long list of heartbreak.

*   *   *

Amrik Bamotra – known to everyone as 'Bob' – was a radiology support worker at King George Hospital in East London.

Bob arrived in the UK from India in the 1980s. He worked in a glass factory, a car factory, as a bus driver, and as a hospital porter before eventually moving to the radiology department. Bob made thousands of friends along the way and was greatly loved by his wife, Charley, his daughter, Jag, and his son, Harry.

'Dad was the most lovable character,' says his proud son. 'Family was everything for him, but he would go the extra mile for anyone. He was the guy that you went to with a problem, the man who had time for you and took care of everyone who he came into contact with.'

Bob became ill after returning from a family wedding in India in February. He developed a fever and his breathing became more and more laboured. Bob was in his sixties and had underlying health conditions that meant he was fighting a losing battle.

'It all happened so quickly,' recalls Harry. 'When he went to hospital the second time in the ambulance, that was the last time we saw him.'

Harry works at the same hospital as his dad. So does his mum and his brother-in-law. They all had security cards but none of them were able to visit Bob on the Covid ward. They only ever saw him on Facetime. Bob died on Friday 10 April, two days before his sixty-third birthday. His family had to go through the grim process of saying goodbye on a video call.

'I convinced myself that he could still fight,' says Harry. 'That morning the phone rang at 5.30; it was the hospital saying that

Dad's next of kin had to get there quickly. My sister went to be at his bedside, and it was her job to call us all.'

What do you say to your father, knowing it's the last time you will speak to him before he dies? 'When I got on the call to him, he was quite drowsy,' says his emotional son. 'My sister was trying to tell Dad who it was. I told him I loved him. I told him to hurry up and get better and reminded him it was his birthday in two days' time. He waved at me but, in the end, his body gave up on him and that was the end.'

It took Harry months to start being able to actually grieve over his dad. He had to be there for the family, so he tried not to let it get to him. When he finally returned to work, his dad's colleagues were incredible.

'They really helped me to process his death. They put money into a charity in his name and every day I kept hearing stories about the difference he made to so many people. I would ask them how they knew him, and they would all say they just met him in the corridor one day and it went from there. That is what Dad was like. When he was alive, he would have long conversations with people wherever we went. I would ask him where he knew them from, and he would laugh and say they came in for a scan a few weeks ago and he got to know them. You don't get many people like my dad. It's not just us who are going to miss him . . . the world will miss him. He was a good man.'

Harry wants to be a music producer. His dad persuaded him to chase his dreams before he died so that is Harry's plan once the world returns to something like normal.

'Two thousand and twenty is a write off for me,' says his

son. 'I lost my dad to this awful virus but, if I look hard enough, there are some positives. Our family have come closer together; I think a lot of families have. I think back to Dad's funeral. Normally we would have the body in the house but, because of the virus, we had to keep it in the hearse outside. There were so many people who came, standing in the rain. Even in death, my dad managed to bring friends and family together.'

When I spoke to Harry he was in the middle of decorating. 'This is another reminder of Dad,' he laughs. 'Look at me, painting the house. This used to be his job and now it falls to me. I often find myself asking "what would Dad do?" when I'm in a tough situation. There are so many things I miss about him. I miss my mum calling him down for dinner. I miss asking him if he wanted a cup of tea. There is nothing I don't miss about him.'

Bob's death got plenty of attention because he touched so many people. The issue of care homes was also at the forefront of many minds during the pandemic.

There were questions about the provision of personal protective equipment, restrictions on visits, death rates and plenty of pressure on the government who promised to put a 'protective ring' around them.

In some places, members of staff actually moved into the care homes to protect the residents and their families back at home. One of those was a teenager from Preston called Kia Tobin. She, together with a war veteran by the name of Ken Benbow, provided one of the most uplifting stories of lockdown.

Kia moved into Thistleton Lodge Care Home back in April 2020. In total, she and the other members of staff, stayed there for seven weeks. Ken was one of the homes big characters. He was always talking, always friendly and always telling anyone who would listen how much he missed his wife, Ada, who had been in the home with him until she passed away in August 2019.

'Ken and I just seemed to get on from day one,' says Kia. 'Once you start him, he won't stop.'

Kia was seventeen when she started working at the care home. Before that she looked after the horses on the promenade in Blackpool. 'My family are all based in care work. My nan was a manager in adult learning difficulties, and I've got aunties and uncles who work in mental health.'

Kia was brought up by her grandparents – Nan and Pap. She decided it was the best thing for her at an early age and she thinks that's why she holds to what she calls 'old fashioned' values. It's also one of the reasons why she gets on so well with Ken.

Ken married Ada in November 1948. They were together for seventy-one years before she died. It's hard for Ken to talk about his wife without getting emotional. 'She was the most wonderful, caring wife and she pushed me all the way through life. I wouldn't have achieved anything without her. She was a great encourager.'

Ken couldn't read or write when he left school. He joined the forces when he was seventeen and a half. Ken has so many stories to tell. We spoke about his life for almost two hours. His memory for detail is incredible.

'I joined the Royal Navy on 13 January 1943,' he says, with a deep sense of pride. 'Training finished in the spring of that year and I was there with a lot of other young lads. One of them was a boy from Chester called Jeff Potten. Can I tell you a bit about Jeff?

'It's quite remarkable really ... we were both in the forces for four years and ten months. We went everywhere together, me and Jeff. We joined in the same room as civilians, we were at the same camp, we shared the same mess, we did our three months of training together, we took our first leave together, we did our first service together, we were both posted to a brand new ship together and, at the end, we came home on the same troop ship, were put in the same barracks, got our civvy suits on the same day from the same place, came home on the same train and we stayed friends until he died in 2012.'

I told Ken it sounded like he could write a book about the time he spent with Jeff. He thought that was hilarious and said there weren't enough pages in the world to tell it.

Ken – and Jeff – travelled the world with the Royal Navy. One of their early jobs was protecting the North Atlantic Convoy from German U-boats. 'We worked in no man's land,' says Ken, lowering his voice. 'You know, where there was no cover from the planes.' Ken tells another amazing story of a day an estimated one hundred German submarines were waiting for them. He was involved in the invasions of Sicily, Italy and Japan and worked in the Bay of Biscay on U-boat patrols. Ken also has vivid memories of D-Day. His ship patrolled the English Channel for three months before 6 June 1944.

'I was down in the belly of the ship and I had to put a shell on every step of a machine that took them up to the guns. I looked after B-gun. Hours a day making sure they had the shells upstairs. I was a proud seaman that day.'

When Ken eventually came back, he found it hard to settle back in his hometown of Oswestry. In the past he'd worked on a farm, but he wanted adventure and thought about rejoining the navy. He got all the way to Chatham Barracks before deciding it wasn't for him.

'When I got home that night, I didn't really know what to do with my life. My aunt was staying with us and she was from Liverpool. She asked me what the problem was, and I told her about the lack of jobs, opportunity and entertainment. "Why don't you come home with me and make your home in Liverpool?" she said. I thought "that sounds like a good idea" and I'm so glad I did. I was only there a week when I met this beautiful girl called Ada ... ' Ken laughs, '. . . and before you ask,' he says, 'yes, the Ada I married.' The laughter stops and Ken starts to cry again. He apologises and tells me it's still so hard to not see her every day.

Ken and Ada used to go dancing four or five nights a week. They 'courted' for two years and then married on 27 November 1948 – the start of many happy years together.

In later life, Ken was the treasurer of the Blackpool branch of the D-Day and Normandy Veterans. He used to visit people in care homes and Ken didn't like what he saw. It convinced him that it was never a place he wanted to be.

'After seeing those lads in the homes, I promised Ada I would never let her live in one. I told her I would take care of her but, as we got on, things got harder and my son and daughter asked us if we would try out Thistleton Lodge for a fortnight;

to see if we liked it. We were only in there for three days when Ada turned to me and said, "Ken, I do like it here. I think this could be our home." It has been our home ever since.'

Ken took his wife's death very hard in 2019. He had one giant picture of her in a frame that he used to keep beside his bed. Each night, he would take the picture, and cuddle it before he went to sleep. Kia worried that he was going to break the glass in the frame and hurt himself. She had heard all the stories about how much he loved his wife and, even though she had joined the care home after Ada had died, she wanted to do something for Ken.

Kia took the picture of Ada and had it made into a cushion. The moment she gave it to Ken was captured on video by another member of staff at the care home. If you haven't seen it yet, may I suggest that you quickly put 'Ken and Kia' into a search engine and watch the magic.

It's easy to see why the video went viral. Once he sees the cushion, it doesn't take long for the emotion to kick in and Ken sits in the chair and weeps over the picture of his wife.

I ask Kia why she thinks it made such an impact on so many people around the world. 'I don't know. It was so crazy. Maybe it was a generational thing. At that time I was seventeen, and when he was seventeen he was fighting a real war. Many years on, I was fighting a war of a very different kind. It was a complete contrast. He was ninety-four at the time so there were seventy-odd years between us.'

The video was watched by millions of people and both Kia and Ken were all over the TV and radio – including an appearance on *BBC Breakfast* – where Ken was clutching the cushion.

'It was a bit overwhelming, but it was a bit scary as well,' says Kia. 'I didn't really know how to handle it. The recognition came out of nowhere. I suffer from anxiety, so it felt a bit strange and a bit worrying at times. I didn't know what to do. I wanted to thank everyone, and I felt so guilty that I couldn't respond to all the messages. That first day, after we came on your show, it was non-stop. I was at work, so it was hard to concentrate. I'll be honest, it was actually quite a difficult time for me but, with all the things being said, and all the positive reaction, that really helped to calm me down. The best thing about it was that people were seeing how important it is to have young carers and it was great to be part of that discussion. A lot of people in care feel underappreciated. We don't get the same benefits as NHS staff, but we are doing such an important job. People like Ken put so much trust in us and the job comes with real challenges and responsibilities. Looking back, I'm glad so many people got to see a positive story about the work that we try and do.'

That week was a very strange and emotional one for Kia. Her granny died on the same day and there was a fire at her mum's house. Virus restrictions prevented her from going to her gran's funeral, so she just drove and sat in the car outside.

'It was weird that all that was going on at the same time that everyone was talking about the cushion. I certainly won't forget 2020 in a hurry. I'm just so happy that it made such a difference to Ken.'

Ken likes talking about the cushion almost as much as he enjoys talking about U-boats. 'I have got to say, it was one of the most wonderful moments of my life. It's much easier to cuddle than an old picture frame. I was told that there were 30 million people who have seen that clip! Kia is an angel; they all are who work here. It is just like a family. I went down to the laundry this morning to see the lady who is down there. She works on her own, so I think it's always good to pop in and check she's okay.'

Ken is just in the middle of telling me about his plans for a big family reunion when he remembers that he has a folder next to his chair with some of the letters he received from some of those who saw the video.

'Can I read you one of them?' he asks. 'This is from a lady' says Ken. 'She starts off very formal.' He coughs, to clear his throat, and then starts.

Dear Mr Benbow . . . 'That's me,' he says.

If I may be informal, Ken. I suffer from bi-polar. 'That's a mental health problem,' interjects Ken.

I have learned to manage it with exercise, medication and other things. This dreadful situation has almost brought me to my knees.

When I saw you and Kia today, I cannot express the impact you had on me.

Ken has to stop. Reading the letter again has made him emotional. He has a little cry and apologies for being a 'big softie'.

I want to thank you from the bottom of my heart. Ken, you have helped me very much. For that you will always have my gratitude. I cannot get rid of my bi-polar, but you have lifted my spirits.

'Isn't that lovely?' says Ken with pride. 'Do you know, that lady travelled 189 miles to come up here and say "hi"? We had a lovely chat that day and now we speak to each other twice a week on the phone. Oh, hold on,' Ken searches in his folder. 'I've got another one here from America. Listen to this, Dan.'

Dear Ken and Kia

I hope this day is serving you well. I saw you're article in the local news in the US. Ken interjects, 'In America! Can you believe that?'

What a great surprise and what a story. You are very special people . . . warming hearts all over the world.

Kia did something wonderful for Ken and made a huge difference to one lovely old man and – thanks to a viral video – many others. While Ken is busy working on his family reunion, Kia also has big plans for the future.

'I want to go to Africa and do international aid work. It is something that I always thought would be amazing. I also have plans to go to Thailand and work in an animal sanctuary. There are two things that really affect me; people who need help and animals. When I see adverts on the TV about WaterAid or the RSPCA, that is something I feel I can commit my life to.'

Kia's grandparents have always encouraged her to go out there and change the world; to have a positive influence on the people around her. She is an incredibly inspirational young woman. We all know that many young people in the UK have a bad reputation. If you are feeling like that . . . listen to Kia.

'I don't blame others for the way that they see people of my age. I see some of the stuff that young people get up to and it makes me feel sick. I can't bear all the self-obsession and the lack of respect. Ken always says that when you walked past a police officer in his day you would always nod to them. Maybe it's the way I've been brought up. My pap is a farmer. He gets up, goes to work, does his best, comes home and loves those around him. My life has been built around respect. Where I'm from, I see many people from my generation who are doing well. Children going out there and making a difference.'

I ask Kia what she has learned from working through a global pandemic. 'I have learned to appreciate everyone around me, and I've learned a lot about myself. I have missed my family, but I have also understood how much I love the job. Being away from home for such a long time, I've also had the opportunity to mature and think about a lot of things. The whole thing with Ken has helped me to see the value of dignity. I think anyone who works in care understands that. You have got to look out for people. You've got to want to do this sort of job. I think that is why it's so meaningful. You've got to put other people first. It's such a rewarding thing to see someone smile. You have repaired that dignity, showed them respect . . . and helped to see some of their character. That is invaluable.'

I love the fact that Kia still thinks the media attention was a lot of fuss about nothing. For her, it was just a normal, nice thing to do for an old man she was looking after. That is what makes her so special. They still see each other most days. They are separated by seventy-seven years but are great friends. Ken will never forget what Kia did for him and it's clear he has also made a big impact on her. He keeps telling her, and anyone else, about U-boats . . . and she continues to listen. Ken still misses

Ada every day, but Kia has made sure that his days without her, are as happy as they can be.

The final person I want to tell you about in this chapter, is a young fella by the name of Tony Hudgell. Tony was one of the many people inspired by Captain Tom during lockdown.

He was fostered by Paula and Mark when he was just four months old. They went on to fully adopt him a year later and he now lives with them and their seven other children.

'When we had Lacey, our youngest,' says Paula, 'Mark still wanted to have more children, but I was done. We felt like we had more to give and there are a lot of children out there who need help. It was never our intention to adopt at the start, but we were keen to foster for as long as we could. Tony fitted into the family very well. He was tiny and almost completely withdrawn when he came to us. He would often just sit there, like his mind was somewhere else, but we did all we could to make him a part of the family.'

The thing that changed everything for Paula was a visit to the consultant paediatrician for Tony's adoption medical. That is the meeting where they run you through all the issues that a child has, before putting them on the adoption list.

'I don't think the doctor meant it in the way that it came out, but they looked through Tony's issues and said, "Who on earth would want to adopt this child?" My heart broke at that point and I thought, "We would."'

Tony was deaf in his right ear and had a mass on the brain

caused by trauma. His physical and cognitive development was impaired, and he suffered from a heart infection and multiple fractures. He was likely to be in a wheelchair for his entire life.

He had suffered horrific abuse at the hands of his birth parents. When he arrived at hospital just before Christmas 2014, Tony was only forty-one days old. He had sepsis, toxic shock and multiple organ failure. His legs had been broken and dislocated for ten days. He was never expected to survive. He was in such a bad way that the hospital thought they had no choice but to withdraw his care, but Tony was a ward of court so they couldn't do that without an order from a judge. The process was delayed because it was the Christmas holidays, and that saved Tony's life. While they were waiting for the order to come through, Tony started to show signs of improvement.

'That is why you should never give up on anyone,' says Paula. 'What he had been through came back to me when the doctor asked who would want him, and I couldn't face the idea of Tony being lost in the system and moving from home to home. We made the decision as a whole family. The older children all agreed. We were going to make him a part of us. We applied for adoption.'

The adoption went through in March 2016, but Paula had another fight on her hands. The Crown Prosecution Service ruled that there was not enough evidence to charge Tony's birth parents. Paula launched a campaign to get justice for Tony and after hundreds of phone calls, petitions, letters and meetings; the decision was overturned and, in February 2018, Tony's birth parents were given the maximum sentence of ten years in jail.

'We were doing that for Tony,' says Paula with passion. 'I

love him just like my own children. If someone had hurt my other kids, I would fight until the end of the earth to get justice for them. I didn't want him to ask me later in life about what happened to his parents and for me to have say that I didn't do all that I could to protect him. I want to be able to look him in the eye and tell him that we fought for him.'

I ask Paula how much Tony knows about the abuse. 'We tell him they were unable to look after him. He hears what happened every time we go to a hospital appointment. He knows they are in prison and he knows he was very poorly because of them. In terms of seeing them one day, that will be up to him when he gets to eighteen. If he wants to meet them, I will support him 100 per cent. It would hurt because, for me, they gave up their rights to him when they nearly killed him. My job now is just to surround him with love and help him to make the most out of his life.'

Tony's injuries were so bad he had both his legs amputated in 2017. Paula always hoped that he would be able to keep his legs, but they were just too badly damaged. There were so many breaks and they had formed false joints.

'Tony also has part of his hip missing. It is permanently dislocated so prosthetics don't really work for him. We tried stubbies to start but it looked like he was going to have to be in a wheelchair. His medical team decided to try one more thing: legs which would have feet at the bottom. I remember Tony saying, "Can I have trainers like Jaden?", his brother. He was so excited, and we finally had those fitted just before lockdown started in 2020.'

Tony has always had a fascination with older people. He was watching television one day and saw the story of Captain

Tom walking in his back garden and raising money for charity. 'I could do that,' the five-year-old said to his mum.

'We thought we would set ourselves a challenge,' remembers Paula. 'We started on 1 June and said we would just try and walk every day and get to 10,000 metres. The first day was so hard. Just 300 metres took us an hour and I thought we had set ourselves too big a challenge. All we wanted to do was raise £500 for the Evelina London Children's Hospital which looked after Tony.'

The local community in Kings Hill threw themselves into it. People started sharing it on social media and, every day, they would come out to clap Tony and cheer him on.

'We got to about £3,000 and it was amazing,' remembers Paula. 'By Friday night of that week, we were on £17,000 and the following morning, we appeared on *BBC Breakfast*. By the end of the day it was £100,000. It was incredible. I must have refreshed the computer about a thousand times that weekend!'

When Tony finally completed his 10,000 metres there was a huge crowd to see him do it and, unbelievably, one little five-year-old, raised over £1.5 million. When Paula first came up with the idea, her husband felt that everyone had had enough of fundraising and wasn't sure it would work.

'None of us can really believe it,' says Paula. 'It's all down to Tony. If he hadn't been born at Christmas . . . he wouldn't be here. People were ready to give up on him, but he never gave up. He knows that what he has done is amazing, but I'm keeping everything in a big box because, when he gets older, I want him to know how many people he managed to touch. I want him to know how special he is. I know for most people that 2020 has been a year to forget but, for us and for Tony, it's been incredibly life-affirming.'

Paula is convinced that Tony has a great life ahead of him. She is also sure that his birth parents have seen what the precious little baby they tried to kill has gone on to achieve.

'I hope they regret what they did to him,' says Paula. 'I know they have seen the footage. I hope it gives them a chance to think about what they did to him. They nearly stole his life away, but Tony is the perfect example of why you should never give up on anyone.'

2020 has been an awful year for so many reasons. We have lost friends and loved ones and our lives have been turned upside down. I don't know about you, but I have needed a little sunshine at times and Tony, Ken and Kia, Bob, Leona and Hylton have all provided that.

I have found the pandemic a valuable lesson in humility. It has reminded me of my limitations and, as a Christian, the importance of putting my trust in God. It has confounded experts and those who are convinced they have the answers.

It has been an important reminder of how little we know and also allowed us to see how many people express themselves with far more confidence than they probably should. There have been quite a few individuals who, even though their knowledge of virology or epidemiology doesn't extend beyond a quick Twitter search, are willing to contradict health experts.

We can all fall into the trap of speaking as though we have

already worked out the best approach or best policy. I don't envy those who have had to make life-changing decisions based on imperfect information.

That is why the testimonies in this chapter are so important. These are some of the people who have had to deal with all that this virus has thrown at them. I could have included so many more people in this chapter and I'm sure there are some in your mind right now as you read this.

They serve both as a challenge and an encouragement. I am inspired by their example, but I am also reminded of a trap I often fall into: complaining about something rather than trying to make it better. If there is one thing I will keep in my mind from the people in this chapter, and in this book, it's that it is possible to have a positive effect on those around me.

It doesn't matter how old you are, what your background is, how much money you have in the bank, who you know, who you don't know or the size of your social media following . . . we can all have an impact on the people we spend time with, even if it's just a few seconds.

The nurses saved Hylton's life, Paula improved the lot of hundreds of people with her iPads, Bob put a smile on a thousand faces, Kia touched Ken and millions of others with her kindness and Paula has transformed Tony by showering him in the love that his life was so desperately missing.

None of us will forget the overwhelming experience of this pandemic. It is something we will talk about for generations to come. I hope we are also keen to remember those who provided some much-needed light in the darkness.

ACKNOWLEDGEMENTS

There you have it. I hope you enjoyed reading this as much as I enjoyed writing it. When I first agreed to pen this tome, I was aware of the tight timeline, but it has been an overwhelming positive experience for me.

My job is very fast moving so it's been wonderful to go back and spend time with some of the people who made a big impression on me the first time I met them. It's been great to be able to stop and look at their stories in more detail and try to understand what makes them tick and what keeps them going.

Once again I would like to show my appreciation to everyone who was kind enough to give me some of their precious time.

I want to thank Tony and Terrence for opening up about their lives and being part of two amazing bits of television. It's been so heart-warming to see all the different people who have been touched by their stories.

Thank you to Ilse and Figen for being willing to bare their souls and share their inner-most feelings. Both have lost a child; but both have achieved so much and inspired so many, despite the grief which leaves them broken.

I am already looking forward to my next interaction with

John Sutherland and, even though I don't think I'll be back in Afghanistan any time soon, I want to thank the men and women I met there who challenged my preconceptions and opened my eyes to the true nature of service and sacrifice.

I want to take the opportunity to thank Lisa Ashton for her unwavering dedication to others, and the legacy of the amazing Winnie Mabaso, and to Maria for making me laugh and bringing so much joy to our show at the Rio Olympics and her chapter in this book.

Thank you to all those who were willing to feature in the chapter about THE story of 2020 – coronavirus. Their accounts are incredible and, when there has been so much to drag us down, they did their best to get us back to where we needed to be.

I am grateful to everyone who has spoken about things that scare them, inspire them, crush them and define them. I particularly want to thank Tommy and Eddie Speed for talking so openly about their dad for the first time since his death. They have certainly helped me come to terms with what happened, and I think many others will be able to take something from their testimony. That was the chapter which took me the longest to write because I felt a deep responsibility to tell their story sensitively.

I want to thank the brilliant team at the BBC. It is a real pleasure to work across different departments with so many talented individuals. Many of my colleagues at *BBC Breakfast* have already been mentioned in these pages but a special thank you should also go to Liam Blyth, Charlotte Simpson and Laura Yates.

I also want to thank God for giving me the opportunity to

write this book. My faith has been challenged and strengthened through this process. I have met some amazing Christians throughout my life who have been a huge encouragement to me over the years. When I think about some of the situations people on these pages have faced, I know there is no way I could have dealt with them without my faith in God. At several points during the course of writing this book, I have come back to the words of a song we often sing in church by Nathan Stiff and called 'O Lord, My Rock and My Redeemer'. There is one verse that goes like this:

My song, when enemies surround me
My hope, when tides of sorrow rise
My joy, when trials are abounding
Your faithfulness, my refuge in the night

There are many people in this book who have faced the storms of life. I have spent many hours sat here thinking about how they have responded to those challenges and it flies in the face of the concept of perfection we often see in the world around us.

So many of the great encouragements in this book have come from people experiencing trauma or grief. It is amazing to see what we are able to achieve in the most troubling of circumstances. One of the many things I will take away from the accounts here is the determination of individuals to make things better and to not allow negativity and hate to eat away and destroy them. They are struggling, but they are not failing.

I think that rings true with so many people in this world. Life can be a struggle and that struggle comes in many different shapes and sizes. For some the battleground is grief, for others it's illness, persecution, stress, family breakdown, death, abuse . . . the list could go on and on. What I hope you've been able to see from this book, is that it's possible to be broken and brilliant at the same time.

I am sitting here writing early on a Saturday morning. I have just seen the news that Chadwick Boseman – the star of the movie *Black Panther* – has died at the age of forty-three. Here is a man who made *Civil War, Marshall, Black Panther, Infinity War, Endgame, 21 Bridges* and *Da 5 Bloods* – all while he was going through multiple bouts of chemotherapy to treat stage three cancer. I think there is an interesting parallel between his ability to inspire so many others while he was suffering in silence.

The other thing I keep coming back to when I read some of these accounts is the need for us to keep communicating with each other. I have lost count of the number of times people have spoken to me about Tony and Terrence. Both their stories are so uplifting and made a deep impact on millions of people around the world. Both of their stories came from a simple conversation which started with the words 'are you okay?' I wonder how many other amazing people I have walked past because I was buried in my phone or thinking about something else rather than what was right in front of me. They have taught me to talk less and to listen more.

I have been challenged, encouraged and inspired by so many

of these stories and I hope that having also now met these *Remarkable People,* you too will feel the same way. I trust you are able to find them a source of inspiration for some of the things you are facing and, in reading about them, see how we can all make a positive impact on the people we see every day.

I can't say it better than Sophie did when she signed up to be a volunteer after singing for Terrence.

'We might not all grow up and change the world, but we can make a little difference. What better time to start than right now?'

One final 'thank you' to the team at Headline Publishing – and particularly Jonathan Taylor, for his guidance along the way – and to Jonny McWilliams, at Crown Media Management, for the encouragement to keep putting pen to page.

I'm off to have a large slice of cake.